# Exercises
# for Effective
# Counseling &
# Psychotherapy

## Les Parrott III, Ph.D.
*Seattle Pacific University*

## Siang-Yang Tan, Ph.D.
*Fuller Theological Seminary*

The McGraw-Hill Companies, Inc.

New York  St. Louis  San Francisco  Auckland  Bogotá  Caracas  Lisbon
London  Madrid  Mexico City  Milan  Montreal  New Delhi
San Juan  Singapore  Sydney  Tokyo  Toronto

**McGraw·Hill**

*A Division of The McGraw·Hill Companies*

**EXERCISES FOR EFFECTIVE COUNSELING
AND PSYCHOTHERAPY**

This book is printed on acid-free paper.

ISBN 0-07-048582-8

1 2 3 4 5 6 7 8 9 0   FGR FGR   9 0 9 8 7 6

The editor was Brian McKean;
the production supervisor was Denise L. Puryear.
Quebecor Printing/Fairfield was printer and binder.

http://www.mhcollege.com

# Contents

# *Preface*

This is an action-oriented book of exercises designed for use with *Counseling and Psychotherapy* by Les Parrott III. It is intended to help you master the content of that text and to practice a variety of counseling techniques derived from the theories covered in it.

The chapters in this workbook are divided into two parts. Part One serves as a study guide to the text's informational and theoretical content. The first four chapters of Part One serve as general study guide to the introductory chapters' content — with a unique set of exercises and activities in each section.

The remaining chapters of Part One include a summary of a particular theoretical approach covered in *Counseling and Psychotherapy*. This summary is followed by a "Guided Study" which consists of a series of about a dozen essay questions and space for you to write your answers. Each question coincides with a specific section from the text's chapter and by comparing your answers to these questions you will be able to assess your conceptual knowledge of the chapter. Next is the "Chapter Review." It consists of numerous fill-in-the-blank questions categorized by the chapter headings. These questions will help you assess how well you have internalized the chapter's specific content on a factual level. This is followed by a list of the chapter's "Key Terms" and an accompanying "Matching Exercise." This will help you assess your knowledge of the chapter's specific vocabulary. Finally, the chapter concludes with "Questions for Discussion and Reflection." These questions can be used on your own or to generate discussions with fellow students. They are meant to help you review the chapter's content as a whole and help you assess what you will take with you from the chapter on a more personal level.

Part Two of this workbook provides a programmed approach to learning and practicing some of the counseling techniques discussed in the theory chapters of *Counseling and Psychotherapy*. From the nine theories discussed in the text, we have lifted out several major techniques and provided a programmed learning model for you to gain first-hand experience in practicing these methods. Activity units in this section include a brief review of a specific theory's methods and techniques and a programmed approach in applying a variety of related skills.

**v**

Each activity unit is based partially on the microcounseling concept of teaching one skill at a time. You will be presented with a typical counseling problem or issue and then asked to respond to a question about how you would apply a specific theoretical perspective. If your answer is correct, we will explain why it is correct and then you will be directed to the next exchange. If your answer is incorrect, we will explain why it is wrong and ask you to reconsider it and select another answer. It is important that you do not move ahead to the next exchange until you have successfully completed each step in the program.

Following the programmed approach to learning counseling skills, you will be presented with an activity unit which will involve role playing a brief counseling exchange with two other people — alternating the client, counselor, and observer roles. You will record each of these exchanges on audio- or video-tape and then use them to refine your application of the specific skills practiced. Using this approach, you will better learn the skills discussed in each of the theory chapters of *Counseling and Psychotherapy*.

This step-by-step programmed approach will help you grasp more fully the application of specific counseling techniques from a variety of theoretical approaches. However, it is important to note that this learning model will, in no way, equip you to be proficient in the practice of any particular school of counseling. The application of a theoretical perspective requires in-depth training and supervision in that approach. This method of practice is designed only to further your knowledge of the application of each theory at an introductory level.

We commend you at the outset for not merely reading about the various theoretical approaches to counseling, but also practicing the skills and techniques which each of these theories foster. We hope you will use this action-oriented workbook as a means for mastering the fundamentals of counseling and psychotherapy. We wish you our very best.

—Les Parrott III and Siang-Yang Tan

# Acknowledgments

My thanks to Lori Nouguier for her careful assistance in helping me with many of the details in this workbook. And to Dr. Siang-Yang Tan I owe a great debt for contributing his creative energies to this project. His skill in helping students apply theoretical techniques is masterful.

— Les Parrott III

I would like to thank Mrs. Linda Rojas for her excellent secretarial help. I would also like to express my deepest gratitude and love for my wife Angela, and my children, Carolyn and Andrew for their faithful support, encouragement, love and prayers as I continue to write. Finally, I want to thank Dr. Les Parrott and McGraw-Hill for inviting me to be co-author of this book.

—Siang-Yang Tan

# PART I

# Exercises for Mastering Content

## CHAPTER 1

# The Realm of Counseling

## PRELIMINARY SELF-EXPLORATION

Before you delve into this chapter, take a moment to consider the following questions. Write down the first thing that comes to your mind for each item. You may then find it helpful to come back to your responses once you have completed your study of this chapter and see if and how you might alter your responses.

- Why do you want to study professional counseling?

  _____

  _____

  _____

  _____

- How willing are *you* to seek professional help from a counselor or psychotherapist?

  _____

  _____

  _____

  _____

- If you are planning a career as a professional counselor what kind of training and work setting do you envision for yourself?

  _____

  _____

  _____

  _____

- How would you continue to grow and develop as a professional once you are working in the field?

  _____

  _____

  _____

  _____

## CHAPTER OVERVIEW

While the realm of counseling has been dominated by a few heads of state like Freud and Adler, and governed by several prime ministers like Rogers and May, and served well by a number of ambassadors like Berne and Glasser, the greatest and most productive servants in the realm of counseling have been virtual unknowns by the thousands who have made the healing profession of psychotherapy their passion. These counselors have seldom been known far beyond the communities where they have used their skills to save marriages, offer hope to struggling adolescents, salvage the bruised personalities of abused children, and enter the pilgrimage of clients who respond to the warmth of a professional who has the heart and the understanding to guide them in solving their problems and redirecting their lives.

The goal of this chapter is to provide a panoramic view of professional therapy by exploring what counseling is, where it came from, and what it takes to become a counselor or psychotherapist. The deep roots of counseling which transcend European-American thought will be excavated and examined. Counseling's struggle to define itself will be revealed. The comparisons between counseling and psychotherapy will be made and shown to be more similar than different. The functions of counselors in their ever evolving roles will be delineated, as will their therapeutic training sites and settings.

The students who study this text will learn what it is like to live and serve in the realm of counseling. Not many will become heads of state, for few are needed. Some may become prime ministers or ambassadors. But most will be fulfilled, even to overflowing, with the rewards of a profession that makes a difference.

# GUIDED STUDY

These questions are meant to guide you through the major sections of the chapter. Write your answer in the space provided and then compare it with the marked section of the text.

1. Describe the significance and influence of Vienna in the historical development of counseling and psychotherapy.

 

 

 

 

2. The roots of counseling go much deeper than Western cultures. Discuss the early non-European influences that shaped contemporary counseling.

 

 

 

 

3. Explain, in your own words, what counseling is. What are its common elements?

 

 

 

 

4. While counseling and psychotherapy are often seen as the same thing, explain how they are sometimes viewed with different emphases.

 

 

 

 

5. Contemporary counselors do more than counsel. Discuss the various function and delivery modes of today's counselors.

_____

_____

_____

_____

6. Mental health practitioners are classified by their training and specialty. Discuss the varieties of professional counselors and the settings in which they work.

_____

_____

_____

_____

7. Competent counselors are dedicated to life-long professional development. Explain how they continue to learn and grow even after completing their advanced degrees.

_____

_____

_____

_____

## CHAPTER REVIEW

The following items will help you master the specific content of the chapter. Complete each of the following sentences by filling in the blanks.

### Vienna and Beyond

1. Vienna, on the south bank of the Danube at the foot of the Austrian Alps, is considered by many to be the birthplace of _____.

2. Sigmund Freud and _____ lived in Vienna, where they both attended medical school and honed their therapeutic skills.

3. An early disciple of Freud, _____ received his medical degree from The University of Zurich and began his practice and research in Basel.

## The Deep Roots of Counseling

1. The desire to help other, to counsel, is as old as time and not limited to _____ cultures.

2. The American Indian and other tribal groups relied on the shaman, believing much more in _____ and _____ healing than in a conventional counselor.

3. It was Josef Breuer, a well-known Viennese physician fourteen years older than Freud, who taught him about _____, a method of removing hysterical symptoms through talking them out."

4. Early in the evolution of psychoanalysis, _____ developed new understanding that went beyond the early psychoanalytic focus on sexuality.

## What is Counseling?

1. Professional counseling is more than merely the art of giving

   _____.

2. Common features of many counseling definitions include the counselor having a personal _____ to help clients and offering a framework for _____ by providing an explanatory scheme.

3. Another common notion is that counseling is a(n) _____ as well as a science.

4. Professional counselors maintain high _____ standards in their practices.

## Counseling or Psychotherapy?

1. Counseling has traditionally been viewed as less _____ than psychotherapy.

2. Some consider the number of interventions to be a deciding factor; meaning that about _____ to _____ sessions constitute counseling, whereas interventions beyond that point are psychotherapy.

3. Clear-cut distinctions between counseling and psychotherapy are virtually impossible to _____.

## Functions of Counselors

1. Along with traditional one-to-one counseling, counselors provide assistance to their clients through _____ therapy, which has become increasingly popular.

2. _____ is another rapidly growing delivery mode used by counselors in working with a wide variety of individuals, groups and organizations.

3. Clients' emotional struggles are often the result of not practicing the basic coping strategies and skill. When this is the case, an effective counselor may serve as a _____.

4. _____ allows established counselors to advance their profession by training new and less experienced counselors.

## Therapeutic Training and Settings

1. Counselors in training typically demonstrate growth and proficiency in self-development, skill development and _____ development.

2. _____ are medical doctors who have advanced training in mental health and psychopathology.

3. _____ psychologists are usually trained at the doctoral level to help people solve psychological problems related to such areas as personal adjustment, marriage, family, career, and school.

4. Social workers practice in a number of environments for both the mentally and _____ challenged.

## Professional Growth and Development

1. While academic milestones are important, proficient counselors maintain involvement in organizations that keep them accountable and _____ in their profession.

2. One of the best resources for professional development is _____ in a counseling organization.

3. Established more than 100 years ago, the _____ _____ Association is the oldest organization of its kind and is made up of more than 70,000 members.

4. With more than 55,000 members from all fields of counseling, the _____ _____ Association is made up of sixteen divisions.

# ADDITIONAL EXERCISES
## ON THE REALM OF COUNSELING

- **Defining Counseling in Your Own Words**

  Some have said that it is easier to practice counseling than it is to describe it. The variety of definitions provided by scholars seems to prove the point. After reviewing the common features that many writers have noted in the text, do your best to write a definition in your own words that makes sense to you.

  _____

  _____

  _____

  _____

- **Are You Reluctant to Seek Help?**

  In one of the sidebars of this chapter in the textbook is a self-test for assessing your willingness to see a counselor. After completing this assessment, take a moment to score your test and read the interpretation provided in the text. With this self-understanding, take a few moments to talk with people you know who are not studying the field of counseling. Interview a half dozen people (in person or on the phone) about how they feel about seeing a professional counselor. If they are single, you might ask them how they would feel about dating someone who is seeing a counselor. Does that matter to them? If they are married with children, ask them how they would feel about their children going to a counselor or how they would feel if their children played with another child who is getting professional help? Do what you can to uncover how people really feel about seeking professional help. Record your discoveries below and compare them with other students who have conducted similar interviews.

  _____

  _____

  _____

  _____

  _____

  _____

  _____

  _____

- **Preparing for Tomorrow Today**

  The text discusses the importance of professional growth and development for the effective counselor. In this context, it mentions the American Psychological Association and the American Counseling Association. Take a moment to contact these two organizations and have them send you information on student memberships. Here are the addresses for you to contact:

  APA                                    ACA
  750 First St., N.E.                    5999 Stevenson Ave.
  Washington, DC 20002-4242              Alexandria, VA 22304-3303

  In addition, you may want to request specific information from these two organizations about their different divisions. What follows is a listing of the various divisions in both organizations.

## Divisions of the American Counseling Association

American College Personnel Association (ACPA)
Association for Counselor Education and Supervision (ACES)
National Career Development Association (NCDA)
Association for Humanistic Education and Development (AHEAD)
American School Counselor Association (ASCA)
American Rehabilitation Counseling Association (ARCA)
Association for Measurement and Evaluation in Counseling &
    Development (AMECD)
National Employment Counselors Association (NECA)
Association for Multicultural Counseling and Development (AMCD)
Association for Religious and Value Issues in Counseling (ARVIC)
Association for Specialists in Group Work (ASGW)
International Association of Addictions and Offender Counselors (IAAOC)
American Mental Health Counselors Association (AMHCA)
Military Educators and Counselors Association (MECA)
Association for Adult Development and Aging (AADA)
International Association of Marriage and Family Counselors (IAMFC)
American College Counseling Association (AACA)

## Divisions of the American Psychological Association

Division 1: General Psychology
Division 2: Teaching of Psychology
Division 3: Experimental Psychology
Division 5: Evaluation, Measurement and Statistics

Division 6: Physiological and Comparative Psychology
Division 7: Developmental Psychology
Division 8: The Society of Personality and Social Psychology
Division 9: Society for the Psychological Study of Social Issues
Division 10: Psychology and the Arts
Division 12: Clinical Psychology
Division 13: Consulting Psychology
Division 14: The Society for Industrial and Organizational Psychology
Division 15: Educational Psychology
Division 16: School Psychology
Division 17: Counseling Psychology
Division 18: Psychologists in Public Service
Division 19: Military Psychology
Division 20: Adult Development and Aging
Division 21: Applied Experimental and Engineering Psychologists
Division 22: Rehabilitation Psychology
Division 23: Consumer Psychology
Division 24: Theoretical and Philosophical Psychology
Division 25: Experimental Analysis of Behavior
Division 26: History of Psychology
Division 27: Community Psychology
Division 28: Psychopharmacology and Substance Abuse
Division 29: Psychotherapy
Division 30: Psychological Hypnosis
Division 31: State Psychological Association Affairs
Division 32: Humanistic Psychology
Division 33: Mental Retardation and Developmental Disabilities
Division 34: Population and Environmental Psychology
Division 35: Psychology of Women
Division 36: Psychologists Interested in Religious Issues
Division 37: Child, Youth and Family Services
Division 38: Health Psychology
Division 39: Psychoanalysis
Division 40: Clinical Neuropsychology
Division 41: The American Psychology-Law Society
Division 42: Psychologists in Independent Practice
Division 43: Family Psychology
Division 44: Society for the Psychological Study of Lesbian and Gay Issues
Division 45: Society for the Psychological Study of Ethnic Minority Issues
Division 46: Media Psychology
Division 47: Exercise and Sport Psychology
Division 48: Peace Psychology
Division 49: Group Psychology and Group Psychotherapy

• **Periodicals Related to Counseling and Psychotherapy**

An excellent way to learn more about the field of counseling is to discover its journals. The following is not an exhaustive list of periodicals related to counseling and psychotherapy. It is intended to indicate the scope of the field and it includes many of the professional resources available in university libraries. Journals are the main disseminators of counseling research, news, and professional development. Read through this list and take time to peruse a few issues in your library. The more you study these various outlets of counseling information, the more informed and competent you will become in this profession.

American Journal of Psychiatry
American Journal of Psychotherapy
American Psychological Association Monitor
American Psychologist
American Vocational Journal
Career Development Quarterly
Clinical Psychology Review
Counseling and Values
Counseling Psychologist
Counselor Education and Supervision
Elementary School Guidance and Counseling
International Journal of Family Counseling
Journal for Specialists in Group Work
Journal of Clinical Psychology
Journal of Consulting and Clinical Psychology
Journal of Counseling and Development
Journal of Counseling Psychology
Journal of Cross Cultural Counseling
Journal of Employment Counseling
Journal of Family Counseling
Journal of Marriage and the Family
Journal of Multicultural Counseling and Development
Journal of Offender Counseling
Journal of Psychology and Theology
Measurement and Evaluation in Counseling and Development
Psychotherapy: Theory, Research & Practice
Rehabilitation Counseling Bulletin
School Counselor
Women and Therapy

# ANSWERS TO CHAPTER REVIEW

## Vienna and Beyond

1. psychiatry (or psychoanalysis or psychotherapy)
2. Alfred Adler
3. Carl Jung

## The Deep Roots of Counseling

1. Western
2. spiritual, holistic
3. catharsis
4. women

## What Is Counseling?

1. advice
2. commitment, change
3. art
4. ethical

## Counseling or Psychotherapy?

1. intensive
2. twelve, fifteen
3. defend

## Functions of Counselors

1. group
2. consultation
3. trainer
4. supervision

## Therapeutic Training and Settings

1. process
2. psychiatrists
3. counseling
4. physically

## Professional Growth and Development

1. current
2. membership
3. American Psychological
4. American Counseling

## CHAPTER 2

# Becoming an Effective Counselor

## PRELIMINARY SELF EXPLORATION

Before you delve into this chapter, take a moment to consider the following questions. Write down the first thing that comes to your mind for each of the items. You may then find it helpful to come back to your responses once you have completed your study of this chapter and see if and how you might alter your responses.

- What specific fears do you have about being a counselor?

_____

_____

_____

_____

- When you picture an effective counselor, what comes to mind? In other words, what is your concept of a successful counselor?

_____

_____

_____

_____

- What happens inside you when you hear the words: mistake, error, slip-up, or blunder? Do you expect to make mistakes in learning to counsel?

_____

_____

_____

_____

- Can you recognize any unreasonable expectations you have placed on yourself as a beginning counselor?

_____

_____

_____

_____

## CHAPTER OVERVIEW

Methods and theories do not in any way guarantee success in therapy. A counselor's personal characteristics are vital to effective intervention and this chapter focuses on those qualities. It examines the importance of psychological health, genuine interest in others, empathic ability, personal warmth, self-awareness, tolerance of ambiguity, and awareness of values.

In addition, the common pitfalls of beginning counselors are explored and guarded against. These include premature problem solving, not setting limits, fear of silence, interrogating, impatience, moralizing and reluctance to refer.

The overarching goal of this chapter is to introduce some of the most important qualities shared by effective counselors and to help you dodge common counselor-training problems.

## GUIDED STUDY

These questions are meant to guide you through the major sections of the chapter. Write your answer in the space provided and then compare it with the marked section of the text.

1. Discuss the importance of personal qualities as compared to expert knowledge in the effectiveness of psychotherapy.

_____

_____

_____

_____

2. While no one expects professional counselors to be paragons of psychological health, it is crucial for the counselor to have a secure sense of personal well-being and be growing as a person. Why is this so vital?

_____

_____

_____

_____

3. Describe the importance for counselors having a genuine interest in others.

_____

_____

_____

_____

4. In specific terms, what is meant by empathic abilities and what do they do for the counselor?

_____

_____

_____

_____

5. If a counselor did not possess a good sense of personal warmth, why would that be detrimental to his or her practice of therapy?

_____

_____

_____

_____

6. How does the ancient dictum of Socrates to "know thyself" apply to the process of becoming an effective counselor?

_____

_____

_____

_____

7. Describe the importance for counselors being tolerant of ambiguity.

_____

_____

_____

_____

8. What are values and how do they impact the counseling process?

_____

_____

_____

_____

9. One of the most common pitfalls of beginning counselors is premature problem solving. Why does this occur?

_____

_____

_____

_____

10. In addition to premature problem solving, what are some of the other most common hurdles for beginning counselors?

_____

_____

_____

_____

# CHAPTER REVIEW

The following items will help you master the specific content of the chapter. Complete each of the following sentences by filling in the blanks.

## Personal Qualities of Effective Counselors

1. Theoretical orientation, interviewing skills, and even professional experience are not the critical determinants for effective therapy. The counselor's _____ is the single most important criterion for effectiveness.

2. A person's _____ cannot compensate for inadequate knowledge or poor therapeutic skills.

3. If counselors do not demonstrate psychological _____ they become part of the problem, rather than part of the solution.

4. Some experts view an avoidance of personal _____ as the essence of all emotional disturbance.

5. Effective counselors are _____; they are genuinely interested in helping people gain better mental health.

6. _____ is the ability to put oneself in the shoes of another person and see the world from his or her perspective.

7. A counselor with personal warmth shows interest, concern, and attention but allows for personal _____ as well.

8. The purpose of nonpossessive warmth is to preserve clients' _____ and to provide a trusting and safe atmosphere.

9. Self-knowledge allows counselors to identify personal limits and become more objective. Counselors in training can become more self-aware by keeping a _____.

10. A counselor's feelings may vacillate daily without reason; they may complain of vague, indefinable symptoms. For this reason, the effective counselor must cultivate a tolerance for _____.

11. Values are the _____ which determine our goals and how we attempt to meet them.

12. The counselor's _____ will be part of the therapeutic work, either consciously or unconsciously.

## Pitfalls of Beginning Counselors

1. Trying to solve a problem before it fully _____ is one of the most common therapeutic mistakes.

2. A seasoned counselor knows it's normally not easy, in one or two sessions, to _____ the underlying problems in a dysfunctional situation.

3. In an effort to be understanding and tolerant, most beginning counselors have difficulty setting _____.

4. In counseling, _____ is not a sign that the counselor needs to say something.

5. Some of counseling's most therapeutic moments occur during periods of quiet _____.

6. The counselor in training needs to learn to refrain from subjecting clients to a barrage of _____.

7. Although there are certain "Aha" moments in counseling, most therapeutic improvement is _____.

8. Research has shown that the counselor who is not _____ continues to believe incorrect things about clients, even in light of new and different information.

9. While holding firm to personal convictions, the effective counselor does not mistake _____ for counseling.

10. The beginning counselor must learn, early on, that _____ to another competent counselor is a part of doing good therapeutic work.

## THE SELF-ACTUALIZING THERAPIST

Effective counselors are on a quest toward self-actualization to better help others in their self-actualizing journey. Use the following list of self-actualizing characteristics to work on qualities you may need to more intentionally cultivate (a detailed description of each is found in a sidebar of this chapter in the text). Rate how much each of these qualities describes you.

| Not Reality-based | | | | | | | | Reality-based | |
|---|---|---|---|---|---|---|---|---|---|
| 1 | 2 | 3 | 4 | 5 | 6 | 7 | 8 | 9 | 10 |

| Not accepting of self and others | | | | | | | Accepting of self and others | | |
|---|---|---|---|---|---|---|---|---|---|
| 1 | 2 | 3 | 4 | 5 | 6 | 7 | 8 | 9 | 10 |

| Not Spontaneous | | | | | | | | Spontaneous | |
|---|---|---|---|---|---|---|---|---|---|
| 1 | 2 | 3 | 4 | 5 | 6 | 7 | 8 | 9 | 10 |

| Not Problem-centered | | | | | | | | Problem-centered | |
|---|---|---|---|---|---|---|---|---|---|
| 1 | 2 | 3 | 4 | 5 | 6 | 7 | 8 | 9 | 10 |

| Not a need for privacy | | | | | | | | A need for privacy | |
|---|---|---|---|---|---|---|---|---|---|
| 1 | 2 | 3 | 4 | 5 | 6 | 7 | 8 | 9 | 10 |

| Not Autonomous | | | | | | | | Autonomous | |
|---|---|---|---|---|---|---|---|---|---|
| 1 | 2 | 3 | 4 | 5 | 6 | 7 | 8 | 9 | 10 |

| Not a freshness of appreciation | | | | | | | Freshness of appreciation | | |
|---|---|---|---|---|---|---|---|---|---|
| 1 | 2 | 3 | 4 | 5 | 6 | 7 | 8 | 9 | 10 |

| Not Mystical | | | | | | | | Mystical | |
|---|---|---|---|---|---|---|---|---|---|
| 1 | 2 | 3 | 4 | 5 | 6 | 7 | 8 | 9 | 10 |

| Not Compassionate | | | | | | | | Compassionate | |
|---|---|---|---|---|---|---|---|---|---|
| 1 | 2 | 3 | 4 | 5 | 6 | 7 | 8 | 9 | 10 |

| Not Relational | | | | | | | | Relational | |
|---|---|---|---|---|---|---|---|---|---|
| 1 | 2 | 3 | 4 | 5 | 6 | 7 | 8 | 9 | 10 |

| Not non-discriminatory | | | | | | | | Non-discriminatory | |
|---|---|---|---|---|---|---|---|---|---|
| 1 | 2 | 3 | 4 | 5 | 6 | 7 | 8 | 9 | 10 |

| Not highly ethical | | | | | | | | Highly ethical | |
|---|---|---|---|---|---|---|---|---|---|
| 1 | 2 | 3 | 4 | 5 | 6 | 7 | 8 | 9 | 10 |

| Not a sense of humor | | | | | | | | Sense of humor | |
|---|---|---|---|---|---|---|---|---|---|
| 1 | 2 | 3 | 4 | 5 | 6 | 7 | 8 | 9 | 10 |

| Not creative | | | | | | | | Creative | |
|---|---|---|---|---|---|---|---|---|---|
| 1 | 2 | 3 | 4 | 5 | 6 | 7 | 8 | 9 | 10 |

Once you have taken the time to rate each quality, circle the three you marked as least like you and the three you marked as most like you. If you feel comfortable doing so, compare your results with another student and discuss what each of you might do to cultivate those qualities which you ranked as least like you.

## WHAT DO YOU VALUE

Values define who we are. They are the cylinders that drive the engine of our lives. Take a moment to make a list of the ten things you value most. Granted, this is not a flippant exercise you can do in a hurry. Set aside some serious time to consider those things that matter most — the things you hold with conviction. If you cannot come up with ten, list as many as you can.

1. _____

2. _____

3. _____

4. _____

5. _____

6. _____

7. _____

8. _____

9. _____

10. _____

After completing your list, review it and note how each of them will influence your work as a counselor. If you feel comfortable doing so, discuss your list with another student.

## ANSWERS TO CHAPTER REVIEW

### Personal Qualities of Effective Counselors

1. personality
2. traits
3. health
4. responsibility
5. authentic
6. empathy
7. space
8. self-respect
9. journal
10. ambiguity
11. convictions (or beliefs)
12. values

### Pitfalls of Beginning Counselors

1. understood
2. identify (or solve)
3. limits
4. silence
5. contemplation
6. questions
7. gradual (or slow)
8. open-minded
9. preaching
10. referral

## CHAPTER 3

# Legal and Ethical Issues for the Beginning Counselor

## PRELIMINARY SELF EXPLORATION

Before you delve into this chapter, take a moment to consider the following questions. Write down the first thing that comes to your mind for each of the items. You may then find it helpful to come back to your responses once you have completed your study of this chapter and see if and how you might alter your responses.

- If a client were in desperate need of help for a problem outside your expertise, what would you do? Why?

  _____

  _____

  _____

  _____

- How do you feel about reporting private information a client confesses to you in therapy? What if it could save another person's life?

  _____

  _____

  _____

  _____

- Would you warn the partner of a sexually active client who has AIDS?

_____

_____

_____

_____

# CHAPTER OVERVIEW

The goal of this chapter is to characterize and explain the significance of counselor attitudes and behavior that support the legal and ethical concerns generally accepted among professional counselors. It begins by laying a foundation
of legal and ethical practice with an understanding of virtue. Next, the client/
counselor relationship is examined through the lens of trust. Confidentiality
and privileged communication are explored within the context of specific ethical dilemmas.

# GUIDED STUDY

These questions are meant to guide you through the major sections of the chapter. Write your answer in the space provided and then compare it with the
marked section of the text.

# CHAPTER REVIEW

The following items will help you master the specific content of the chapter.
Complete each of the following sentences by filling in the blanks.

## Foundations of Legal & Ethical Practice

1. A legal and ethical counseling practice is grounded on something counselors _____, not something counselors _____.

2. The bedrock of legal and ethical counseling is _____ — a term
rarely heard in psychology.

3. A sound counseling practice is built on knowing the law and understanding client _____.

4. Effective counselors are transparent and fully honest with themselves
about the _____ of their own expertise.

## The Client/Counselor Relationship

1. The essential element in a therapeutic relationship is _____.

2. _____ _____ is the basis of a trusting relationship and a cornerstone of counselor ethics.

3. A relationship with a client outside of the therapeutic context will almost always _____ treatment.

## Confidentiality & Privileged Communication

1. Problems of _____ are the most frequent source of ethical dilemmas for counselors.

2. There is no _____ for inadvertent slips that reveal information shared in confidence.

3. Legally, confidentiality is known as _____ _____. It spells out the legal conditions for breaking confidence with a client.

4. Counselors have a duty to _____ by disclosing information that can prevent a threatened danger.

5. _____, like counselors, are obligated to respect the confidentiality of client communication.

## When in Doubt

1. Misjudgment occurs when counselors do not utilize _____ for understanding and practicing the legal and ethical standard of counseling.

2. Legal and ethical considerations can be complex and confusing, so effective counselors regularly _____ with other professionals on issues that are unclear.

3. _____ can be appropriate and helpful in a number of situations, both for ancillary work with the primary counselor as well as a final referral when the counselor is doubtful about their ability to effectively meet the needs of the client effectively.

# Ethical Principles of Psychologists and Code of Conduct

## CONTENTS

## INTRODUCTION

## PREAMBLE

## GENERAL PRINCIPLES

## ETHICAL STANDARDS

*4. Therapy*

4.01  Structuring the Relationship

4.02  Informed Consent to Therapy

4.03  Couple and Family Relationships

4.04  Providing Mental Health Services to Those Served by Others

4.05  Sexual Intimacies with Current Patients or Clients

4.06  Therapy with Former Sexual Partners

4.07  Sexual Intimacies with Former Therapy Patients

4.08  Interruption of Services

4.09  Terminating the Professional Relationship

*5. Privacy and Confidentiality*

5.01  Discussing the Limits of Confidentiality

5.02  Maintaining Confidentiality

5.03  Minimizing Intrusions on Privacy

5.04  Maintenance of Records

5.05  Disclosures

5.06  Consultations

5.07  Confidential Information in Databases

5.08  Use of Confidential Information for Didactic or Other Purposes

5.09  Preserving Records and Data

5.10  Ownership of Records and Data

5.11  Withholding Records for Nonpayment

*6. Teaching, Training, Supervision, Research, and Publishing*

6.01  Design of Education and Training Programs

6.02  Descriptions of Education and Training Programs

6.03  Accuracy and Objectivity in Teaching

6.04  Limitation on Teaching

6.05  Assessing Student and Supervisee Performance

6.06  Planning Research

6.07  Responsibility

6.08  Compliance with Law and Standards

6.09  Institutional Approval

6.10  Research Responsibilities

6.11  Informed Consent to Research

6.12  Dispensing with Informed Consent

6.13  Informed Consent in Research Filming or Recording

6.14  Offering Inducements for Research Participants

6.15  Deception in Research

6.16  Sharing and Utilizing Data

6.17  Minimizing Invasiveness

6.18  Providing Participants with Information about the Study

6.19  Honoring Commitments

6.20  Care and Use of Animals in Research

6.21  Reporting of Results

6.22  Plagiarism

6.23  Publication Credit

6.24  Duplicate Publication of Data

6.25  Sharing Data

6.26  Professional Reviewers

*7. Forensic Activities*

7.01  Professionalism

7.02  Forensic Assessment

7.03  Clarification of Role

7.04  Truthfulness and Candor

7.05  Prior Relationships

7.06  Compliance with Law and Rules

*8. Resolving Ethical Issues*

8.01  Familiarity with Ethics Code

8.02  Confronting Ethical Issues

8.03  Conflicts between Ethics and Organizational Demands

8.04  Informal Resolution of Ethical Violations

8.05  Reporting Ethical Violations

8.06  Cooperating with Ethics Committees

8.07  Improper Complaints

# INTRODUCTION

The American Psychological Association's (APA's) Ethical Principles of Psychologists and Code of Conduct (hereinafter referred to as the Ethics Code) consists of an Introduction, a Preamble, six General Principles (A-F), and specific Ethical Standards. The Introduction discusses the intent, organization, procedural considerations, and scope of application of the Ethics Code. The Preamble and General Principles are *aspirational* goals to guide psychologists toward the highest ideals of psychology. Although the Preamble and General Principles are not themselves enforceable rules, they should be considered by psychologists in arriving at an ethical course of action and may be considered by ethics bodies in interpreting the Ethical Standards. The Ethical Standards set forth *enforceable* rules for conduct as psychologists. Most of the Ethical Standards are written broadly, in order to apply to psychologists in varied roles, although the application of an Ethical Standard may vary depending on the context. The Ethical Standards are not exhaustive. The fact that a given conduct is not specifically addressed by the Ethics Code does not mean that it is necessarily either ethical or unethical.

Membership in the APA commits members to adhere to the APA Ethics Code and to the rules and procedures used to implement it. Psychologists and students, whether or not they are APA members, should be aware that the Ethics Code may be applied to them by state psychology boards, courts, or other public bodies.

This Ethics Code applies only to psychologists' work-related activities, that is, activities that are part of the psychologists' scientific and professional functions or that are psychological in nature. It includes the clinical or counseling practice of psychology, research, teaching, supervision of trainees, development of assessment instruments, conducting assessments, educational counseling, organizational consulting, social intervention, administration, and other activities as well. These work-related activities can be distinguished from the purely private conduct of a psychologist, which ordinarily is not within the purview of the Ethics Code.

The Ethics Code is intended to provide standards of professional conduct that can be applied by the APA and by other bodies that choose to adopt them. Whether or not a psychologist has violated the Ethics Code does not by itself determine whether he or she is legally liable in a court action, whether a contract is enforceable, or whether other legal consequences occur. These results are based on legal rather than ethical rules. However, compliance with or violation of the Ethics Code may be admissible as evidence in some legal proceedings, depending on the circumstances.

In the process of making decisions regarding their professional behavior, psychologists must consider this Ethics Code, in addition to applicable laws and psychology board regulations. If the Ethics Code establishes a higher standard of conduct than is required by law, psychologists must meet the higher ethical standard. If the Ethics Code standard appears to conflict with the requirements of law, then psychologists make known their commitment to the Ethics Code and take steps to resolve the conflict in a responsible manner. If neither law nor the Ethics Code resolves an issue, psychologists should consider other professional materials and the dictates of their own conscience, as well as seek consultation with others within the field when this is practical.

The procedures for filing, investigating, and resolving complaints of unethical conduct are described in the current Rules and Procedures of the APA Ethics Committee. The actions that APA may take for violation of the Ethics Code include actions such as reprimand, censure, termination of APA membership, and referral of the matter to other bodies. Complainants who seek remedies such as monetary damages in alleging ethical violations by a psychologist must resort to private negotiation, administrative bodies, or the courts. Actions that violate the Ethics Code may lead to the imposition of sanctions on a psychologist by bodies other than the APA, including state psychological associations, other professional groups, psychology boards, other state or federal agencies, and payers for health services. In addition to actions for violation of the Ethics Code, the APA Bylaws provide that APA may take action against a member after his or her conviction of a felony, expulsions or suspension for an affiliated state psychological association, or suspension or loss of licensure.

This version of the APA Ethics Code was adopted by the American Psychological Association's Council of Representatives during its meeting, August 13 and 16, 1992, and is effective beginning December 1, 1992. Inquiries concerning the substance or interpretation of the APA Ethics Code should be addressed to the Director, Office of Ethics, American Psychological Association, 750 First Street, NE, Washington, DC 2002-4242.

This Code will be used to adjudicate complaints brought concerning alleged conduct occurring on or after the effective date. Complaints regarding conduct occurring prior to the effective date will be adjudicated on the basis of the version of the Code that was in effect at the time the conduct occurred, except that no provisions repealed in June 1989, will be enforced, even if an earlier version contains the provision. The Ethics Code will undergo continuing review and study for future revisions; comments on the Code may be sent to the above address.

The APA has previously published its Ethical Standards as follows:

American Psychological Association. (1953). *Ethical standards of psychologists.* Washington, DC.: Author.

American Psychological Association. (1958). Standards of ethical behavior for psychologists. *American Psychologist, 13,* 268-271.

American Psychological Association. (1963). Ethical standards of psychologists. *American Psychologist, 18,* 56-60.

American Psychological Association. (1968). Ethical standards of psychologist. *American Psychologist, 23,* 357-361.

American Psychological Association. (1977, March). Ethical standards of psychologists. *APA Monitor*, pp. 22-23.

American Psychological Association. (1979). *Ethical Standards of Psychologists.* Washington, DC: Author

American Psychological Association. (1981). Ethical principles of psychologists. *American Psychologist, 26*, 633-638.

American Psychological Association. (1990). Ethical principles of psychologists (Amended June 2, 1989). *American Psychologist, 45*, 390-395.

Request copies of the APA's Ethical Principles of Psychologists and Code of Conduct from the APA Order Department, 750 First Street, NE, Washington, DC 20002-4242, or phone (202) 336-5510.

1. Professional materials that are most helpful in this regard are guidelines and standards that have been adopted or endorsed by professional psychological organizations. Such guidelines and standards, whether adopted by the American Psychological Association (APA) or its Divisions, are not enforceable as such by this Ethics Code, but are of educative value to psychologist, courts, and professional bodies. Such materials include, but are not limited to, the APA's *General Guidelines for Providers of Psychological Services* (1987), *Specialty Guidelines for the Delivery of Services by Clinical Psychologists, Counseling Psychologists, Industrial/ Organizational Psychologists, and School Psychologists* (1981), *Guidelines for Computer Based Tests and Interpretations* (1987), *Standards for Educational and Psychological Testing* (1985), *Ethical Principles in the Conduct of Research With Human Participants* (1982), *Guidelines for Ethical Conduct in the Care and Use of Animals* (1986), *Guidelines for Providers of Psychological Service to Ethnic, Linguistic, and Culturally Diverse Populations* (1990), and *Publication Manual of the American Psychological Association* (3$^{rd}$ ed., 1983) Materials not adopted by the APA as a whole include the APA Division 41 (Forensic Psychology)/American Psychology-Law Society's *Specialty Guidelines for Forensic Psychologists* (1991).

## PREAMBLE

Psychologists work to develop a valid and reliable body of scientific knowledge based on research. They may apply that knowledge to human behavior in a variety of contexts. In doing so, they perform many roles, such as researcher, educator, diagnostician, therapist, supervisor, consultant, administrator, social interventionist, and expert witness.

Their goal is to broaden knowledge of behavior and, where appropriate, to apply it pragmatically to improve the condition of both the individual and society. Psychologists respect the central importance of freedom of inquiry and expression in research, teaching, and publication. They also strive to help the public in developing informed judgments and choices concerning human behavior. This Ethics Code provides a common set of values upon which psychologists build their professional and scientific work.

This Code is intended to provide both the general principles and the decision rules to cover most situations encountered by psychologists. It has as its primary goal the welfare and protection of the individuals and groups with whom psychologists work. It is the individual responsibility of each psychologist to aspire to the highest possible standards of conduct. Psychologists respect and protect human and civil rights, and do not knowingly participate in or condone unfair discriminatory practices.

The development of a dynamic set of ethical standards for a psychologist's work-related conduct requires personal commitment to a lifelong effort to act ethically; to encourage ethical behavior by students, supervisees, employees, and colleagues, as appropriate; and to consult with others, as needed, concerning ethical problems. Each psychologist supplements, but does not violate, the Ethics Code's values and rules on the basis of guidance drawn from personal values, culture, and experience.

## GENERAL PRINCIPLES

### Principle A: Competence

Psychologists strive to maintain high standards of competence in their work. They recognize the boundaries of their particular competencies and the limitations of their expertise. They provide only those services and use only those techniques for which they are qualified by education, training, or experience. Psychologist are cognizant of the fact that the competencies required in serving, teaching, and/or studying groups of people vary with the distinctive characteristics of those groups. In those areas in which recognized professional standards do not yet exist, psychologists exercise careful judgment and take appropriate precautions to protect the welfare of those with whom they work. They maintain knowledge of relevant scientific and professional information related to the services they render, and they recognize the need to ongoing education. Psychologists make appropriate use of scientific, professional, technical, and administrative resources.

### Principle B. Integrity

Psychologists seek to promote integrity in the science, teaching, and practice of psychology. In these activities psychologists are honest, fair, and respectful of others. In describing or reporting their qualifications, services, products, fees, research, or teaching, they do not make statements that are false, misleading, or deceptive. Psychologists strive to be aware of their own belief systems, values, needs, and limitations and the effect of these on their work. To the extent feasible, they are performing and to function appropriately in accordance with these roles. Psychologists avoid improper and potentially harmful dual relationships.

## Principle C: Professional and Scientific Responsibility

Psychologists uphold professional standards of conduct, clarify their professional roles and obligations, accept appropriate responsibility for their behavior, and adapt their methods to the needs of different populations. Psychologists consult with, refer to, or cooperate with other professionals and institutions to the extent needed to serve the best interests of their patients, clients, or other recipients of their services.

Psychologists' moral standards and conduct are personal matters to the same degree as is true for any other person, except as psychologists' conduct may compromise their professional responsibilities or reduce the public's trust in psychology and psychologists. Psychologists are concerned about the ethical compliance of their colleagues' scientific and professional conduct. When appropriate, they consult with colleagues in order to prevent or avoid unethical conduct.

## Principle D: Respect for People's Rights and Dignity

Psychologists accord appropriate respect to the fundamental rights, dignity, and worth of all people. They respect the rights of individuals to privacy, confidentiality, self-determination, and autonomy, mindful that legal and other obligations may lead to the inconsistency and conflict with the exercise of these rights. Psychologists are aware of cultural, individual, and role differences, including those due to age, gender, race, ethnicity, national origin, religion, sexual orientation, disability, language, and socioeconomic status.

Psychologists try to eliminate the effect on their work of biases based on those factors, and they do not knowingly participate in or condone unfair discriminatory practices.

## Principle E: Concern for Others' Welfare

Psychologists seek to contribute to the welfare of those with whom they interact professionally. In their professional actions, psychologists weigh the welfare and rights of their patients or clients, students, supervisees, human research participants, and other affected persons, and the welfare of animal subjects of research. When conflicts occur among psychologists' obligations or concerns, they attempt to resolve these conflicts and to perform their roles in a responsible fashion that avoids or minimizes harm. Psychologists are sensitive to real and ascribed differences in power between themselves and others, and they do not exploit or mislead other people during or after professional relationships.

## Principle F: Social Responsibility

Psychologists are aware of their professional and scientific responsibilities to the community and the society in which they work and live. They apply and make public their knowledge of psychology in order to contribute to human welfare. Psychologists are concerned about and work to mitigate the causes of human suffering. When undertaking research, they strive to advance human welfare and the science of psychology. Psychologists try to avoid misuse of their word. Psychologists comply with the law and encourage the development of law and social policy that serve the interests of their patients and clients and the public. They are encouraged to contribute a portion of their professional time for little or no personal advantage.

## ETHICAL STANDARDS

## 1. General Standards

These General Standards are potentially applicable to the professional and scientific activities of all psychologists.

*1.01 Applicability of the Ethics Code*
The activity of a psychologist subject to the Ethics Code may be reviewed under these Ethical Standards only if the activity is part of his or her work-related functions or the activity is psychological in nature. Personal activities having no connection to or effect on psychologists' roles are not subject to the Ethics Code.

*1.02 Relationship of Ethics and Law*
If psychologists' ethical responsibilities conflict with law, psychologists make known their commitment to the Ethics Code and take steps to resolve the conflict in a responsible manner.

*1.03 Professional and Scientific Relationship*
Psychologists provide diagnostic, therapeutic, teaching, research, supervisory, consultative, or other psychological services only in the context of a defined professional or scientific relationship or role. (See also Standards 2.01, Evaluation, Diagnosis, and Interventions in Professional Context, and 7.02, Forensic Assessments).

*1.04 Boundaries of Competence*
  (a) Psychologists provide services, teach, and conduct research only within the boundaries of their competence, based on their education, training, supervised experience, or appropriate professional experience.
  (b) Psychologists provide services, teach, or conduct research in new areas or involving new techniques only after first undertaking appropriate study, training, supervision, and/or consultation from persons who are competent in those areas or techniques.

In those emerging areas in which generally recognized standards for preparatory training do not yet exist, psychologists nevertheless take reasonable steps to ensure the competence of their work and to protect patients, clients, students, research participants, and others from harm.

## 1.05 Maintaining Expertise

Psychologists who engage in assessment, therapy, teaching, research, organizational consulting, or other professional activities maintain a reasonable level of awareness of current scientific and professional information in their fields of activity, and undertake ongoing efforts to maintain competence in the skills they use.

## 1.06 Basis for Scientific and Professional Judgments

Psychologists rely on scientifically and professionally derived knowledge when making scientific or professional judgments or when engaging in scholarly or professional endeavors.

## 1.07 Describing the Nature and Results of Psychological Services

(a) When psychologists provide assessment, evaluation, treatment, counseling, supervision, teaching, consultation, research, other psychological services to an individual, a group, or an organization, they provide, using language that is reasonably understandable to the recipient of those services, appropriate information beforehand about the nature of such services and appropriate information later about results and conclusions. (See also Standard 2.09, Explaining Assessment Results.)

(b) If psychologists will be precluded by law or by organizational roles from providing such information to particular individuals or groups, they so inform those individuals or groups at the outset of the service.

## 1.08 Human Differences

Where differences of age, gender, race, ethnicity, national origin, religion, sexual orientation, disability, language, or socioeconomic status significantly affect psychologists' work concerning particular individuals or groups, psychologists obtain the training, experience, consultation, or supervision necessary to ensure the competence of their services, or they make appropriate referrals.

## 1.09 Respecting Others

In their work-related activities, psychologists respect the rights of others to hold values, attitudes, and opinions that differ from their own.

## 1.10 Nondiscrimination

In their work-related activities, psychologists do not engage in unfair discrimination based on age, gender, race, ethnicity, national origin, religion, sexual orientation, disability, socioeconomic status, or any basis proscribed by law.

### 1.11 Sexual Harassment

(a) Psychologists do not engage in sexual harassment. Sexual harassment is sexual solicitation, physical advances, or verbal or nonverbal conduct that is sexual in nature, that occurs in connection with the psychologist's activities or roles as a psychologist, and that either (l) is unwelcome, is offensive, or creates a hostile workplace environment, and the psychologist knows or is told this; or (2) is sufficiently severe or intense to be abusive to a reasonable person in the context. Sexual harassment can consist of a single intense or severe act or of multiple persistent or pervasive acts.

(b) Psychologists accord sexual-harassment complainants and respondents dignity and respect. Psychologists do not participate in denying a person academic admittance or advancement, employment, tenure, promotion, based solely upon their having made, or their being the subject of, sexual harassment charges. This does not preclude taking action based upon the outcome of such proceedings or consideration of other appropriate information.

### 1.12 Other Harassment

Psychologists do not knowingly engage in behavior that is harassing or demeaning to persons with whom they interact in their work based on factors such as those persons' age, gender, race, ethnicity, national origin, religion, sexual orientation, disability, language, or socioeconomic status.

### 1.13 Personal Problems and Conflicts

(a) Psychologists recognize that their personal problems and conflicts may interfere with their effectiveness. Accordingly, they refrain from undertaking an activity when they know or should know that their personal problems are likely to lead to harm to a patient, client, colleague, student, research participant, or other person to whom they may owe a professional or scientific obligation.

(b) In addition, psychologists have an obligation to be alert to signs of, and to obtain assistance for, their personal problems at an early stage, in order to prevent significantly impaired performance.

When psychologists become aware of personal problems that may interfere with their performing work-related duties adequately, they take appropriate measures such as obtaining professional consultation or assistance, and determine whether they should limit, suspend, or terminate their work-related duties.

### 1.14 Avoiding Harm

Psychologists take reasonable steps to avoid harming their patients or clients, research participants, students and others with whom they work and to minimize harm where it is unforeseeable and unavoidable.

*1.15 Misuse of Psychologists' Influence*
Because psychologists' scientific and professional judgments and actions may affect the lives of others, they are alert to and guard against personal, financial, social, organizational, or political factors that might lead to misuse of their influence.

*1.16 Misuse of Psychologists' Work*
Psychologists do not participate in activities in which it appears likely that their skills or data will be misused by others, unless corrective mechanisms are available. (See also Standard 7.04, Truthfulness and Candor).

   If psychologists learn of misuse or misrepresentation of their work, they take reasonable steps to correct or minimize the misuse or misrepresentation.

*1.17 Multiple Relationships*
In many communities and situations, it may not be feasible or reasonable for psychologists to avoid social or other nonprofessional contacts with persons such as patients, clients, students, supervisees, or research participants.

   Psychologists must always be sensitive to the potential harmful effects of other contacts on their work and on those persons with whom they deal. A psychologist refrains from entering into or promising another personal, scientific, professional, financial, or other relationship with such persons if it appears likely that such a relationship reasonably might impair the psychologist's objectivity or otherwise interfere with the psychologist's effectively performing his or her functions as a psychologist, or might harm or exploit the other party.

   Likewise, whenever feasible, a psychologist refrains from taking on professional or scientific obligations when preexisting relationships would create a risk of such harm.

   If a psychologist finds that, due to unforeseen factors, a potentially harmful multiple relationship has arisen, the psychologist attempts to resolve it with due regard for the best interests of the affected person and maximal compliance with the Ethics Code.

*1.18 Barter (With Patients or Clients)*
Psychologists ordinarily refrain from accepting goods, services, or other non-monetary remuneration from patients in return for psychological services because such can create inherent potential for conflicts, exploitation, and distortion of the professional relationship. A psychologist may participate in bartering only if (1) it is not clinically contraindicated, and (2) the relationship is not exploitative. (See also Standards 1.17, Multiple Relationships, and 1.25, Fees and Financial Arrangements.)

*1.19 Exploitative Relationships*
(a) Psychologists do not exploit persons over whom they have supervisory, evaluative, or other authority such as students, supervisees, employees, research participants, and clients or patients. (See also Standards 4.05-4.07 regarding sexual involvement with clients or patients.)

(b) Psychologists do not engage in sexual relationships with students or supervisees in training over whom the psychologist has evaluative or direct authority, because such relationships are so likely to impair judgment or be exploitative.

### 1.20 Consultations and Referrals

(a) Psychologists arrange for appropriate consultations and referrals based principally on the best interests of their patients or clients, with appropriate consent, and subject to other relevant considerations, including applicable law and contractual obligations. (See also Standards 5.01, Discussing the Limits of Confidentiality, and 5.06, Consultations.)

(b) When indicated and professionally appropriate, psychologists cooperate with other professionals in order to serve their patients or clients effectively and appropriately.

Psychologists' referral practices are consistent with law.

### 1.21 Third-Party Requests for Services

(a) When a psychologist agrees to provide services to a person or entity at the request of a third party, the psychologist clarifies to the extent feasible, at the outset of the service, the nature of the relationship with each party. This clarification includes the role of the psychologist (such as therapist, organizational consultant, diagnostician, or expert witness), the probable uses of the services provided or the information obtained, and the fact that there may be limits to confidentiality.

(b) If there is a foreseeable risk of the psychologist's being called upon to perform conflicting roles because of the involvement of a third party, the psychologist clarifies the nature and direction of his or her responsibilities, keeps all parties appropriately informed as matters develop, and resolves the situation in accordance with this Ethics Code.

### 1.22 Delegation to and Supervision of Subordinates

(a) Psychologists delegate to their employees, supervisees, and research assistants only those responsibilities that such persons can reasonably be expected to perform competently, on the basis of their education, training, or experience, either independently or with the level of supervision being provided.

(b) Psychologists provide proper training and supervision to their employees or supervisees and take reasonable steps to see that such persons perform services responsibly, competently, and ethically.

If institutional policies, procedures, or practices prevent fulfillment of this obligation, psychologists attempt to modify their role or to correct the situation to the extent feasible.

*1.23 Documentation of Professional and Scientific Work*

(a) Psychologists appropriately document their professional and scientific work in order to facilitate provision of services later by them or by other professionals, to ensure accountability, and to meet other requirements of institutions or the law.

(b) When psychologists have reason to believe that records of their professional services will be used in legal proceedings involving recipients of or participants in their work, they have a responsibility to create and maintain documentation in the kind of detail and quality that would be consistent with reasonable scrutiny in an adjudicative forum. (See also Standard 7.01, Professionalism, under Forensic Activities.)

*1.24 Records and Data*

Psychologists create, maintain, disseminate, store, retain, and dispose of records and data relating to their research, practice, and other work in accordance with law and in a manner that permits compliance with the requirements of this Ethics Code. (See also Standard 5.04, Maintenance of Records.)

*1.25 Fees and Financial Arrangements*

(a) As early as is feasible in a professional or scientific relationship, the psychologist and the patient, client, or other appropriate recipient of psychological services reach an agreement specifying the compensation and the billing arrangements.

(b) Psychologists do not exploit recipients of services or payers with respect to fees.

(c) Psychologists' fee practices are consistent with law.

(d) Psychologists do not misrepresent their fees.

(e) If limitations to services can be anticipated because of limitations in financing, this is discussed with the patient, client, or other appropriate recipient of services as early as is feasible. (See also Standard 4.08, Interruption of Services.)

(f) If the patient, client, or other recipient of services does not pay for services as agreed, and if the psychologist wishes to use collection agencies or legal measures to collect the fees, the psychologist first informs the person that such measures will be taken and provides that person an opportunity to make prompt payment. (See also Standard 5.11, Withholding Records for Nonpayment.)

*1.26 Accuracy in Reports to Payers and Funding Sources*

In their reports to payers for services or sources of research funding, psychologists accurately state the nature of the research or service provided, the fees or charges, and where applicable, the identity of the provider, the findings, and the diagnosis. (See also Standard 5.05, Disclosures.)

*1.27 Referrals and Fees*
When a psychologist pays, receives payment from, or divides fees with another professional other than in an employer-employee relationship, the payment to each is based on the services (clinical, consultative, administrative, or other) provided and is not based on the referral itself.

## 2. Evaluation, Assessment, or Intervention

*2.01 Evaluation, Diagnosis, and Interventions in Professional Context*
(a) Psychologists perform evaluations, diagnostic services, or interventions only within the context of a defined professional relationship. (See also Standard 1.03, Professional and Scientific Relationship.)

(b) Psychologists' assessments, recommendations, reports, and psychological diagnostic or evaluative statements are based on information and techniques (including personal interviews of the individual when appropriate) sufficient to provide appropriate substantiation for their findings. (See also Standard 7.02, Forensic Assessment.)

*2.02 Competence and Appropriate Use of Assessments and Interventions*
(a) Psychologists who develop, administer, score, interpret, or use psychological assessment techniques, interviews, tests, or instruments do so in a manner and for purposes that are appropriate in light of the research on or evidence of the usefulness and proper application of the techniques.

(b) Psychologists refrain from misuse of assessment techniques, interventions, results, and interpretations, and take reasonable steps to prevent others from misusing the information these techniques provide. This includes refraining from releasing raw test results or raw cats to persons, other than to patients or clients as appropriate, who are not qualified to use such information. (See also Standards 1.02, Relationship of Ethics and Law, and 1.04, Boundaries of Competence.)

*2.02 Competence and Appropriate Use of Assessments and Interventions*
(a) Psychologists who develop, administer, score, interpret, or use psychological assessment techniques, interviews, tests, or instruments, do so in a manner and for purposes that are appropriate in light of the research on or evidence of the usefulness and proper application of the techniques.

(b) Psychologists refrain from misuse of assessment techniques, interventions, results, and interpretations and take reasonable steps to prevents others from misusing the information these techniques provide. This includes refraining from releasing raw test results or raw data to persons, other than to patients or clients as appropriate, who are not qualified to use such information. (See also Standards 1.02, Relationship of Ethics and Law, and 1.04, Boundaries of Competence.)

*2.03 Test Construction*
Psychologists who develop and conduct research with tests and other assessment techniques use scientific procedures and current professional knowledge for test design, standardization, validation, reduction or elimination of bias, and recommendations for use.

*2.04 Use of Assessment in General and with Special Populations*
Psychologists who perform interventions or administer, score, interpret, or use assessment techniques are familiar with the reliability, validation, and related standardization or outcome studies of, and proper applications and uses of, the techniques they use.

Psychologists recognize limits to the certainty with which diagnoses, judgments, or predictions can be made about individuals.

Psychologists attempt to identify situations in which particular interventions or assessment techniques or norms may not be applicable or may require adjustment in administration or interpretation because of factors such as individuals' gender, age, race, ethnicity, national origin, religion, sexual orientation, disability, language, or socioeconomic status.

*2.05 Interpreting Assessment Results*
When interpreting assessment results, including automated interpretations, psychologists take into account the various test factors and characteristics of the person being assessed that might affect psychologists' judgments or reduce the accuracy of their interpretations. They indicate any significant reservations they have about the accuracy or limitations of their interpretations.

*2.06 Unqualified Persons*
Psychologists do not promote the use of psychological assessment techniques by unqualified persons. (See also Standard 1.22, Delegation to and Supervision of Subordinates.)

*2.07 Obsolete Tests and Outdated Test Results*
Psychologists do not base their assessment or intervention decisions or recommendations on data or test results that are outdated for the current purpose.

Similarly, psychologists do not base such decisions or recommendations on tests and measures that are obsolete and not useful for the current purpose.

*2.08 Test Scoring and Interpretation Services*
(a) Psychologists who offer assessment or scoring procedures to other professionals accurately describe the purpose, norms, validity, reliability, and applications of the procedures and any special qualifications applicable to their use.

(b) Psychologists select scoring and interpretation services (including automated services) on the basis of evidence of the validity of the program and procedures as well as on other appropriate considerations.

(c) Psychologists retain appropriate responsibility for the appropriate application, interpretation, and use of assessment instruments, whether they score and interpret such tests themselves or use automated or other services.

*2.09 Explaining Assessment Results*
Unless the nature of the relationship is clearly explained to the person being assessed in advance and precludes provision of an explanation of results (such as in some organizational consulting, preemployment or security screenings, and forensic evaluations), psychologists ensure that an explanation of the results is provided using language that is reasonably understandable to the person assessed or to another legally authorized person on behalf of the client. Regardless of whether the scoring and interpretation are done by the psychologist, by assistants, or by automated or other outside services, psychologists take reasonable steps to ensure that appropriate explanations of results are given.

*2.10 Maintaining Test Security*
Psychologists make reasonable efforts to maintain the integrity and security of tests and other assessment techniques consistent with law, contractual obligations, and in a manner that permits compliance with the requirements of this Ethics Code. (See also Standard 1.02, Relationship of Ethics and Law.)

## 3. Advertising and Other Public Statements

*3.01 Definition of Public Statements*
Psychologists comply with this Ethics Code in public statements relating to their professional services, products, or publications or to the field of psychology. Public statements include but are not limited to paid or unpaid advertising brochures, printed matter, directory listings, personal resumes or curricula vitae, interviews, or comments for use in media, statements in legal proceedings, lectures and public oral presentations, and published materials.

*3.02 Statements by Others*
(a) Psychologists who engage others to create or place public statements that promote their professional practice, products, or activities retain professional responsibility for such statements.
(b) In addition, psychologists make reasonable efforts to prevent others whom they do not control (such as employees, publishers, sponsors, organizational clients, and representatives of the print or broadcast media) from making deceptive comments concerning psychologists' practice or professional or scientific activities.
(c) If psychologists learn of deceptive statements about their work made by others, psychologists make reasonable efforts to correct such statements.

(d) Psychologists do not compensate employees of press, radio, television, or other communication media in return for publicity in a news item.

A paid advertisement relating to the psychologist's activities must be identified as such, unless it is already apparent from the context.

### 3.03 Avoidance of False or Deceptive Statements

Psychologists do not make public statements that are false, deceptive, misleading, or fraudulent, either because of what they state, convey, or suggest or because of what they omit, concerning their research, practice, or other work activities or those of persons or organizations with which they are affiliated.

As examples (and not in limitation) of this standard, psychologists do not make false or deceptive statements concerning (1) their training, experience, or competence; (2) their academic degrees; (3) their credentials; (4) their institutional or association affiliations; (5) their services; (6) the scientific or clinical basis for, or results or degree of success of, their services; (7) their fees; or (8) their publications or research findings. (See also Standards 6.1S, Deception in Research, and 6.18, Providing Participants with Information about the Study.)

Psychologists claim as credentials for their psychological work, only degrees that (1) were earned from a regionally accredited educational institution or (2) were the basis for psychology licensure by the state in which they practice.

### 3.04 Media Presentations

When psychologists provide advice or comment by means of public lectures, demonstrations, radio or television programs, prerecorded tapes, printed articles, mailed material, or other media, they take reasonable precautions to ensure that (1) the statements are based on appropriate psychological literature and practice, (2) the statements are otherwise consistent with this Ethics Code, and (3) the recipients of the information are not encouraged to infer that a relationship has been established with them personally.

### 3.05 Testimonials

Psychologists do not solicit testimonials from current psychotherapy clients or patients or other persons who because of their particular circumstances are vulnerable to undue influence.

### 3.06 In-Person Solicitation

Psychologists do not engage, directly, or through agents, in uninvited in-person solicitation of business from actual or potential psychotherapy patients or clients or other persons who because of their particular circumstances are vulnerable to undue influence. However, this does not preclude attempting to implement appropriate collateral contacts with significant others for the purpose of benefiting an already engaged therapy patient.

## 4. Therapy

*4.01 Structuring the Relationship*
 (a) Psychologists discuss with clients or patients as early as is feasible in the therapeutic relationship appropriate issues, such as the nature and anticipated course of therapy, fees, and confidentiality. (See also Standards 1.25, Fees and Financial Arrangements, and 5.01, Discussing the Limits of Confidentiality.)

 (b) When the psychologist's work with clients or patients will be supervised, the above discussion includes that fact and the name of the supervisor, when the supervisor has legal responsibility for the case.

 (c) When the therapist is a student intern, the client or patient is informed of that fact.

 (d) Psychologists make reasonable efforts to answer patients' questions and to avoid apparent misunderstandings about therapy. Whenever possible, psychologists provide oral and/or written information, using language that is reasonably understandable to the patient or client.

*4.02 Informed Consent to Therapy*
 (a) Psychologists obtain appropriate informed consent to therapy or related procedures, using language that is reasonably understandable to participants. The content of informed consent will vary depending on many circumstances; however, informed consent generally implies that the person (1) has the capacity to consent, (2) has been informed of significant information concerning the procedure, (3) has freely and without undue influence expressed consent, and (4) consent has been appropriately documented.

 (b) When persons are legally incapable of giving informed consent, psychologists obtain informed permission from a legally authorized person, if such substitute consent is permitted by law.

   In addition, psychologists ( 1) inform those persons who are legally incapable of giving informed consent about the proposed interventions in a manner commensurate with the persons' psychological capacities, (2) seek their assent to those interventions, and (3) consider such persons' preferences and best interests.

*4.03 Couple and Family Relationships*
When a psychologist agrees to provide services to several persons who have a relationship (such as husband and wife or parents and children), the psychologist attempts to clarify at the outset (1) which of the individuals are patients or clients and (2) the relationship the psychologist will have with each person. This clarification includes the role of the psychologist and the probable uses of the services provided or the information obtained. (See also Standard 5.01, Discussing the Limits of Confidentiality.)

As soon as it becomes apparent that the psychologist may be called on to perform potentially conflicting roles (such as marital counselor to husband and wife, and then witness for one party in a divorce proceeding), the psychologist attempts to clarify and adjust, or withdraw from, jobs appropriately. (See also Standard 7.03, Clarification of Role, under Forensic Activities.)

### 4.04 Providing Mental Health Services to Those Served by Others

In deciding whether to offer or provide services to those already receiving mental health services elsewhere, psychologists carefully consider the treatment issues and the potential patient's or client's welfare. The psychologist discusses these issues with the patient or client, or another legally authorized person on behalf of the client, in order to minimize the risk of confusion and conflict, consults with the other service providers when appropriate, and proceeds with caution and sensitivity to the therapeutic issues.

### 4.05 Sexual Intimacies with Current Patients or Clients

Psychologists do not engage in sexual intimacies with current patients or clients.

### 4.06 Therapy with Former Sexual Partners

Psychologists do not accept as therapy patents or clients persons with whom they have engaged sexual intimacies.

### 4.07 Sexual Intimacies with Former Therapy Patients

(a) Psychologists do not engage in sexual intimacies with a former therapy patient or client for at least two years after cessation or termination of professional services.

(b) Because sexual intimacies with a former therapy patient or client are so frequently harmful to the patient or client, and because such intimacies undermine public confidence in the psychology profession and thereby deter the public's use of needed services, psychologists do not engage in sexual intimacies with former therapy patients and clients even after a two-year interval except in the most unusual circumstances. The psychologist who engages in such activity after the two years following cessation or termination of treatment bears the burden of demonstrating that there has been no exploitation, in light of all relevant factors, including (1) the amount of time that has passed since therapy terminated, (2) the nature and duration of the therapy, (3) the circumstances of termination, (4) the patient's or clients personal history, (5) the patient's or client's current mental status, (6) the likelihood of adverse impact on the patient or client and others, and (7) any statements or actions made by the therapist during the course of therapy suggesting or inviting the possibility of posttermination sexual or romantic relationship with patient or client. (See also Standard 1.17, Multiple Relationships.)

### 5.07 Confidential Information in Databases

If confidential information concerning recipients of psychological services is to be entered into databases or systems of records available to persons whose access has not been consented to by the recipient, then psychologists use coding or other techniques to avoid the inclusion of personal identifiers.

If a research protocol approved by an institutional review board or similar body requires the inclusion of personal identifiers, such identifiers are deleted before the information is made accessible to persons other than those of whom the subject was advised. If such deletion is not feasible, then before psychologists transfer such data to others or review such data collected by others, they take reasonable steps to determine that appropriate consent of personally identifiable individuals has been obtained.

### 5.08 Use of Confidential Information for Didactic or Other Purposes

Psychologists do not disclose in their writings, lectures, or other public media, confidential, personally identifiable information concerning their patients, individual or organizational clients, students, research participants, or other recipients of their services that they obtained during the course of their work, unless the person or organization has consented in writing or unless there is other ethical or legal authorization for doing so.

Ordinarily, in such scientific and professional presentations, psychologists disguise confidential information concerning such persons or organizations so that they are not individually identifiable to others and so that discussions do not cause harm to subjects who might identify themselves.

### 5.09 Preserving Records and Data

A psychologist makes plans in advance so that confidentiality of records and data is protected in the event of the psychologist's death, incapacity, or withdrawal from the position or practice.

### 5.10 Ownership of Records and Data

Recognizing that ownership of records and data is governed by legal principles, psychologists take reasonable and lawful steps so that records and data remain available to the extent needed to serve the best interests of patients, individual or organizational clients, research participants, or appropriate others.

### 5.11 Withholding Records for Nonpayment

Psychologists may not withhold records under their control that are requested and imminently needed for a patient's or client's treatment solely because payment had not been received, except as otherwise provided by law.

## 6. Teaching, Training, Supervision, Research, and Publishing

### 6.01 Design of Education and Training Programs

Psychologists who are responsible for education and training programs seek to ensure that the programs are competently designed, provide the proper experiences, and meet the requirements for licensure, certification, or other goals for which claims are made by the program.

### 6.02 Descriptions of Education and Training Programs
Psychologists responsible for education and training programs seek to ensure that there is a current and accurate description of the program content, timing goals and objectives, and requirements that must be met for satisfactory completion of the program. This information must be made readily available to all interested parties.

Psychologists seek to ensure that statements concerning their course outlines are accurate and not misleading, particularly regarding the subject matter to be covered, bases for evaluating progress, and the nature of course experiences. (See also Standard 3.03, Avoidance of False or Deceptive Statements.) To the degree to which they exercise control, psychologists responsible for announcements, catalogs, brochures, or advertisements describing workshops, seminars, or other non-degree-granting educational programs ensure that they accurately describe the audience for which the program is intended, the educational objectives, the presenters, and the fees involved.

### 6.03 Accuracy and Objectivity in Teaching
When engaged in teaching or training, psychologists present psychological information accurately and with a reasonable degree of objectivity. When engaged in teaching or training, psychologists recognize the power they hold over students or supervisees and therefore make reasonable efforts to avoid engaging in conduct that is personally demeaning to students or supervisees. (See also Standards 1.09, Respecting Others, and 1.12, Other Harassment.)

### 6.04 Limitation on Teaching
Psychologists do not teach the use of techniques or procedures that require specialized training, licensure, or expertise, including but not limited to hypnosis, biofeedback, and projective techniques, to individuals who lack the prerequisite training, legal scope of practice, or expertise.

### 6.05 Assessing Student and Supervisee Performance
In academic and supervisory relationships, psychologists establish an appropriate process for providing feedback to students and supervisees. Psychologists evaluate students and supervisees on the basis of their actual performance on relevant and established program requirements.

### 6.06 Planning Research
Psychologists design, conduct, and report research in accordance with recognized standards of scientific competence and ethical research.

Psychologists plan their research so as to minimize the possibility that results will be misleading.

In planning research, psychologists consider their research's ethical accept-
ability under the Ethics Code. If an ethical issue is unclear, psychologists seek
to resolve the issue through consultation with institutional review boards, animal care and use committees, peer consultations, or other proper mechanisms.

Psychologists take reasonable steps to implement appropriate protections
for the rights and welfare of human participants, other persons affected by the
research, and the welfare of animal subjects.

*6.07 Responsibility*
Psychologists conduct research competently and with due concern for the dignity and welfare of the participants.

Psychologists are responsible for the ethical conduct of research conducted
by them or by others under their supervision or control.

Researchers and assistants are permitted to perform only those tasks for
which they are appropriately trained and prepared.

As part of the process of development and implementation of research projects, psychologists consult those with expertise concerning any special population under investigation or most likely to be affected.

*6.08 Compliance with Law and Standards*
Psychologists plan and conduct research in a manner consistent with federal
and state law and regulations, as well as professional standards governing the
conduct of research, and particularly those standards governing research with
human participants and animal subjects.

*6.09 Institutional Approval*
Psychologists obtain from host institutions or organizations appropriate
approval prior to conducting research , and they provide accurate information
about their research proposals. They conduct the research in accordance with
the approved research protocol.

*6.10 Research Responsibilities*
Prior to conducting research (except research involving only anonymous sur-
veys, naturalistic observations, or similar research), psychologists enter into an
agreement with participants that clarifies the nature of the research and the
responsibilities of each party.

*6.11 Informed Consent to Research*
Psychologists use language that is reasonable and understandable to research
participants in obtaining their appropriate informed consent (except as provided
in Standard 6.12, Dispensing with Informed Consent). Such informed consent is
appropriately documented.) Using language that is reasonably understandable
to participants, psychologists inform participants of the nature of the research;
they inform participants that they are free to participate or to decline to participate or to withdraw from the research; they explain the foreseeable conse-

quences of declining or withdrawing; they inform participants of significant factors that may be expected to influence their willingness to participate (such as risks, discomfort, adverse effects, or limitations on confidentiality, except as provided in Standard 6.15, Deception in Research); and they explain other aspects about which the prospective participants inquire.

When psychologists conduct research with individuals such as students or subordinates, psychologists take special care to protect the prospective participant from adverse consequences of declining or withdrawing from participation. When research participation is a course requirement or opportunity for extra credit, the prospective participant is given the choice of equitable alternative activities. For persons who are legally incapable of giving informed consent, psychologists nevertheless (1) provide an appropriate explanation, (2) obtain the participant's consent, and (3) obtain appropriate permission from a legally authorized person, if such substitute consent is permitted by law.

### 6.12 Dispensing with Informed Consent
Before determining that planned research (such as research involving only anonymous questionnaires, naturalistic observations, or certain kinds of archival research) does not require the informed consent of research participants, psychologists consider applicable regulations and institutional review board requirements, and they consult with colleagues as appropriate.

### 6.13 Informed Consent in Research Filming or Recording
Psychologists obtain informed consent from research participants prior to filming or recording them in any form, unless the research involves simply naturalistic observations in public places and it is not anticipated that the recording will be used in a manner that could cause personal identification or harm.

### 6.14 Offering Inducements for Research Participants
In offering professional services as inducement to obtain research participants, psychologists must make clear the nature of the services, as well as the risks, obligations, and limitations. (See also Standard 1.18, Barter [with Patients or Clients].) Psychologists do not offer excessive or inappropriate financial or other inducements to obtain research participants, particularly when it might tend to coerce participation.

### 6.15 Deception in Research
Psychologists do not conduct a study involving deception unless they have determined that the use of deceptive techniques is justified by the study's prospective scientific, educational, or applied value and that equally effective alternative procedures that do not use deception are not feasible.

Psychologists never deceive research participants about significant aspects that would affect their willingness to participate, such as physical risks, discomfort, or unpleasant emotional experiences.

Any other deception that is an integral feature of the design and conduct of an experiment must be explained to participants as early as is feasible, preferably at the conclusion of their participation, but no later than at the conclusion of the research. (See also Standard 6.18, Providing Participants with Information about the Study.)

*6.16 Sharing and Utilizing Data*
Psychologists inform research participants of their anticipated sharing or further use of personally identifiable research data and of the possibility of unanticipated future uses.

*6.17 Minimizing Invasiveness*
In conducting research, psychologists interfere with the participants or milieu from which data are collected only in a manner that is warranted by an appropriate research design and that is consistent with psychologists' roles as scientific investigators.

*6.18 Providing Participants with Information about the Study*
Psychologists provide a prompt opportunity for participants to obtain appropriate information about the name, results, and conclusions of the research, and psychologists attempt to correct any misconceptions that participants may have.

If scientific or humane values justify delaying or withholding this information, psychologists take reasonable measures to reduce the risk of harm.

*6.19 Honoring Commitments*
Psychologists take reasonable measures to honor all commitments they have made to research participants.

*6.20 Care and Use of Animals in Research*
Psychologists who conduct research involving animals treat them humanely.

Psychologists acquire, care for, use, and dispose of animals in compliance with current federal, state, and local laws and regulations, and with professional standards.

Psychologists trained in research methods and experienced in the care of laboratory animals supervise all procedures involving animals and are responsible for ensuring appropriate consideration of their comfort, health, and humane treatment.

Psychologists ensure that all individuals using animals under their supervision have received instruction in research methods and in the care, maintenance, and handling of the species being used, to the extent appropriate to their role.

Responsibilities and activities of the individuals assisting in a research project are consistent with their respective competencies.

Psychologists make reasonable efforts to minimize the discomfort, infection, illness, and pain of animal subjects.

A procedure subjecting animals to pain, stress, or privation is used only when an alternative procedure is unavailable and the goal is justified by its prospective scientific, educational, or applied value.

Surgical procedures are performed under appropriate anesthesia; techniques to avoid infection and minimize pain are followed during and after surgery.

When it is appropriate that the animal's life be terminated, it is done rapidly, with an effort to minimize pain, and in accordance with accepted procedures.

### 6.21 Reporting of Results

Psychologists do not fabricate data or falsify results in their publications.

If psychologists discover significant errors in their published data, they take reasonable steps to correct such errors in a correction, retraction, erratum, or other appropriate publication means.

### 6.22 Plagiarism

Psychologists do not present substantial portions or cements of another's work or data as their own, even if the other work or data source is cited occasionally.

### 6.23 Publication Credit

Psychologists take responsibility and credit, including authorship credit, only for work they have actually performed or to which they have contributed.

Principal authorship and other publication credits accurately reflect the relative scientific or professional contributions of the individuals involved, regardless of their relative status. Mere possession of an institutional position, such as Department Chair, does not justify authorship credit. Minor contributions to the research or to the writing for publications are appropriately acknowledged, such as in footnotes or in an introductory statement.

A student is usually listed as principal author on any multiple-authored article that is substantially based on the student's dissertation or thesis.

### 6.24 Duplicate Publication of Data

Psychologists do not publish, as original data, data that have been previously published. This does not preclude republishing data when they are accompanied by proper acknowledgment.

### 6.25 Sharing Data

After research results are published, psychologists do not withhold the data on which their conclusions are based from other competent professionals who seek to verify the substantive claims through reanalysis and who intend to use such data only for that purpose, provided that the confidentiality of the participants can be protected and unless legal rights concerning proprietary data preclude their release.

*6.26 Professional Reviewers*
Psychologists who review material submitted for publication, grant, or other research proposal review, respect the confidentiality of and the proprietary rights in such information of those who submitted it.

## 7. Forensic Activities

*7.01 Professionalism*
Psychologists who perform forensic functions, such as assessments, interviews, consultations, reports, or expert testimony, must comply with all the provisions of this Ethics Code to the extent that they apply to such activities. In addition, psychologists base their forensic work on appropriate knowledge of and competence in the areas underlying such work, including specialized knowledge concerning special populations. (See also Standards 1.06, Basis for Scientific and Professional Judgments; 1.08, Human Differences; 1.15, Misuse of Psychologists' Influence; and 1.23, Documentation of Professional and Scientific Work.)

*7.02 Forensic Assessment*
(a) Psychologists' forensic assessments, recommendations, and reports are based on information and techniques (including personal interviews of the individual, when appropriate) sufficient to provide appropriate substantiation for their findings. (See also Standards 1.03, Professional and Scientific Relationship; 1.23, Documentation of Professional and Scientific Work; 2.01, Evaluation, Diagnosis, and Interventions in Professional Context; and 2.05, Interpreting Assessment Results.)

(b) Except as noted in (c), below, psychologists provide written or oral forensic reports or testimony of the psychological characteristics of an individual only after they have conducted an examination of the individual adequate to support their statements or conclusions.

(c) When, despite reasonable efforts, such an examination is not feasible, psychologists clarify the impact of their limited information on the reliability and validity of their reports and testimony, and they appropriately limit the nature and extent of their conclusions or recommendations.

*7.03 Clarification of Role*
In most circumstances, psychologists avoid performing multiple and potentially conflicting roles in forensic matters. When psychologists may be called on to serve in more than one role in a legal proceeding—for example, as consultant or expert for one party or for the court and a fact witness—they clarify role expectations and the extent of confidentiality in advance to the extent feasible, and thereafter as changes occur, in order to avoid compromising their professional judgment and objectivity and in order to avoid misleading others regarding their role.

*7.04 Truthfulness and Candor*

(a) In forensic testimony and reports, psychologists testify truthfully, honesty, and candidly and, consistent with applicable legal procedures, describe fairly the bases for their testimony and conclusions.

(b) Whenever necessary to avoid misleading, psychologists acknowledge the limit of their data or conclusions.

*7.05 Prior Relationships*

A prior professional relationship with a party does not preclude psychologists from testifying as fact witnesses or from testifying to their services to the extent permitted by applicable law. Psychologists appropriately take into account ways in which the prior relationship might affect their professional objectivity or opinions and disclose the potential conflict to the relevant parties.

*7.06 Compliance with Law and Rules*

In performing forensic roles, psychologists are reasonably familiar with the rules governing their roles. Psychologists are aware of the occasionally competing demands placed upon them by these principles and the requirements of the court system, and attempt to resolve these conflicts by making known their commitment to this Ethics Code and taking steps to resolve the conflict in a responsible manner. (See also Standard 1.02, Relationship of Ethics and Law.)

## 8. Resolving Ethical Issues

*8.01 Familiarity with Ethics Code*

Psychologists have an obligation to be familiar with this Ethics Code, other applicable codes, and their application to psychologists' work. Lack of awareness or misunderstanding of an ethical standard is not itself a defense to a charge of unethical conduct.

*8.02 Confronting Ethical Issues*

When a psychologist is uncertain whether a particular situation or course of action would violate this Ethics Code, the psychologist ordinarily consults with other psychologists knowledgeable about ethical issues, with state or national psychology ethics committees, or with other appropriate authorities in order to choose a proper response.

*8.03 Conflicts between Ethics and Organizational Demands*

If the demands of an organization with which psychologists are affiliated conflict with this Ethics Code, psychologists clarify the nature of the conflict, make known their commitment to the Ethics Code, and to the extent feasible, seek to resolve the conflict in a way that permits the fullest adherence to the Ethics Code.

*8.04 Informal Resolution of Ethical Violations*
When psychologists believe that there may have been an ethical violation by another psychologist, they attempt to resolve the issue by bringing it to the attention of that individual if an informal resolution appears appropriate and the intervention does not violate any confidentiality rights that may be involved.

*8.05 Reporting Ethical Violations*
If an apparent ethical violation is not appropriate for informal resolution under Standard 8.04 or is not resolved properly in that fashion, psychologists take further action appropriate to the situation, unless such action conflicts with confidentiality rights in ways that cannot be resolved. Such action might include referral to state or national committees on professional ethics or to state licensing boards.

*8.06 Cooperating with Ethics Committees*
Psychologists cooperate in ethics investigations, proceedings, and resulting requirements of the APA or any affiliated state psychological association to which they belong. In doing so, they make reasonable efforts to resolve any issues as to confidentiality. Failure to cooperate is itself an ethics violation.

*8.07 Improper Complaints*
Psychologists do not file or encourage the filing of ethics complaints that are frivolous and are intended to harm the respondent rather than to protect the public.

# *Ethical Standards of the*
# *American Counseling Association*

## PREAMBLE

The American Counseling Association is an educational, scientific and professional organization whose members are dedicated to the enhancement of human development throughout the life span. Association members recognize diversity in our society and embrace a cross-cultural approach in support of the worth, dignity, potential, and uniqueness of each individual.

The specification of a code of ethics enables the association to clarify to current and future members, and to those served by members, the nature of the ethical responsibilities held in common by its members. As the code of ethics of the association, this document establishes principles that define the ethical behavior of association members. All members of the American Counseling Association are required to adhere to the Code of Ethics and the Standards of Practice. The Code of Ethics will serve as the basis for processing ethical complaints initiated against members of the association.

## SECTION A: THE COUNSELING RELATIONSHIP

### A.1. Client Welfare

*a. Primary Responsibility.*
The primary responsibility of counselors is to respect the dignity and to promote the welfare of clients.

*b. Positive Growth and Development.*
Counselors encourage client growth and development in ways that foster the clients' interest and welfare; counselors avoid fostering dependent counseling relationships.

*c. Counseling Plans.*
Counselors and their clients work jointly in devising integrated, individual counseling plans that offer reasonable promise of success and are consistent with abilities and circumstances of clients. Counselors and clients regularly review counseling plans to ensure their continued viability and effectiveness, respecting clients' freedom of choice. (See A.3.b.)

*d. Family Involvement.*
Counselors recognize that families are usually important in clients' lives and strive to enlist family understanding and involvement as a positive resource, when appropriate.

*e. Career and Employment Needs.*
Counselors work with their clients in considering employment in jobs and circumstances that are consistent with the clients' overall abilities, vocational limitations, physical restrictions, general temperament, interest and aptitude patterns, social skills, education, general qualifications, and other relevant characteristics and needs. Counselors neither place nor participate in placing clients in positions that will result in damaging the interest and the welfare of clients, employers, or the public.

## A.2. Respecting Diversity

*a. Nondiscrimination.*
Counselors do not condone or engage in discrimination based on age, color, culture, disability, ethnic group, gender, race, religion, sexual orientation, marital status, or socioeconomic status. (See C.5.a., C.5.b., and D.1.i.)

*b. Respecting Differences.*
Counselors will actively attempt to understand the diverse cultural backgrounds of the clients with whom they work. This includes, but is not limited to, learning how the counselor's own cultural/ethnic/racial identity impacts her/his values and beliefs about the counseling process. (See E.8. and F.2.i.)

## A.3. Client Rights

*a. Disclosure to Clients.*
When counseling is initiated, and throughout the counseling process as necessary, counselors inform clients of the purposes, goals, techniques, procedures, limitations, potential risks and benefits of services to be performed, and other pertinent information. Counselors take steps to ensure that clients understand the implications of diagnosis, the intended use of tests and reports, fees, and billing arrangements. Clients have the right to expect confidentiality and to be provided with an explanation of its limitations, including supervision and/or treatment team professionals; to obtain clear information about their case records; to participate in the ongoing counseling plans; and to refuse any recommended services and be advised of the consequences of such refusal. (See E.5.a. and G.2.)

*b. Freedom of Choice.*
Counselors offer clients the freedom to choose whether to enter into a counseling relationship and to determine which professional(s) will provide counseling. Restrictions that limit choices of clients are fully explained. (See A.1.c.)

*c. Inability to Give Consent.*
When counseling minors or persons unable to give voluntary informed consent, counselors act in these clients' best interests. (See B.3.)

## A.4. Clients Served by Others

If a client is receiving services from another mental health professional, counselors, with client consent, inform the professional persons already involved and develop clear agreements to avoid confusion and conflict for the client. (See C.6.c.)

## A.5. Personal Needs and Values

*a. Personal Needs.*
In the counseling relationship, counselors are aware of the intimacy and responsibilities inherent in the counseling relationship, maintain respect for clients, and avoid actions that seek to meet their personal needs at the expense of clients.

*b. Personal Values.*
Counselors are aware of their own values, attitudes, beliefs, and behaviors and how these apply in a diverse society, and avoid imposing their values on clients. (See C.5.a.)

## A.6. Dual Relationships

*a. Avoid when Possible.*
Counselors are aware of their influential positions with respect to clients, and they avoid exploiting the trust and dependency of clients. Counselors make every effort to avoid dual relationships with clients that could impair professional judgment or increase the risk of harm to clients. (Examples of such relationships include, but are not limited to, familial, social, financial, business, or close personal relationships with clients.) When a dual relationship cannot be avoided, counselors take appropriate professional precautions such as informed consent, consultation, supervision, and documentation to ensure that judgment is not impaired and no exploitation occurs. (See F.1.b.)

*b. Superior/Subordinate Relationships.*
Counselors do not accept as clients superiors or subordinates with whom they have administrative, supervisory, or evaluative relationships.

## A.7. Sexual Intimacies with Clients

*a. Current Clients.*
Counselors do not have any type of sexual intimacies with clients and do not counsel persons with whom they have had a sexual relationship.

*b. Former Clients.*
Counselors do not engage in sexual intimacies with former clients within a minimum of two years after terminating the counseling relationship. Counselors who engage in such relationship after two years following termination have the responsibility to thoroughly examine and document that such relations did not have an exploitative nature, based on factors such as duration of counseling, amount of time since counseling, termination circumstances, client's personal history and mental status, adverse impact on the client, and actions by the counselor suggesting a plan to initiate a sexual relationship with the client after termination.

## A.8. Multiple Clients

When counselors agree to provide counseling services to two or more persons who have a relationship (such as husband and wife, or parents and children), counselors clarify at the outset which person or persons are clients and the nature of the relationships they will have with each involved person. If it becomes apparent that counselors may be called upon to perform potentially conflicting roles, they clarify, adjust, or withdraw from roles appropriately. (See B.2. and B.4.d.)

## A.9. Group Work

*a. Screening.*
Counselors screen prospective group counseling/therapy participants. To the extent possible, counselors select members whose needs and goals are compatible with goals of the group, who will not impede the group process, and whose well-being will not be jeopardized by the group experience.

*b. Protecting Clients.*
In a group setting, counselors take reasonable precautions to protect clients from physical or psychological trauma.

## A.10. Fees and Bartering (See D.3.A. and D.3.B.)

*a. Advance Understanding.*
Counselors clearly explain to clients, prior to entering the counseling relationship, all financial arrangements related to professional services including the use of collection agencies or legal measures for nonpayment. (A.11.c.)

*b. Establishing Fees.*
In establishing fees for professional counseling services, counselors consider the financial status of clients and locality. In the event that the established fee structure is inappropriate for a client, assistance is provided in attempting to find comparable services of acceptable cost. (See A.10.d., D.3.a., and D.3.b.)

*c. Bartering Discouraged.*
Counselors ordinarily refrain from accepting goods or services from clients in return for counseling services because such arrangements create inherent

potential for conflicts, exploitation, and distortion of the professional relation-ship. Counselors may participate in bartering only if the relationship is not exploitive, if the client requests it, if a clear written contract is established, and if such arrangements are an accepted practice among professionals in the com-munity. (See A.6.a.)

*d. Pro Bono Service.*
Counselors contribute to society by devoting a portion of their professional activity to services for which there is little or no financial return (pro bono).

## A.11. Termination and Referral

*a. Abandonment Prohibited.*
Counselors do not abandon or neglect clients in counseling. Counselors assist in making appropriate arrangements for the continuation of treatment, when necessary, during interruptions such as vacations, and following termination.

*b. Inability to Assist Clients.*
If counselors determine an inability to be of professional assistance to clients, they avoid entering or immediately terminate a counseling relationship. Counselors are knowledgeable about referral resources and suggest appropri-ate alternatives. If clients decline the suggested referral, counselors should dis-continue the relationship.

*c. Appropriate Termination.*
Counselors terminate a counseling relationship, securing client agreement when possible, when it is reasonably clear that the client is no longer benefit-ing, when services are no longer required, when counseling no longer serves the client's needs or interests, when clients do not pay fees charged, or when agency or institution limits do not allow provision of further counseling ser-vices. (See A.10.b. and C.2.g.)

## A.12. Computer Technology

*a. Use of Computers.*
When computer applications are used in counseling services, counselors ensure that: (1) the client is intellectually, emotionally, and physically capable of using the computer application; (2) the computer application is appropriate for the needs of the client; (3) the client understands the purpose and operation of the computer applications; and (4) a follow-up of client use of a computer application is provided to correct possible misconceptions, discover inappro-priate use, and assess subsequent needs.

*b. Explanation of Limitations.*
Counselors ensure that clients are provided information as a part of the counsel-ing relationship that adequately explains the limitations of computer technology.

*c. Access to Computer Applications.*
Counselors provide for equal access to computer applications in counseling services. (See A.2.a.)

# SECTION B: CONFIDENTIALITY

## B.1. Right to Privacy

*a. Respect for Privacy.*
Counselors respect their clients' right to privacy and avoid illegal and unwarranted disclosures of confidential information. (See A.3.a. and B.6.a.)

*b. Client Waiver.*
The right to privacy may be waived by the client or their legally recognized representative.

*c. Exceptions.*
The general requirement that counselors keep information confidential does not apply when disclosure is required to prevent clear and imminent danger to the client or others or when legal requirements demand that confidential information be revealed. Counselors consult with other professionals when in doubt as to the validity of an exception.

*d. Contagious, Fatal Diseases.*
A counselor who receives information confirming that a client has a disease commonly known to be both communicable and fatal is justified in disclosing information to an identifiable third party, who by his or her relationship with the client is at high risk of contracting the disease. Prior to making a disclosure the counselor should ascertain that the client has not already informed the third party about his or her disease and that the client is not intending to inform the third party in the immediate future. (See B.1.c and B.1.f)

*e. Court Ordered Disclosure.*
When court orders release of confidential information without a client's permission, counselors request to the court that the disclosure not be required due to potential harm to the client or counseling relationship. (See B.1.c.)

*f. Minimal Disclosure.*
When circumstances require the disclosure of confidential information, only essential information is revealed. To the extent possible, clients are informed before confidential information is disclosed.

*g. Explanation of Limitations.*
When counseling is initiated and throughout the counseling process as necessary, counselors inform clients of the limitations of confidentiality and identify foreseeable situations in which confidentiality must be breached. (See G.2.a.)

*h. Subordinates.*
Counselors make every effort to ensure that privacy and confidentiality of clients are maintained by subordinates including employees, supervisees, clerical assistants, and volunteers. (See B.l.a.)

*i. Treatment Teams.*
If client treatment will involve a continued review by a treatment team, the client will be informed of the team's existence and composition.

## B.2. Groups and Families

*a. Group Work.*
In group work, counselors clearly define confidentiality and the parameters for the specific group being entered, explain its importance, and discuss the difficulties related to confidentiality involved in group work. The fact that confidentiality cannot be guaranteed is clearly communicated to group members.

*b. Family Counseling.*
In family counseling, information about one family member cannot be disclosed to another member without permission. Counselors protect the privacy rights of each family member. (See A.8., B.3., and B.4.d.)

## B.3. Minor or Incompetent Clients

When counseling clients who are minors or individuals who are unable to give voluntary, informed consent, parents or guardians may be included in the counseling process as appropriate. Counselors act in the best interests of clients and take measures to safeguard confidentiality. (See A.3.c.)

## B.4. Records

*a. Requirement of Records.*
Counselors maintain records necessary for rendering professional services to their clients and as required by laws, regulations, or agency or institution procedures.

*b. Confidentiality of Records.*
Counselors are responsible for securing the safety and confidentiality of any counseling records they create, maintain, transfer, or destroy whether the records are written, taped, computerized, or stored in any other medium. (See B.1.a.)

*c. Permission to Record or Observe.*
Counselors obtain permission from clients prior to electronically recording or observing sessions. (See A.3.a.)

*d. Client Access.*
Counselors recognize that counseling records are kept for the benefit of clients, and therefore provide access to records and copies of records when requested by competent clients, unless the records contain information that may be misleading and detrimental to the client. In situations involving multiple clients, access to records is limited to those parts of records that do not include confidential information related to another client. (See A.8., B.1.a., and B.2.b.)

*e. Disclosure or Transfer.*
Counselors obtain written permission from clients to disclose or transfer records to legitimate third parties unless exceptions to confidentiality exist as listed in Section B.1. Steps are taken to ensure that receivers of counseling records are sensitive to their confidential nature.

## B.5. Research and Training

*a. Data Disguise Required.*
Use of data derived from counseling relationships for purposes of training, research, or publication is confined to content that is disguised to ensure the anonymity of the individuals involved. (See B.1.g. and G.3.d.)

*b. Agreement for Identification.*
Identification of a client in a presentation or publication is permissible only when the client has reviewed the material and has agreed to its presentation or publication. (See G.3.d.)

## B.6. Consultation

*a. Respect for Privacy.*
Information obtained in a consulting relationship is discussed for professional purposes only with persons clearly concerned with the case. Written and oral reports present data germane to the purposes of the consultation, and every effort is made to protect client identity and avoid undue invasion of privacy.

*b. Cooperating Agencies.*
Before sharing information, counselors make efforts to ensure that there are defined policies in other agencies serving the counselor's clients that effectively protect the confidentiality of information.

## SECTION C: PROFESSIONAL RESPONSIBILITY

## C.1. Standards Knowledge

Counselors have a responsibility to read, understand, and follow the Code of Ethics and the Standards of Practice.

## C.2. Professional Competence

*a. Boundaries of Competence.*
Counselors practice only within the boundaries of their competence, based on their education, training, supervised experience, state and national professional credentials, and appropriate professional experience. Counselors will demonstrate a commitment to gain knowledge, personal awareness, sensitivity, and skills pertinent to working with a diverse client population.

*b. New Specialty Areas of Practice.*
Counselors practice in specialty areas new to them only after appropriate education, training, and supervised experience. While developing skills in new specialty areas, counselors take steps to ensure the competence of their work and to protect others from possible harm.

*c. Qualified for Employment.*
Counselors accept employment only for positions for which they are qualified by education, training, supervised experience, state and national professional credentials, and appropriate professional experience. Counselors hire for professional counseling positions only individuals who are qualified and competent.

*d. Monitor Effectiveness.*
Counselors continually monitor their effectiveness as professionals and take steps to improve when necessary. Counselors in private practice take reasonable steps to seek out peer supervision to evaluate their efficacy as counselors.

*e. Ethical Issues Consultation.*
Counselors take reasonable steps to consult with other counselors or related professionals when they have questions regarding their ethical obligations or professional practice. (See H.1)

*f. Continuing Education.*
Counselors recognize the need for continuing education to maintain a reasonable level of awareness of current scientific and professional information in their fields of activity. They take steps to maintain competence in the skills they use, are open to new procedures, and keep current with the diverse and/or special populations with whom they work.

*g. Impairment.*
Counselors refrain from offering or accepting professional services when their physical, mental or emotional problems are likely to harm a client or others. They are alert to the signs of impairment, seek assistance for problems, and, if necessary, limit, suspend, or terminate their professional responsibilities. (See A.11.c.)

## C.3. Advertising and Soliciting Clients

*a. Accurate Advertising.*
There are no restrictions on advertising by counselors except those that can be specifically justified to protect the public from deceptive practices. Counselors advertise or represent their services to the public by identifying their credentials in an accurate manner that is not false, misleading, deceptive, or fraudulent. Counselors may only advertise the highest degree earned which is in counseling or a closely related field from a college or university that was accredited when the degree was awarded by one of the regional accrediting bodies recognized by the Council on Postsecondary Accreditation.

*b. Testimonials.*
Counselors who use testimonials do not solicit them from clients or other persons who, because of their particular circumstances, may be vulnerable to undue influence.

*c. Statements by Others.*
Counselors make reasonable efforts to ensure that statements made by others about them or the profession of counseling are accurate.

*d. Recruiting through Employment.*
Counselors do not use their places of employment or institutional affiliation to recruit or gain clients, supervisees, or consultees for their private practices. (See C.5.e.)

*e. Products and Training Advertisements.*
Counselors who develop products related to their profession or conduct workshops or training events ensure that the advertisements concerning these products or events are accurate and disclose adequate information for consumers to make informed choices.

*f. Promoting to Those Served.*
Counselors do not use counseling, teaching, training, or supervisory relationships to promote their products or training events in a manner that is deceptive or would exert undue influence on individuals who may be vulnerable. Counselors may adopt textbooks they have authored for instruction purposes.

*g. Professional Association Involvement.*
Counselors actively participate in local, state, and national associations that foster the development and improvement of counseling.

## C.4. Credentials

*a. Credentials Claimed.*
Counselors claim or imply only professional credentials possessed and are responsible for correcting any known misrepresentations of their credentials

by others. Professional credentials include graduate degrees in counseling or closely related mental health fields, accreditation of graduate programs, national voluntary certifications, government-issued certifications or licenses, ACA professional membership, or any other credential that might indicate to the public specialized knowledge or expertise in counseling.

*b. ACA Professional Membership.*
ACA professional members may announce to the public their membership status. Regular members may not announce their ACA membership in a manner that might imply they are credentialed counselors.

*c. Credential Guidelines.*
Counselors follow the guidelines for use of credentials that have been established by the entities that issue the credentials.

*d. Misrepresentation of Credentials.*
Counselors do not attribute more to their credentials than the credentials represent, and do not imply that other counselors are not qualified because they do not possess certain credentials.

*e. Doctoral Degrees from Other Fields.*
Counselors who hold a master's degree in counseling or a closely related mental health field, but hold a doctoral degree from other than counseling or a closely related field do not use the title, "Dr." in their practices and do not announce to the public in relation to their practice or status as a counselor that they hold a doctorate.

## C.5. Public Responsibility

*a. Nondiscrimination.*
Counselors do not discriminate against clients, students, or supervisees in a manner that has a negative impact based on their age, color, culture, disability, ethnic group, gender, race, religion, sexual orientation, or socioeconomic status, or for any other reason. (See A.2.a.)

*b. Sexual Harassment.*
Counselors do not engage in sexual harassment. Sexual harassment is defined as sexual solicitation, physical advances, or verbal or nonverbal conduct that is sexual in nature, that occurs in connection with professional activities or roles, and that either: (1) is unwelcome, is offensive, or creates a hostile workplace environment, and counselors know or are told this; or (2) is sufficiently severe or intense to be perceived as harassment to a reasonable person in the context. Sexual harassment can consist of a single intense or severe act or multiple persistent or pervasive acts.

*c. Reports to Third Parties.*
Counselors are accurate, honest, and unbiased in reporting their professional activities and judgments to appropriate third parties including courts, health insurance companies, those who are the recipients of evaluation reports, and others. (See B.1.g.)

*d. Media Presentations.*
When counselors provide advice or comment by means of public lectures, demonstrations, radio or television programs, prerecorded tapes, printed articles, mailed material, or other media, they take reasonable precautions to ensure that (1) the statements are based on appropriate professional counseling literature and practice; (2) the statements are otherwise consistent with the Code of Ethics and the Standards of Practice; and (3) the recipients of the information are not encouraged to infer that a professional counseling relationship has been established. (See C.6.b.)

*e. Unjustified Gains.*
Counselors do not use their professional positions to seek or receive unjustified personal gains, sexual favors, unfair advantage, or unearned goods or services. (See C.3.d.)

## C.6. Responsibility to Other Professionals

*a. Different Approaches.*
Counselors are respectful of approaches to professional counseling that differ from their own. Counselors know and take into account the traditions and practices of other professional groups with which they work.

*b. Personal Public Statements.*
When making personal statements in a public context, counselors clarify that they are speaking from their personal perspectives and that they are not speaking on behalf of all counselors or the profession. (See C.5.d.)

*c. Clients Served by Others.*
When counselors learn that their clients are in a professional relationship with another mental health professional, they request release from clients to inform the other professionals and strive to establish positive and collaborative professional relationships. (See A.4.)

## SECTION D: RELATIONSHIPS WITH OTHER PROFESSIONALS

## D.1. Relationships with Employers and Employees

*a. Role Definition.*
Counselors define and describe for their employers and employees the parameters and levels of their professional roles.

*b. Agreements.*
Counselors establish working agreements with supervisors, colleagues, and subordinates regarding counseling or clinical relationships, confidentiality, adherence to professional standards, distinction between public and private material, maintenance and dissemination of recorded information, workload, and accountability. Working agreements in each instance are specified and made known to those concerned.

*c. Negative Conditions.*
Counselors alert their employers to conditions that may be potentially disruptive or damaging to the counselor's professional responsibilities or that may limit their effectiveness.

*d. Evaluation.*
Counselors submit regularly to professional review and evaluation by their supervisor or the appropriate representative of the employer.

*e. In-Service.*
Counselors are responsible for in-service development of self and staff.

*f. Goals.*
Counselors inform their staff of goals and programs.

*g. Practices.*
Counselors provide personnel and agency practices that respect and enhance the rights and welfare of each employee and recipient of agency services. Counselors strive to maintain the highest levels of professional services.

*h. Personnel Selection and Assignment.*
Counselors select competent staff and assign responsibilities compatible with their skills and experiences.

*i. Discrimination.*
Counselors, as either employers or employees, do not engage in or condone practices that are inhumane, illegal, or unjustifiable (such as considerations based on age, color, culture, disability, ethnic group, gender, race, religion, sexual orientation, or socioeconomic status) in hiring, promotion, or training. (See A.2.a. and C.5.b.)

*j. Professional Conduct.*
Counselors have a responsibility both to clients and to the agency or institution within which services are performed to maintain high standards of professional conduct.

*k. Exploitive Relationships.*
Counselors do not engage in exploitive relationships with individuals over whom they have supervisory, evaluative, or instructional control or authority.

*l. Employer Policies.*
The acceptance of employment in an agency or institution implies that counselors are in agreement with its general policies and principles. Counselors strive to reach agreement with employers as to acceptable standards of conduct that allow for changes in institutional policy conducive to the growth and development of clients.

## D.2. Consultation (See B.6.)

*a. Consultation as an Option.*
Counselors may choose to consult with any other professionally competent persons about their clients. In choosing consultants, counselors avoid placing the consultant in a conflict of interest situation that would preclude the consultant being a proper party to the counselor's efforts to help the client. Should counselors be engaged in a work setting that compromises this consultation standard, they consult with other professionals whenever possible to consider justifiable alternatives.

*b. Consultant Competency.*
Counselors are reasonably certain that they have or the organization represented has the necessary competencies and resources for giving the kind of consulting services needed and that appropriate referral resources are available.

*c. Understanding with Clients.*
When providing consultation, counselors attempt to develop with their clients a clear understanding of problem definition, goals for change, and predicted consequences of interventions selected.

*d. Consultant Goals.*
The consulting relationship is one in which client adaptability and growth toward self-direction are consistently encouraged and cultivated. (See A.l.b.)

## D.3. Fees for Referral

*a. Accepting Fees from Agency Clients.*
Counselors refuse a private fee or other remuneration for rendering services to persons who are entitled to such services through the counselor's employing agency or institution. The policies of a particular agency may make explicit provisions for agency clients to receive counseling services from members of its staff in private practice. In such instances, the clients must be informed of other options open to them should they seek private counseling services. (See A.10.a., A.1l.b., and C.3.d.)

*b. Referral Fees.*
Counselors do not accept a referral fee from other professionals.

## D.4. Subcontractor Arrangements

When counselors work as subcontractors for counseling services for a third party, they have a duty to inform clients of the limitations of confidentiality that the organization may place on counselors in providing counseling services to clients. The limits of such confidentiality ordinarily are discussed as part of the intake session. (See B.l.e. and B.l.f.)

## SECTION E: EVALUATION, ASSESSMENT, AND INTERPRETATION

## E.1. General

*a. Appraisal Techniques.*
The primary purpose of educational and psychological assessment is to provide measures that are objective and interpretable in either comparative or absolute terms. Counselors recognize the need to interpret the statements in this section as applying to the whole range of appraisal techniques, including test and nontest data.

*b. Client Welfare.*
Counselors promote the welfare and best interests of the client in the development, publication, and utilization of educational and psychological assessment techniques. They do not misuse assessment results and interpretations and take reasonable steps to prevent others from misusing the information these techniques provide. They respect the client's right to know the results, the interpretations made, and the bases for their conclusions and recommendations.

## E.2. Competence to Use and Interpret Tests

*a. Limits of Competence.*
Counselors recognize the limits of their competence and perform only those testing and assessment services for which they have been trained. They are familiar with reliability, validity, related standardization, error of measurement, and proper application of any technique utilized. Counselors using computer-based test interpretations are trained in the construct being measured and the specific instrument being used prior to using this type of computer application. Counselors take reasonable measures to ensure the proper use of psychological assessment techniques by persons under their supervision.

*b. Appropriate Use.*
Counselors are responsible for the appropriate application, scoring, interpretation, and use of assessment instruments, whether they score and interpret such tests themselves or use computerized or other services.

*c. Decisions Based on Results.*
Counselors responsible for decisions involving individuals or policies that are based on assessment results have a thorough understanding of educational and psychological measurement, including validation criteria, test research, and guidelines for test development and use.

*d. Accurate Information.*
Counselors provide accurate information and avoid false claims or misconceptions when making statements about assessment instruments or techniques. Special efforts are made to avoid unwarranted connotations of such terms as IQ and grade equivalent scores. (See C.5.c.)

## E.3. Informed Consent

*a. Explanation to Clients.*
Prior to assessment, counselors explain the nature and purposes of assessment and the specific use of results in language the client (or other legally authorized person on behalf of the client) can understand, unless an explicit exception to this right has been agreed upon in advance. Regardless of whether scoring and interpretation are completed by counselors, by assistants, or by computer or other outside services, counselors take reasonable steps to ensure that appropriate explanations are given to the client.

*b. Recipients of Results.*
The examinee's welfare, explicit understanding, and prior agreement determine the recipients of test results. Counselors include accurate and appropriate interpretations with any release of individual or group test results. (See B.1.a. and C.5.c.)

## E.4. Release of Information to Competent Professionals

*a. Misuse of Results.*
Counselors do not misuse assessment results, including test results, and interpretations, and take reasonable steps to prevent the misuse of such by others. (See C.5.c.)

*b. Release of Raw Data.*
Counselors ordinarily release data (e.g., protocols, counseling or interview notes, or questionnaires) in which the client is identified only with the consent of the client or the client's legal representative. Such data are usually released only to persons recognized by counselors as competent to interpret the data. (See B.1.a.)

## E.5. Proper Diagnosis of Mental Disorders

*a. Proper Diagnosis.*
Counselors take special care to provide proper diagnosis of mental disorders. Assessment techniques (including personal interview) used to determine client

care (e.g., locus of treatment, type of treatment, or recommended follow-up)
are carefully selected and appropriately used. (See A.3.a. and C.5.c.)

*b. Cultural Sensitivity.*
Counselors recognize that culture affects the manner in which clients' problems are defined. Clients' socioeconomic and cultural experience is considered
when diagnosing mental disorders.

## E.6. Test Selection

*a. Appropriateness of Instruments.*
Counselors carefully consider the validity, reliability, psychometric limitations,
and appropriateness of instruments when selecting tests for use in a given situation or with a particular client.

*b. Culturally Diverse Populations.*
Counselors are cautious when selecting tests for culturally diverse populations
to avoid inappropriateness of testing that may be outside of socialized behavioral or cognitive patterns.

## E.7. Conditions of Test Administration

*a. Administration Conditions.*
Counselors administer tests under the same conditions that were established
in their standardization. When tests are not administered under standard conditions or when unusual behavior or irregularities occur during the testing session, those conditions are noted in interpretation, and the results may be
designated as invalid or of questionable validity.

*b. Computer Administration.*
Counselors are responsible for ensuring that administration programs function
properly to provide clients with accurate results when a computer or other
electronic methods are used for test administration. (See A.12.b.)

*c. Unsupervised Test-Taking.*
Counselors do not permit unsupervised or inadequately supervised use of
tests or assessments unless the tests or assessments are designed, intended,
and validated for self-administration and/or scoring.

*d. Disclosure of Favorable Conditions.*
Prior to test administration, conditions that produce most favorable test results
are made known to the examinee.

## E.8. Diversity in Testing

Counselors are cautious in using assessment techniques, making evaluations,
and interpreting the performance of populations not represented in the norm

group on which an instrument was standardized. They recognize the effects of age, color, culture, disability, ethnic group, gender, race, religion, sexual orientation, and socioeconomic status on test administration and interpretation and place test results in proper perspective with other relevant factors. (See A.2.a.)

## E.9. Test Scoring and Interpretation

*a. Reporting Reservations.*
In reporting assessment results, counselors indicate any reservations that exist regarding validity or reliability because of the circumstances of the assessment or the inappropriateness of the norms for the person tested.

*b. Research Instruments.*
Counselors exercise caution when interpreting the results of research instruments possessing insufficient technical data to support respondent results. The specific purposes for the use of such instruments are stated explicitly to the examinee.

*c. Testing Services.*
Counselors who provide test scoring and test interpretation services to support the assessment process confirm the validity of such interpretations. They accurately describe the purpose, norms, validity, reliability, and applications of the procedures and any special qualifications applicable to their use. The public offering of an automated test interpretations service is considered a professional-to-professional consultation. The formal responsibility of the consultant is to the consultee, but the ultimate and overriding responsibility is to the client.

## E.10. Test Security

Counselors maintain the integrity and security of tests and other assessment techniques consistent with legal and contractual obligations. Counselors do not appropriate, reproduce, or modify published tests or parts thereof without acknowledgment and permission from the publisher.

## E.11. Obsolete Tests and Outdated Test Results

Counselors do not use data or test results that are obsolete or outdated for the current purpose. Counselors make every effort to prevent the misuse of obsolete measures and test data by others.

## E.12. Test Construction

Counselors use established scientific procedures, relevant standards, and current professional knowledge for test design in the development, publication, and utilization of educational and psychological assessment techniques.

## SECTION F: TEACHING, TRAINING, AND SUPERVISION

## F.1. Counselor Educators and Trainers

*a. Educators as Teachers and Practitioners.*
Counselors who are responsible for developing, implementing, and supervising educational programs are skilled as teachers and practitioners. They are knowledgeable regarding the ethical, legal, and regulatory aspects of the profession, are skilled in applying that knowledge, and make students and supervisees aware of their responsibilities. Counselors conduct counselor education and training programs in an ethical manner and serve as role models for professional behavior. Counselor educators should make an effort to infuse material related to human diversity into all courses and/or workshops that are designed to promote the development of professional counselors.

*b. Relationship Boundaries with Students and Supervisees.*
Counselors clearly define and maintain ethical, professional, and social relationship boundaries with their students and supervisees. They are aware of the differential in power that exists and the student's or supervisee's possible incomprehension of that power differential. Counselors explain to students and supervisees the potential for the relationship to become exploitive.

*c. Sexual Relationships.*
Counselors do not engage in sexual relationships with students or supervisees and do not subject them to sexual harassment. (See A.6. and C.5.b.)

*d. Contributions to Research.*
Counselors give credit to students or supervisees for their contributions to research and scholarly projects. Credit is given through coauthorship, acknowledgment, footnote statement, or other appropriate means, in accordance with such contributions. (See G.4.b. and G.4.c.)

*e. Close Relatives.*
Counselors do not accept close relatives as students or supervisees.

*f. Supervision Preparation.*
Counselors who offer clinical supervision services are adequately prepared in supervision methods and techniques. Counselors who are doctoral students serving as practicum or internship supervisors to master's level students are adequately prepared and supervised by the training program.

*g. Responsibility for Services to Clients.*
Counselors who supervise the counseling services of others take reasonable measures to ensure that counseling services provided to clients are professional.

*h. Endorsement.*
Counselors do not endorse students or supervisees for certification, licensure, employment, or completion of an academic or training program if they believe

students or supervisees are not qualified for the endorsement. Counselors take reasonable steps to assist students or supervisees who are not qualified for endorsement to become qualified.

## F.2. Counselor Education and Training Programs

*a. Orientation.*
Prior to admission, counselors orient prospective students to the counselor education or training program's expectations, including but not limited to the following: (1) the type and level of skill acquisition required for successful completion of the training, (2) subject matter to be covered, (3) basis for evaluation, (4) training components that encourage self-growth or self-disclosure as part of the training process, (5) the type of supervision settings and requirements of the sites for required clinical field experiences, (6) student and supervisee evaluation and dismissal policies and procedures, and (7) up-to-date employment prospects for graduates.

*b. Integration of Study and Practice.*
Counselors establish counselor education and training programs that integrate academic study and supervised practice.

*c. Evaluation.*
Counselors clearly state to students and supervisees, in advance of training, the levels of competency expected, appraisal methods, and timing of evaluations for both didactic and experiential components. Counselors provide students and supervisees with periodic performance appraisal and evaluation feedback throughout the training program.

*d. Teaching Ethics.*
Counselors make students and supervisees aware of the ethical responsibilities and standards of the profession and the students and supervisees' ethical responsibilities to the profession. (See C.1. and F.3.e.)

*e. Peer Relationships.*
When students or supervisees are assigned to lead counseling groups or provide clinical supervision for their peers, counselors take steps to ensure that students and supervisees placed in these roles do not have personal or adverse relationships with peers and that they understand they have the same ethical obligations as counselor educators, trainers, and supervisors. Counselors make every effort to ensure that the rights of peers are not compromised when students or supervisees are assigned to lead counseling groups or provide clinical supervision.

*f. Varied Theoretical Positions.*
Counselors present varied theoretical positions so that students and supervisees may make comparisons and have opportunities to develop their own positions.
    Counselors provide information concerning the scientific bases of professional practice. (See C.6.a.)

*g. Field Placements.*
Counselors develop clear policies within their training program regarding field placement and other clinical experiences. Counselors provide clearly stated roles and responsibilities for the student or supervisee, the site supervisor, and the program supervisor. They confirm that site supervisors are qualified to provide supervision and are informed of their professional and ethical responsibilities in this role.

*h. Dual Relationships as Supervisors.*
Counselors avoid dual relationships such as performing the role of site supervisor and training program supervisor in the student's or supervisee's training program. Counselors do not accept any form of professional services, fees, commissions, reimbursement, or remuneration from a site for student or supervisee placement.

*i. Diversity in Programs.*
Counselors are responsive to their institution's and program's recruitment and retention needs for training program administrators, faculty, and students with diverse backgrounds and special needs. (See A.2.a.)

## F.3. Students and Supervisees

*a. Limitations.*
Counselors, through ongoing evaluation and appraisal, are aware of the academic and personal limitations of students and supervisees that might impede performance. Counselors assist students and supervisees in securing remedial assistance when needed, and dismiss from the training program supervisees who are unable to provide competent service due to academic or personal limitations. Counselors seek professional consultation and document their decision to dismiss or refer students or supervisees for assistance. Counselors assure that students and supervisees have recourse to address decisions made, to require them to seek assistance, or to dismiss them.

*b. Self-Growth Experiences.*
Counselors use professional judgment when designing training experiences conducted by the counselors themselves that require student and supervisee self-growth or self-disclosure. Safeguards are provided so that students and supervisees are aware of the ramifications their self-disclosure may have on counselors whose primary role as teacher, trainer, or supervisor requires acting on ethical obligations to the profession. Evaluative components of experiential training experiences explicitly delineate predetermined academic standards that are separate and not dependent on the student's level of self-disclosure. (See A.6.)

*c. Counseling for Students and Supervisees.*
If students or supervisees request counseling, supervisors or counselor educators provide them with acceptable referrals. Supervisors or counselor educa-

tors do not serve as counselor to students or supervisees over whom they hold administrative, teaching, or evaluative roles unless this is a brief role associated with a training experience. (See A.6.b.)

*d. Clients of Students and Supervisees.*
Counselors make every effort to ensure that the clients at field placements are aware of the services rendered and the qualifications of the students and supervisees rendering those services. Clients receive professional disclosure information and are informed of the limits of confidentiality. Client permission is obtained in order for the students and supervisees to use any information concerning the counseling relationship in the training process. (See B.1.e.)

*e. Standards for Students and Supervisees.*
Students and supervisees preparing to become counselors adhere to the Code of Ethics and the Standards of Practice. Students and supervisees have the same obligations to clients as those required of counselors. (See H.1.)

# SECTION G: RESEARCH AND PUBLICATION

## G.1. Research Responsibilities

*a. Use of Human Subjects.*
Counselors plan, design, conduct, and report research in a manner consistent with pertinent ethical principles, federal and state laws, host institutional regulations, and scientific standards governing research with human subjects. Counselors design and conduct research that reflects cultural sensitivity appropriateness.

*b. Deviation from Standard Practices.*
Counselors seek consultation and observe stringent safeguards to protect the rights of research participants when a research problem suggests a deviation from standard acceptable practices. (See B.6.)

*c. Precautions to Avoid Injury.*
Counselors who conduct research with human subjects are responsible for the subjects' welfare throughout the experiment and take reasonable precautions to avoid causing injurious psychological, physical, or social effects to their subjects.

*d. Principal Researcher Responsibility.*
The ultimate responsibility for ethical research practice lies with the principal researcher. All others involved in the research activities share ethical obligations and full responsibility for their own actions.

*e. Minimal Interference.*
Counselors take reasonable precautions to avoid causing disruptions in subjects' lives due to participation in research.

*f. Diversity.*

Counselors are sensitive to diversity and research issues with special populations. They seek consultation when appropriate. (See A.2.a. and B.6.)

## G.2. Informed Consent

*a. Topics Disclosed.*

In obtaining informed consent for research, counselors use language that is
understandable to research participants and that: (1) accurately explains the
purpose and procedures to be followed; (2) identifies any procedures that are
experimental or relatively untried; (3) describes the attendant discomforts and
risks; (4) describes the benefits or changes in individuals or organizations that
might be reasonably expected; (5) discloses appropriate alternative procedures
that would be advantageous for subjects; (6) offers to answer any inquiries concerning the procedures; (7) describes any limitations on confidentiality; and (8)
instructs that subjects are free to withdraw their consent and to discontinue
participation in the project at any time. (See B.1.f )

*b. Deception.*

Counselors do not conduct research involving deception unless alternative
procedures are not feasible and the prospective value of the research justifies
the deception. When the methodological requirements of a study necessitate
concealment or deception, the investigator is required to explain clearly the
reasons for this action as soon as possible.

*c. Voluntary Participation.*

Participation in research is typically voluntary and without any penalty for
refusal to participate. Involuntary participation is appropriate only when it can
be demonstrated that participation will have no harmful effects on subjects
and is essential to the investigation.

*d. Confidentiality of Information.*

Information obtained about research participants during the course of an
investigation is confidential. When the possibility exists that others may obtain
access to such information, ethical research practice requires that the possibility, together with the plans for protecting confidentiality, be explained to participants as a part of the procedure for obtaining informed consent. (See B.1.e.)

*e. Persons Incapable of Giving Informed Consent.*

When a person is incapable of giving informed consent, counselors provide an
appropriate explanation, obtain agreement for participation and obtain appropriate consent from a legally authorized person.

*f. Commitments to Participants.*

Counselors take reasonable measures to honor all commitments to research
participants.

*g. Explanations after Data Collection.*
After data are collected, counselors provide participants with full clarification of the nature of the study to remove any misconceptions. Where scientific or human values justify delaying or withholding information, counselors take reasonable measures to avoid causing harm.

*h. Agreements to Cooperate.*
Counselors who agree to cooperate with another individual in research or publication incur an obligation to cooperate as promised in terms of punctuality of performance and with regard to the completeness and accuracy of the information required.

*i. Informed Consent for Sponsors.*
In the pursuit of research, counselors give sponsors, institutions, and publication channels the same respect and opportunity for giving informed consent that they accord to individual research participants. Counselors are aware of their obligation to future research workers and ensure that host institutions are given feedback information and proper acknowledgment.

## G.3. Reporting Results

*a. Information Affecting Outcome.*
When reporting research results, counselors explicitly mention all variables and conditions known to the investigator that may have affected the outcome of a study or the interpretation of data.

*b. Accurate Results.*
Counselors plan, conduct, and report research accurately and in a manner that minimizes the possibility that results will be misleading. They provide thorough discussions of the limitations of their data and alternative hypotheses. Counselors do not engage in fraudulent research, distort data, misrepresent data, or deliberately bias their results.

*c. Obligation to Report Unfavorable Results.*
Counselors communicate to other counselors the results of any research judged to be of professional value. Results that reflect unfavorably on institutions, programs, services, prevailing opinions, or vested interests are not withheld.

*d. Identity of Subjects.*
Counselors who supply data, aid in the research of another person, report research results, or make original data available take due care to disguise the identity of respective subjects in the absence of specific authorization from the subjects to do otherwise. (See B.1.g. and B.5.a.)

*e. Replication Studies.*
Counselors are obligated to make available sufficient original research data to qualified professionals who may wish to replicate the study.

## G.4. Publication

*a. Recognition of Others.*
When conducting and reporting research, counselors are familiar with and give recognition to previous work on the topic, observe copyright laws, and give full credit to those to whom credit is due. (See F.1.d. and G.4.c.)

*b. Contributors.*
Counselors give credit through joint authorship, acknowledgment, footnote statements, or other appropriate means to those who have contributed significantly to research or concept development in accordance with such contributions. The principal contributor is listed first and minor technical or professional contributions are acknowledged in notes or introductory statements.

*c. Student Research.*
For an article that is substantially based on a student's dissertation or thesis, the student is listed as the principal author. (See F.1.d. and G.4.a.)

*d. Duplicate Submission.*
Counselors submit manuscripts for consideration to only one journal at a time. Manuscripts that are published in whole or in substantial part in another journal or published work are not submitted for publication without acknowledgment and permission from the previous publication.

*e. Professional Review.*
Counselors who review material submitted for publication, research, or other scholarly purposes respect the confidentiality and proprietary rights of those who submitted it.

## SECTION H: RESOLVING ETHICAL ISSUES

## H.1. Knowledge of Standards

Counselors are familiar with the Code of Ethics and the Standards of Practice and other applicable ethics codes from other professional organizations of which they are member, or from certification and licensure bodies. Lack of knowledge or misunderstanding of an ethical responsibility is not a defense against a charge of unethical conduct. (See F.3.e.)

## H.2. Suspected Violations

*a. Ethical Behavior Expected.*
Counselors expect professional associates to adhere to Code of Ethics. When counselors possess reasonable cause that raises doubts as to whether a counselor is acting in an ethical manner, they take appropriate action. (See H.2.d. and H.2.e.)

*b. Consultation.*
When uncertain as to whether a particular situation or course of action may be in violation of Code of Ethics, counselors consult with other counselors who are knowledgeable about ethics, with colleagues, or with appropriate authorities.

*c. Organization Conflicts.*
If the demands of an organization with which counselors are affiliated pose a conflict with Code of Ethics, counselors specify the nature of such conflicts and express to their supervisors or other responsible officials their commitment to Code of Ethics. When possible, counselors work toward change within the organization to allow full adherence to Code of Ethics.

*d. Informal Resolution.*
When counselors have reasonable cause to believe that another counselor is violating an ethical standard, they attempt to first resolve the issue informally with the other counselor if feasible, providing that such action does not violate confidentiality rights that may be involved.

*e. Reporting Suspected Violations.*
When an informal resolution is not appropriate or feasible, counselors, upon reasonable cause, take action such as reporting the suspected ethical violation to state or national ethics committees, unless this action conflicts with confidentiality rights that cannot be resolved.

*f. Unwarranted Complaints.*
Counselors do not initiate, participate in, or encourage the filing of ethics complaints that are unwarranted or intend to harm a counselor rather than to protect clients or the public.

## H.3. Cooperation with Ethics Committees

Counselors assist in the process of enforcing Code of Ethics. Counselors cooperate with investigations, proceedings, and requirements of the ACA Ethics Committee or ethics committees of other duly constituted associations or boards having jurisdiction over those charged with a violation. Counselors are familiar with the ACA Policies and Procedures and use it as a reference in assisting the enforcement of the Code of Ethics.

## STANDARDS OF PRACTICE

All members of the American Counseling Association (ACA) are required to adhere to the Standards of Practice and the Code of Ethics. The Standards of Practice represent minimal behavioral statements of the Code of Ethics. Members should refer to the applicable section of the Code of Ethics for further interpretation and amplification of the applicable Standard of Practice.

## Section A: The Counseling Relationship

*Standard of Practice One (Sp-1) Nondiscrimination*
Counselors respect diversity and must not discriminate against clients because of age, color, culture, disability, ethnic group, gender, race, religion, sexual orientation, marital status, or socioeconomic status. (See A.2.a.)

*Standard of Practice Two (Sp-2) Disclosure to Clients*
Counselors must adequately inform clients, preferably in writing, regarding the counseling process and counseling relationship at or before the time it begins and throughout the relationship. (See A.3.a.)

*Standard of Practice Three (Sp-3) Dual Relationships*
Counselors must make every effort to avoid dual relationships with clients that could impair their professional judgment or increase the risk of harm to clients. When a dual relationship cannot be avoided, counselors must take appropriate steps to ensure that judgment is not impaired and that no exploitation occurs. (See A.6.a. and A.6.b.)

*Standard of Practice Four (Sp4) Sexual Intimacies with Clients*
Counselors must not engage in any type of sexual intimacies with current clients and must not engage in sexual intimacies with former clients within a minimum of two years after terminating the counseling relationship. Counselors who engage in such relationship after two years following termination have the responsibility to thoroughly examine and document that such relations did not have an exploitative nature.

*Standard of Practice Five (Sp-5) Protecting Clients during Group Work*
Counselors must take steps to protect clients from physical or psychological trauma resulting from interactions during group work. (See A.9.b.)

*Standard of Practice Six (Sp-6) Advance Understanding of Fees*
Counselors must explain to clients, prior to their entering the counseling relationship, financial arrangements related to professional services. (See A.10.a-d. and A.11.c.)

*Standard of Practice Seven (Sp7) Termination*
Counselors must assist in making appropriate arrangements for the continuation of treatment of clients, when necessary, following termination of counseling relationships. (See A.11.a.)

*Standard of Practice Eight (Sp8) Inability to Assist Clients*
Counselors must avoid entering or immediately terminate a counseling relationship if it is determined that they are unable to be of professional assistance to a client. The counselor may assist in making an appropriate referral for the client. (See A.11.b.)

## Section B: Confidentiality

*Standard of Practice Nine (Sp-9) Confidentiality Requirement*
Counselors must keep information related to counseling services confidential unless disclosure is in the best interest of clients, is required for the welfare of others, or is required by law. When disclosure is required, only information that is essential is revealed and the client is informed of such disclosure. (See B.1.a- f.)

*Standard of Practice Ten (Sp-10) Confidentiality Requirements for Subordinates*
Counselors must take measures to ensure that privacy and confidentiality of clients are maintained by subordinates. (See B.1.h.)

*Standard of Practice Eleven (Sp11) Confidentiality in Group Work*
Counselors must clearly communicate to group members that confidentiality cannot be guaranteed in group work. (See B.2.a.)

*Standard of Practice Twelve (Sp12) Confidentiality in Family Counseling*
Counselors must not disclose information about one family member in counseling to another family member without prior consent. (See B.2.b.)

*Standard of Practice Thirteen (Sp13) Confidentiality of Records*
Counselors must maintain appropriate confidentiality in creating, storing, accessing, transferring, and disposing of counseling records. (See B.4.b.)

*Standard of Practice Fourteen (Sp14) Permission To Record or Observe*
Counselors must obtain prior consent from clients in order to electronically record or observe sessions. (See B.4.c.)

*Standard of Practice Fifteen (Sp15) Disclosure or Transfer of Records*
Counselors must obtain client consent to disclose or transfer records to third parties, unless exceptions listed in SP-9 exist. (See B.4.e.)

*Standard of Practice Sixteen (Sp16) Data Disguise Required*
Counselors must disguise the identity of the client when using data for training, research, or publication. (See B.5.a.)

## Section C: Professional Responsibility

*Standard of Practice Seventeen (Sp-17) Boundaries of Competence*
Counselors must practice only within the boundaries of their competence. (See C.2.a.)

*Standard of Practice Eighteen (Sp18) Continuing Education*
Counselors must engage in continuing education to maintain their professional competence. (See C.2.f)

*Standard of Practice Nineteen (Sp19) Impairment of Professionals*
Counselors must refrain from offering professional services when their personal problems or conflicts may cause harm to a client or others. (See C.2.g.)

*Standard of Practice Twenty (Sp20) Accurate Advertising*
Counselors must accurately represent their credentials and services when advertising. (See C.3.a.)

*Standard of Practice Twenty-One (Sp-21) Recruiting through Employment*
Counselors must not use their place of employment or institutional affiliation to recruit clients for their private practices. (See C.3.d.)

*Standard of Practice Twenty-Two (Sp-22) Credentials Claimed*
Counselors must claim or imply only professional credentials possessed and must correct any known misrepresentations of their credentials by others. (See C.4.a.)

*Standard of Practice Twenty-Three (SP-23) Sexual Harassment*
Counselors must not engage in sexual harassment. (See C.5.b.)

*Standard of Practice Twenty-Four (Sp-24) Unjustified Gains*
Counselors must not use their professional positions to seek or receive unjustified personal gains, sexual favors, unfair advantage, or unearned goods or services. (See C.5.e.)

*Standard of Practice Twenty-Five (Sp-25) Clients Served by Others*
With the consent of the client, counselors must inform other mental health professionals serving the same client that a counseling relationship between the counselor and client exists. (See C.6.c.)

*Standard of Practice Twenty-Six (SP-26) Negative Employment Conditions*
Counselors must alert their employers to institutional policy or conditions that may be potentially disruptive or damaging to the counselor's professional responsibilities, or that may limit their effectiveness or deny clients' rights. (See D.1.c.)

*Standard of Practice Twenty-Seven (SP-27) Personnel Selection and Assignment*
Counselors must select competent staff and must assign responsibilities compatible with staff skills and experiences. (See D.1.h.)

*Standard Of Practice Twenty-Eight (Sp-28) Exploitive Relationships with Subordinates*
Counselors must not engage in exploitive relationships with individuals over whom they have supervisory, evaluative, instructional control or authority. (See D.1.k.)

## Section D: Relationship with Other Professionals

*Standard of Practice Twenty-Nine (Sp-29) Accepting Fees from Agency Clients*
Counselors must not accept fees or other remuneration for consultation with persons entitled to such services through the counselor's employing agency or institution. (See D.3.a.)

*Standard of Practice Thirty (Sp-30) Referral Fees*
Counselors must not accept referral fees. (See D.3.b.)

## Section E: Evaluation, Assessment, and Interpretation

*Standard of Practice Thirty-One (Sp31) Limits of Competence*
Counselors must perform only testing and assessment services for which they are competent. Counselors must not allow the use of psychological assessment techniques by unqualified persons under their supervision. (See E.2.a.)

*Standard of Practice Thirty-Two (Sp-32) Appropriate Use of Assessment Instruments*
Counselors must use assessment instruments in the manner for which they were intended. (See E.2.b.)

*Standard of Practice Thirty-Three (Sp-33) Assessment Explanations to Clients*
Counselors must provide explanations to clients prior to assessment about the nature and purposes of assessment and the specific uses of results. (See E.3.a.)

*Standard of Practice Thirty-Four (Sp-34) Recipients of Test Results*
Counselors must ensure that accurate and appropriate interpretations accompany any release of testing and assessment information. (See E.3.b.)

*Standard of Practice Thirty-Five (Sp-35) Obsolete Tests and Outdated Test Results*
Counselors must not base their assessment or intervention decisions or recommendations on data or test results that are outdated for the current purpose. (See E.11.)

## Section F: Teaching, Training, and Supervision

*Standard of Practice Thirty-Six (Sp-36) Sexual Relationships with Students or Supervisees*
Counselors must not engage in sexual relationships with their students and supervisees. (See F.1.c.)

*Standard of Practice Thirty-Seven (Sp-37) Credit for Contributions to Research*
Counselors must give credit to students or supervisees for their contributions to research and scholarly projects. (See F.1.d.)

*Standard of Practice Thirty-Eight (Sp-38) Supervision Preparation*
Counselors who offer clinical supervision services must be trained and prepared in supervision methods and techniques. (See F.1.f )

*Standard of Practice Thirty-Nine (Sp-39) Evaluation Information*
Counselors must clearly state to students and supervisees in advance of training, the levels of competency expected, appraisal methods, and timing of evaluations. Counselors must provide students and supervisees with periodic
performance appraisal and evaluation feedback throughout the training program. (See E.2.c.)

*Standard of Practice Forty (Sp-40) Peer Relationships in Training*
Counselors must make every effort to ensure that the rights of peers are not
violated when students and supervisees are assigned to lead counseling
groups or provide clinical supervision. (See F.2.e.)

*Standard of Practice Forty-One (Sp-41) Limitations of Students and Supervisees*
Counselors must assist students and supervisees in securing remedial assistance, when needed, and must dismiss from the training program students and
supervisees who are unable to provide competent service due to academic or
personal limitations. (See F.3.a.)

*Standard of Practice Forty-Two (Sp-42) Self-Growth Experiences*
Counselors who conduct experiences for students or supervisees that include
self-growth or self-disclosure must inform participants of counselors' ethical
obligations to the profession and must not grade participants based on their
nonacademic performance. (See F.3.b.)

*Standard of Practice Forty-Three (Sp-43) Standards for Students and Supervisees*
Students and supervisees preparing to become counselors must adhere to the
Code of Ethics and the Standards of Practice of counselors. (See F.7.e )

## Section G: Research and Publication of Practice Forty-Four

*(Sp-44) Precautions to Avoid Injury in Research*
Counselors must avoid causing physical, social, or psychological harm or
injury to subjects in research (See G.1.c.)

*Standard of Practice Forty-Five (Sp-45) Confidentiality of Research Information*
Counselors must keep confidential information obtained about research participants. (See G.2.d.)

*Standard of Practice Forty-Six (Sp-46) Information Affecting Research Outcome*
Counselors must report all variables and conditions known to the investigator
that may have affected research data or outcomes. (See G.3.a.)

*Standard of Practice Forty-Seven (Sp-47) Accurate Research Results*
Counselors must not distort or misrepresent research data, nor fabricate or intentionally bias research results. (See G.3.b.)

*Standard of Practice Forty-Eight (Sp-48) Publication Contributors*
Counselors must give appropriate credit to those who have contributed to research. (See G.4.a. and G.4.b.)

## Section H: Resolving Ethical Issues

*Standard of Practice Forty-Nine (Sp-49) Ethical Behavior Expected*
Counselors must take appropriate action when they possess reasonable cause that raises doubts as to whether counselors or other mental health professionals are acting in an ethical manner. (See H.2.a.)

*Standard of Practice Fifty (Sp-50) Unwarranted Complaints*
Counselors must not initiate, participate in, or encourage the filing of ethics complaints that are unwarranted or intended to harm a mental health professional rather than to protect clients or the public. (See H.2.f.)

*Standard of Practice Fifty-One (Sp-51) Cooperation with Ethics Committees*
Counselors must cooperate with investigations, proceedings, and requirements of the ACA Ethics Committee or ethics committees of other duly constituted associations or boards having jurisdiction over those charged with a violation. (See H.3.)

## References

The following documents are available to counselors as resources to guide them in their practices. These resources are not a part of the Code of Ethics and the Standards of Practice.

American Association for Counseling and Development/Association for Measurement and Evaluation in Counseling and Development. (1989). The responsibilities of users of standardized tests (revised). Washington, DC: Author.

American Counseling Association. (1988). American Counseling Association Ethical Standards. Alexandria, VA: Author.

American Psychological Association. (1985). Standards for educational and psychological testing (revised). Washington, DC: Author.

American Rehabilitation Counseling Association, Commission on Rehabilitation Counselor Certification, and National Rehabilitation Counseling Association. (1995). Code of professional ethics for rehabilitation counselors. Chicago, IL: Author.

American School Counselor Association. (1992). Ethical standards for school counselors. Alexandria, VA: Author.

Joint Committee on Testing Practices. (1988). Code of fair testing practices in education. Washington, DC: Author.

National Board for Certified Counselors. (1989). National Board for Certified Counselors Code of Ethics. Alexandria, VA: Author.

Prediger, D.J. (Ed.). (1993, March). Multicultural assessment standards. Alexandria, VA: Association for Assessment in Counseling.

## POLICIES AND PROCEDURES FOR RESPONDING TO MEMBERS' REQUESTS FOR INTERPRETATIONS OF THE ETHICAL STANDARDS

*Revised by Governing Council April 1994 Effective July 1, 1994*

### Section A: Appropriate Requests

1. Members may request that the Committee issue formal interpretations of the ACA Code of Ethics for the purpose of guiding the member's own professional behavior.

2. Requests for interpretations will not be considered in the following situations:

   a. The individual requesting the interpretation is not an ACA member, or

   b. The request is intended to determine whether the behavior of another mental health professional is unethical. In the event an ACA member believes the behavior of another mental health professional is unethical, the ACA member should resolve the issue directly with the professional, if possible, and should file an ethical complaint if appropriate.

### Section B: Procedures

1. Members must send written requests for interpretations to the Committee at ACA Headquarters.

2. Questions should be submitted in the following format: "Does (counselor behavior) violate Sections or any other sections of the ACA Ethical Standards?" Questions should avoid unique details, be general in nature to the extent possible, and be brief.

3. The Committee staff liaison will revise the question, if necessary, and submit it to the Committee Co-Chair for approval.

4. The question will be sent to Committee members who will be asked to respond individually.

5. The Committee Co-Chair will develop a consensus interpretation on behalf of the Committee.

6. The consensus interpretation will be sent to members of the Committee for final approval.
7. The formal interpretation will be sent to the member who submitted the inquiry.
8. The question and the formal interpretation will be published in the ACA newsletter, but the identity of the member requesting the interpretation will not be disclosed.

## POLICIES AND PROCEDURES FOR PROCESSING COMPLAINTS OF ETHICAL VIOLATIONS

### Section A: General

1. The American Counseling Association, hereafter referred to as the "Association" or "ACA," is dedicated to enhancing human development throughout the life span and promoting the counseling profession.
2. The Association, in furthering its objectives, administers the Code of Ethics that have been developed and approved by the ACA Governing Council.
3. The purpose of this document is to facilitate the work of the ACA Ethics Committee ("Committee") by specifying the procedures for processing cases of alleged violations of the ACA Code of Ethics, codifying options for sanctioning members, and stating appeals procedures. The intent of the Association is to monitor the professional conduct of its members to promote sound ethical practices. ACA does not, however, warrant the performance of any individual.

### Section B: Ethic Committee Members

1. Ethics Committee is a standing committee of the Association. The Committee consists of six (6) appointed members, including two (2) Co-Chairs whose terms overlap. Two members are appointed annually for three (3) year terms by the PresidentElect; appointments are subject to confirmation by the ACA Governing Council. Any vacancy occurring on the Committee will be filled by the President in the same manner, and the person appointed shall serve the unexpired term of the member whose place he or she took. Committee members may be reappointed to not more than one (1) additional consecutive term.
2. One (1) of the Committee co-chairs is appointed annually by the President-Elect from among the Committee members who have two (2) years of service remaining and serves as co-chair for two (2) years, subject to confirmation by the Governing Council.

## Section C: Role and Function

1. The Ethics Committee is responsible for:

   a. Educating the membership as to the Association's Code of Ethics.

   b. Periodically reviewing and recommending changes in the Code of Ethics of the Association as well as the Policies and Procedures for Processing Complaints of Ethical violations;

   c. Receiving and processing complaints of alleged violations of the Code of Ethics of the Association; and,

   d. Receiving and processing questions.

2. The Committee shall meet in person or by telephone conference a minimum of three (3) times per year for processing complaints.

3. In processing complaints about alleged ethical misconduct, the Committee will compile an objective, factual account of the dispute in question and make the best possible recommendation for the resolution of the case. The Committee, in taking any action, shall do so only for cause, shall only take the degree of disciplinary action that is reasonable, shall utilize these procedures with objectivity and fairness, and in general shall act only to further the interests and objectives of the Association and its membership.

4. Of the six (6) voting members of the Committee, a vote of four (4) is necessary to conduct business. In the event a Co-Chair or any other member of the Committee has a personal interest in the case, he or she shall withdraw from reviewing the case.

5. In the event Committee members recuse themselves from a complaint and insufficient voting members are available to conduct business, the President shall appoint former ACA Committee members to decide the complaint.

## Section D: Responsibilities of the Committee

The Committee members have an obligation to act in an unbiased manner, to work expeditiously, to safeguard the confidentiality of the Committee's activities, and to follow procedures established to protect the rights of all individuals involved.

## Section E: Responsibilities of the Co-chairs Administering the Complaint

1. In the event that one of the Co-Chairs Administering the Complaint; conflict of interest in a particular case, the other Co-Chair shall administer the complaint. The Co-Chair administering the complaint shall not have a vote in the decision.

2. In addition to the above guidelines for members of the Committee, the Co-Chairs, in conjunction with the Headquarters staff liaison, have the responsibilities of:

   a. Receiving, via ACA Headquarters, complaints that have been certified for membership status of the accused;

   b. Determining whether the alleged behavior(s), if true, would violate ACA's Code of Ethics and whether the Committee should review the complaint under these rules;

   c. Notifying the complainant and the accused member of receipt of the case by certified mail return receipt requested;

   d. Notifying the members of the Committee of the case;

   e. Requesting additional information from complainants, accused members and others;

   f. Presiding over the meetings of the Committee;

   g. Preparing and sending, by certified mail, communications to the complainant and accused member on the recommendations and decisions of the Committee; and

   h. Arranging for legal advice with assistance and financial approval of the ACA Executive Director.

## Section F: Jurisdiction

1. The Committee will consider whether individuals have violated the ACA Code of Ethics if those individuals:

   a. Are current members of the American Counseling Association; or

   b. Were ACA members when the alleged violations occurred.

2. Ethics committees of divisions, branches, corporate affiliates, or other ACA entities must refer all ethical complaints involving ACA members to the Committee.

## Section G: Eligibility to File Complaints

1. The Committee will receive complaints that ACA members have violated one or more sections of the ACA Code of Ethics from the following individuals:

   a. Members of the general public who have reason to believe that ACA members have violated the ACA Code of Ethics.

   b. ACA members, or members of other helping professions, who have reason to believe that other ACA members have violated the ACA Code of Ethics.

   c. The Co-Chair of the Committee on behalf of the ACA membership when the Co-Chair has reason to believe through information received by the Committee that ACA members have violated the ACA Code of Ethics.

2. If possible, individuals should attempt to resolve complaints directly with accused members before filing ethical complaints.

## Section H: Time Lines

1. Lines set forth in these standards are guidelines only and have been established to provide a reasonable time framework for processing complaints.

2. Complainants or accused members may request extensions of deadlines when appropriate. Extensions of deadlines will be granted by the Committee only when justified by unusual circumstance.

## Section I: Nature of Communication

1. Only written communications regarding ethical complaints against members will be acceptable. If telephone inquiries from individuals are received regarding the filing of complaints, responding to complaints, or providing information regarding complaints, the individuals calling will be informed of the written communication requirement and asked to comply.

2. All correspondence related to an ethical complaint must be addressed to the Ethics Committee, ACA Headquarters, 5999 Stevenson Avenue, Alexandria, VA, 22304, and must be marked "confidential." This process is necessary to protect the confidentiality of the complainant and the accused member.

## Section J: Filing Complaints

1. Only written complaints, signed by complainants, will be considered.

2. Individuals eligible to file complaints will send a letter outlining the nature of the complaint to the Committee at the ACA Headquarters.

3. The ACA staff liaison to the Committee will communicate in writing with complainants. Receipt of complaints and confirmation of membership status of accused members as defined in Section F.1, above, will be acknowledged to the complainant. Proposed formal complaints will be sent to complainants after receipt of complaints have been acknowledged.

4. If the complaint does not involve member as defined in Section F.1 above, the staff liaison shall inform the complainant.

5. The Committee Co-Chair administering a complaint will determine whether the complaint, if true, would violate one or more sections of the ethical standards or if the complaint could be properly decided if accepted. If not, the complaint will not be accepted and the complainant shall be notified.

6. If the Committee Co-Chair administering the complaint determines that there is insufficient information to make a fair determination of whether the behavior alleged in the complaint would be cause for action by the Committee, the ACA staff liaison to the Committee may request further information from the complainant or others.

7. When complaints are accepted, complainants will be informed that copies of the formal complaints plus evidence and documents submitted in support of the complaint will be provided to the accused member and that the complainant must authorize release of such information to the accused member before the complaint process may proceed.

8. The ACA staff liaison, after receiving approval of the Committee Co-Chair administering a complaint, will formulate a formal complaint which will be presented to the complainants for their signature.

    a. The correspondence from complainants will be received and the staff liaison and Committee Co-Chair administering the complaint will identify all ACA Code of Ethics that might have been violated if the accusations are true.

    b. The formal complaint will be sent to complainants with a copy of these Policies and Procedures, a copy of the ACA Code of Ethics, a verification affidavit form and an authorization and release of information form. Complainants will be asked to sign and return the completed complaint, verification affidavit and authorization and release of information forms. It will be explained to complainants that sections of the codes that might have been violated may be added or deleted by the complainant before signing the formal statement.

    c. If complainants elect to add or delete sections of the ethical standards in the formal complaint, the unsigned formal complaint shall be returned to ACA Headquarters with changes noted and a revised formal complaint will be sent to the complainants for their signature.

9. When the completed formal complaint, verification affidavit form and authorization and release of information form are presented to complainants for their signature, they will be asked to submit all evidence and documents they wish to be considered by the Committee in reviewing the complaint.

## Section K: Notification of Accused Members

1. Once signed formal complaints have been received accused members will be sent a copy of the formal complaint and copies of all evidence and documents submitted in support of the complaint.

2. Accused members will be asked to respond to the complaint against them. They will be asked to address each section of the ACA Code of Ethics they have been accused of having violated. They will be informed that if they wish to respond they must do so in writing within sixty (60) working days.

3. Accused members will be informed that they must submit all evidence and documents they wish to be considered by the Committee in reviewing the complaint within sixty (60) working days.

4. After accused members have received notification that a complaint has been brought against them, they will be given sixty (60) working days to notify the Committee Co-Chair (via ACA Headquarters) in writing, by certified mail, if they wish to request a formal face-to-face hearing before the Committee. Accused members may waive their right to a formal hearing before the Committee. (See Section P: Hearings.)

5. If the Committee Co-Chair determines that there is insufficient information to make a fair determination of whether the behavior alleged in the complaint would be cause for action by the Committee, the ACA staff liaison to the Committee may request further information from the accused member or others. The accused member shall be given thirty (30) working days from receipt of the request to respond.

6. All requests for additional information from others will be accompanied by a verification affidavit form which the information provider will be asked to complete and return.

7. The Committee may, in its discretion, delay or postpone its review of the case with good cause, including if the Committee wishes to obtain additional information. The accused member may request that the Committee delay or postpone its review of the case for good cause if done so in writing.

## Section L: Disposition of Complaints

1. After receiving the responses of accused members, Committee members will be provided copies of: (a) the complaint, (b) supporting evidence and documents sent to accused members, (c) the response, and (d) supporting evidence and documents provided by accused members and others.

2. Decisions will be rendered based on the evidence and documents provided by the complainant and accused member or others.

3. The Committee Co-Chair administering a complaint will not participate in deliberations or decisions regarding that particular complaint.

4. At the next meeting of the Committee held no sooner than fifteen (15) working days after members received copies of documents related to a complaint, the Committee will discuss the complaint, response, and supporting documentation, if any, and determine the outcome of the complaint.

5. The Committee will determine whether each Code of Ethics the member has been accused of having violated was violated based on the information provided.

6. After deliberations, the Committee may decide to dismiss the complaint or to dismiss charges within the complaint.

7. In the event it is determined that any of the ACA Code of Ethics has been violated, the Committee will impose for the entire complaint one or a combination of the possible sanctions allowed.

## Section M: Complaints

If the Complainant and accused member both agree to discontinue the complaint process, the Committee may, at its discretion, complete the adjudication process if available evidence indicates that this is warranted. The Co-Chair of the Committee, on behalf of the ACA membership, shall act as complainant.

## Section N: Possible Sanctions

1. Reprinted remedial requirements may be stipulated by the Committee.
2. Probation for a specified period of time subject to Committee review of compliance. Remedial requirements may be imposed to be completed within a specified period of time.
3. Suspension from ACA membership for a specified period of time subject to Committee review of compliance. Remedial requirements may be imposed to be completed within a specified period of time.
4. Permanent expulsion from ACA membership. This sanction requires a unanimous vote of those voting.
5. The penalty for failing to fulfill in a satisfactory manner a remedial requirement imposed by the Committee as a result of a probation sanction will be automatic suspension until the requirement is met, unless the Committee determines that the remedial requirement should be modified based on good cause shown prior to the end of the probationary period.
6. The penalty for failing to fulfill in a satisfactory manner a remedial requirement imposed by the Committee as a result of a suspension sanction will be automatic permanent expulsion unless the Committee determines that the remedial requirement should be modified based on good cause shown prior to the end of the suspension period.
7. Other corrective action.

## Section O: Notification of Results

1. Accused members shall be notified of Committee decisions regarding complaints against them.
2. Complainants will be notified of Committee decisions after the deadline for accused members to file appeals or, in the event an appeal is filed, after a filed appeal decision has been rendered.
3. After complainants are notified of the results of their complaints as provided in Section O, Paragraph 2, above, if a violation has been found and

accused members have been suspended or expelled, counselor licensure, certification, or registry boards, other mental health licensure, certification, or registry boards, voluntary national certification boards, and appropriate professional associations will also be notified of the results. In addition, ACA divisions, state branches, the ACA Insurance Trust, and other ACA-related entities will also be notified of the results.

4. After complainants have been notified of the results of their complaint as provided in Section O, Paragraph 2, above, if a violation has been found and accused members have been suspended or expelled, a notice of the Committee action that includes the sections of the ACA ethical standards that were found to have been violated and the sanctions imposed will be published in the ACA newsletter.

## Section P: Hearings

1. At the discretion of the Committee, a hearing may be conducted when the results of the Committee's preliminary determination indicate that additional information is needed.

2. When accused members, within sixty (60) working days of notification of the complaint, request a formal face-to-face or telephone conference hearing before the Committee a hearing shall be conducted. (See Section K.6.)

3. The accused shall bear all their expenses associated with attendance at hearings requested by the accused.

4. The Committee Co-Chair shall schedule a formal hearing on the case at the next scheduled Committee meeting and notify both the complainant and the accused member of their right to attend the hearing in person or by telephone conference call.

5. The hearing will be held before a panel made up of the Committee and if the accused member chooses, a representative of the accused member's primary Division. This representative will be identified by the Division President and will have voting privileges.

## Section Q: Hearing Procedures

1. Purpose.
   a. A hearing will be conducted to determine whether a breach of the ethical standards has occurred and, if so, to determine appropriate disciplinary action.
   b. The Committee will be guided in its deliberations by principles of basic fairness and professionalism, and will keep its deliberations as confidential as possible, except as provided herein.

2. Notice.
   a. The accused members shall be advised in writing by the Co-Chair administering the complaint of the time and place of the hearing and the

charges involved at least forty-five (45) working days before the hearing. Notice shall include a formal statement of the complaints lodged against the accused member and supporting evidence.

b. The accused member is under no duty to respond to the notice, but the Committee will not be obligated to delay or postpone its hearing unless the accused so requests in writing, with good cause reviewed at least fifteen (15) working days in advance. In the absence of such 15 day advance notice and postponement by the Committee, if the accused fails to appear at the hearing, the Committee shall decide the complaint on record. Failure of the accused member to appear at the hearing shall not be viewed by the Committee as sufficient grounds alone for taking disciplinary action.

3. Conduct of the Hearing.

a. *Accommodations.* The location of the hearing shall be determined at the discretion of the Committee. The Committee shall provide a private room to conduct the hearing and no observers or recording devices other than a recording device used by the Committee shall be permitted.

b. *Presiding Officer.* The Co-Chair in charge of the case shall preside over the hearing and deliberations of the Committee. At the conclusion of the hearing and deliberations of the Committee, the Co-Chair shall promptly notify the accused member and complainant of the Committee's decision in writing as provided in Section O, Paragraphs 1 and 2, above.

c. *Record.* A record of the hearing shall be made and preserved, together with any documents presented in evidence, at ACA Headquarters for a period of three (3) years. The record shall consist of a summary of testimony received or a verbatim transcript, at the discretion of the Committee.

d. *Right to Counsel.* The accused member shall be entitled to have legal counsel present to advise and represent them throughout the hearing. Legal counsel for ACA shall also be present at the hearing to advise the Committee and shall have the privilege of the floor.

e. *Witnesses.* Either party shall have the right to call witnesses to substantiate his or her version of the case.

f. The Committee shall have the right to call witnesses it believes may provide further insight into the matter. ACA shall, in its sole discretion, determine the number and identity of witnesses to be heard.

g. Witnesses shall not be present during the hearing except when they are called upon to testify and shall be excused upon completion of their testimony and any cross-examination.

h. The Co-Chair administering the complaint shall allow questions to be asked of any witness by the opposition or members of the Committee if such questions and testimony are relevant to the issues in the case.

i. The Co-Chair administering the complaint will determine what questions and testimony are relevant to the case. Should the hearing be disturbed by irrelevant testimony, the Co-Chair administering the complaint may call a brief recess until order can be restored.

j. All expenses associated with counsel on behalf of the parties shall be borne by the respective parties. All expenses associated with witnesses on behalf of the accused shall be borne by the accused when the accused requests a hearing. If the Committee requests the hearing, all expenses associated with witnesses shall be borne by ACA.

4. Presentation of Evidence.

a. The staff liaison, or the Co-Chair administering the complaint shall be called upon first to present the charge(s) made against the accused and to briefly describe the evidence supporting the charge. The person presenting the charges shall also be responsible for examining and cross-examining witnesses on behalf of the complainant and for otherwise presenting the matter during the hearing.

b. The complainant or a member of the Committee shall then be called upon to present the case against the accused. Witnesses who can substantiate the case may be called upon to testify and answer questions of the accused and the Committee.

c. If the accused has exercised the right to be present at the hearing, he or she shall be called upon last to present any evidence which refutes the charges against him or her. This includes witnesses as in Subsection (3) above.

d. The accused will not be found guilty simply for refusing to testify. Once the accused member chooses to testify, however, he or she may be cross-examined by the complainant and members of the Committee.

e. The Committee will endeavor to conclude the hearing within a period of approximately three (3) hours. The parties will be requested to be considerate of this time frame in planning their testimony.

f. Testimony that is merely cumulative or repetitious may, at the discretion of the Co-Chair administering the complaint, be excluded.

5. Relevancy of Evidence.

a. The Hearing Committee is not a court of law and is not required to observe formal rules of evidence. Evidence that would be inadmissible in a court of law may be admissible in the hearing before the Committee, if it is relevant to the case. That is, if the evidence offered tends to explain, clarify, or refute any of the important facts of the case, it should generally be considered.

b. The Committee will not consider evidence or testimony for the purpose of supporting any charge that was not set forth in the notice of the hearing or that is not relevant to the issues of the case.

6. Burden of Proof.

a. The burden of proving a violation of the ethical standards is on the complainant and/or the Committee. It is not up to the accused to prove his or her innocence of any wrongdoing.

b. Although the charge(s) need not be proved "beyond a reasonable doubt," the Committee will not find the accused guilty in the absence of substantial, objective, and believable evidence to sustain the charge(s).

7. Deliberation of the Committee.

a. After the hearing is completed, the Committee shall meet in a closed session to review the evidence presented and reach a conclusion. ACA legal counsel may attend the closed session to advise the Committee if the Committee so desires.

b. The Committee shall be the sole trier of the facts and shall weigh the evidence presented and assess the credibility of the witnesses. The act of a majority of the members of the Committee present shall be the decision of the Committee. A unanimous vote of those voting is required for permanent expulsion from ACA membership.

c. Only members of the Committee who were present throughout the entire hearing shall be eligible to vote.

8. Decision of the Committee.

a. The Committee will first resolve the issue of the guilt or innocence of the accused on each charge. Applying the burden of proof in subsection (5), above, the Committee will vote by secret ballot, unless the members of the Committee consent to an oral vote.

b. In the event a majority of the members of the Committee do not find the accused guilty, the charges shall be dismissed. If the Committee finds the accused member has violated the Code of Ethics, it must then determine what sanctions, in accordance with Section N: Possible Sanctions, shall be imposed.

c. As provided in Section O, above, the Co-Chair administering the complaint shall notify the accused member and complainant of the Committee's decision in writing.

## Section R: Appeals

1. Decisions of the ACA Ethics Committee that members have violated the ACA Code of Ethics may be appealed by the member found to have been in violation based on one or both of the following grounds:

a. The Committee violated its policies and procedures for processing complaints of ethical violations; and/or

b. The decision of the Committee was arbitrary and capricious and was not supported by the materials provided by the complainant and accused member.

2. After members have received notification that they have been found in violation of one or more ACA Code of Ethics, they will be given thirty (30) working days to notify the Committee in writing by certified mail that they are appealing the decision.

3. An appeal may consist only of a letter stating one or both of the grounds of appeal listed in subsection 1 above and the reasons for the appeal.

4. Appealing members will be asked to identify the primary ACA division to which he or she belongs. The ACA President will appoint a three (3) person appeals panel consisting of two (2) former ACA Ethics Committee Chairs and the President of the identified division. The ACA attorney shall serve as legal advisor and have the privilege of the floor.

5. The three (3) member appeals panel will be given copies of the materials available to the Committee when it made its decision, a copy of the hearing transcript if a hearing was held, plus a copy of the letter filed by the appealing member.

6. The appeals panel generally will render its decision regarding an appeal which must receive a majority vote within sixty (60) working days of their receipt of the above materials.

7. The decision of the appeals panel may include one of the following:

   a. The decision of the Committee is upheld.

   b. The decision of the Committee is reversed and remanded with guidance to the Committee for a new decision. The reason for this decision will be given to the Committee in detail in writing.

8. When a Committee decision is reversed and remanded, the complainant and accused member will be informed in writing and additional information may be requested first from the complainant and then from the accused member. The Committee will then render another decision without a hearing.

9. Decisions of the appeals panel to uphold the Committee decision are final.

## Section S: Evidence

1. In the event substantial new evidence is presented in a case in which an appeal was not filed, or in a case which a final decision has been rendered, the case may be reopened by the Committee.

2. The Committee will consider substantial new evidence and if it is found to be substantiated and capable of exonerating a member who was expelled, the Committee will reopen the case and go through the entire complaint process again.

## Section T: Records

1. The records of the Committee regarding complaints are confidential except as provided herein.

2. Original copies of complaint records will be maintained in locked files at ACA Headquarters or at an off-site location chosen by ACA.

3. Members of the Committee will keep copies of complaint records confidential and will destroy copies of records after a case has been closed or when they are no longer members of the Committee.

## Section U: Legal Actions Related to Complaints

1. Complaints and accused members are required to notify the Committee if they learn of any type of legal action (civil or criminal) being filed related to the complaint.
2. In the event any type of legal action is filed regarding an accepted complaint, all actions related to the complaint will be stayed until the legal action has been concluded. The Committee will consult with legal counsel concerning whether the processing of the complaint will be stayed if the legal action does not involve the same complainant and the same facts complained of.
3. If actions on a complaint are stayed, the complainant and accused member will be notified.
4. When actions on a complaint are continued after a legal action has been concluded, the complainant and accused member will be notified.

For information on ordering the ACA Code of Ethics and Standards of Practice write to:

ACA Distribution Center
P.O. Box 531
Annapolis Junction, MD 20701-0531

Or call 301-470-4ACA (301-470-4222) • toll free 1-800-422-2648 • fax (301) 604 0158

# ANSWERS TO CHAPTER REVIEW

## Foundations of Legal & Ethical Practice

1. are, do
2. virtue
3. rights
4. limits

## The Client/Counselor Relationship

1. trust
2. informed consent
3. complicate

## Confidentiality & Privileged Communication

1. confidentiality
2. excuse
3. privileged communication
4. warn
5. supervisors

## When in Doubt

1. resources
2. consult
3. referral

## CHAPTER 4

# Contemporary Issues in Counseling

## PRELIMINARY SELF EXPLORATION

Before you delve into this chapter, take a moment to consider the following questions. Write down the first thing that comes to your mind for each of the items. You may then find it helpful to come back to your responses once you have completed your study of this chapter and see if and how you might alter your responses.

- The practice of counseling and psychotherapy is never static. Changes in our society create shifts in our profession. What changes are you already aware of in this respect?

  _____

  _____

  _____

  _____

- What comes to mind when you think of multicultural counseling? Paint a mental picture of what that means to you.

  _____

  _____

  _____

  _____

- From your perspective, what difference does gender make in the counseling process?

_____

_____

_____

_____

- What feelings do you have about counseling a person who has a different religious orientation from you?

_____

_____

_____

_____

# CHAPTER OVERVIEW

Counseling and cultural differences, gender differences, the differently abled, religious clients, AIDS, and older adults — each area presents a unique set of issues and special needs. But all are calling to the contemporary counselor for help and it is the responsibility of today's counselors to wake up and answer the call. It is also the responsibility of counselors-in-training to help the field of counseling respond professionally to these contemporary concerns. The future of counseling depends on it.

# GUIDED STUDY

These questions are meant to guide you through the major sections of the chapter. Write your answer in the space provided and then compare it with the marked section of the text.

1. Culture consists of everything people have learned to do, believe, value and enjoy in their collective lives. Explain how and why differences of culture must be seriously considered by today's counselors if they are to be effective.

_____

_____

_____

_____

2. Just as cross-cultural issues must be considered so do differences across the genders. Discuss the importance of gender in contemporary counseling.

_____

_____

_____

_____

3. The differently abled person is challenged by a number of significant hurdles. Note the three mentioned in this chapter and how the contemporary counselor can be effective with this population.

_____

_____

_____

_____

4. Counselors are being confronted with calls for help today in areas that were formerly the primary domain of the clergy. Discuss the unique concerns of religious clients and how today's counselors must be prepared to work with them.

_____

_____

_____

_____

5. No disease in modern times has received more attention than AIDS. Explain what today's counselors need to know about this disease and how to work with clients who suffer with it.

_____

_____

_____

_____

6. With growing elderly population, today's counselors must be prepared to work with people 65 years of age and older. What does this entail for the contemporary counselor?

_____

_____

_____

_____

# CHAPTER REVIEW

The following items will help you master the specific content of the chapter. Complete each of the following sentences by filling in the blanks.

## Counseling and Cultural Differences

1. Research indicates that ethnic-minority clients often do not take advantage of counseling services, and when they do, they frequently _____ the therapeutic relationship early.

2. Culturally skilled counselors are comfortable with _____ that exist between themselves and their clients.

3. Culturally skilled counselors acknowledge their own _____ attitude, beliefs, and feelings.

## Counseling and Gender Differences

1. Important differences in the therapeutic treatment received by men and women are often _____.

2. Most counseling theories were developed by males and most therapists are _____.

3. Inadvertently or not, counseling has fostered a societal context that puts women at increased risk for _____.

4. If authoritarian processes are employed as a technique, the therapy should not have the effect of maintaining or reinforcing _____ dependency of women.

## Counseling and the Differently Abled

1. Counselors are too often ill-prepared to provide effective services for the physically challenged because they carry _____ regarding handicapping conditions.

2. Counselors must be aware of the _____ of handicapped children and their parents as well as the skills necessary to advice parents.

## Counseling and Religious Concerns

1. In a recent poll, it was shown that _____ of the population of the United States consider religion to be "important" or "very important" in their lives.

2. Contemporary counselors are being called on for help in areas that were formerly the primary domain of the _____.

3. Counselors need to avoid stereotypical assumptions that religiously devout clients are more _____ than other clients.

## Counseling and AIDS

1. AIDS results when the body's immune system breaks down and is caused by the human _____ virus.

2. People infected with _____ may appear completely healthy, but they may also develop many health problems that signal the onset of AIDS.

3. When a patient learns he or she is HIV positive, _____ counseling has proved to be quite effective as the disease progresses.

## Counseling and Older Adults

1. Erik Erikson has identified the primary developmental task of older persons as "_____ vs. despair."

2. The transitions and role losses in old age greatly affect the _____ of the elderly adult.

3. _____ counseling can help the retiree plan more effectively for a future that is bolstered by good physical and mental health.

## THE FUTURE OF COUNSELING

Take a moment to see yourself as a counselor twenty years from now. Write the year it would be in this space: _____. Imagine where you might be doing your work as a counselor. Describe it:

_____

_____

_____

_____

Next, think about what societal developments at this time may be impacting your practice. Consider technology and sociological influences:

_____

_____

_____

_____

Compare your responses to another student's responses.

# ANSWERS TO CHAPTER REVIEW

## Counseling and Cultural Differences

1. terminate
2. differences
3. prejudicial

## Counseling and Gender Differences

1. overlooked
2. males
3. emotional distress
4. stereotypic

## Counseling and the Differently Abled

1. biases (or prejudices)
2. rights

## Counseling and Religious Concerns

1. two thirds
2. clergy
3. emotionally disturbed (or dysfunctional)

## Counseling and AIDS

1. immunodeficiency
2. HIV
3. group

## Counseling and Older Adults

1. integrity
2. vulnerability
3. Preretirement

## CHAPTER 5

# Introduction: Your Personal Theory of Therapy

Before proceeding to the theory chapters of Part Two, take a moment to answer these two questions.

1. In your own words, why is it important for counseling students to study theories of counseling?

   _____

   _____

   _____

   _____

2. After completing the true/false questions in this introductory chapter to Part Two, summarize your fundamental beliefs about counseling. In a single paragraph describe your personal theory of counseling in elementary terms.

   _____

   _____

   _____

   _____

   _____

   _____

   _____

## CHAPTER 6

# Psychoanalytic Therapy

## CHAPTER OVERVIEW

1. *Biography.* Freud (1856-1939) spent nearly all of his life in Vienna. He was an excellent student but his career choices were restricted because of his Jewish heritage. He settled on medicine and at the age of 26 attained a position at the University of Vienna. By exploring the meaning of his own dreams, he gained insights into the dynamics of personality and he formulated his clinical theory as he observed the work of his patients in analysis. He had very little tolerance for colleagues who diverged from his psychoanalytic doctrines. He died of cancer of the jaw in London.

2. *Historical Development.* The origins of Psychoanalysis are identified with the early 1880s. During this time, Josef Breuer's treatment of hysteria (specifically with Anna O.) influenced Freud's thinking. Freud studied under Jean Charcot where he explored the use of hypnotic techniques. These two experiences, among other, led to Freud first using the term "psychoanalysis" in 1896.

3. *View of Human Nature.* Freud viewed people as being dominated by the instinctual, unconscious, and irrational forces of sex and aggression. For Freud, personality was determined entirely by conditions and events beyond personal control. He viewed consciousness as only a small part of the total psyche. Freud divided personality into three components: id (present at birth, entirely unconscious, and includes all innate instincts), ego (develops out of the id at about 6-8 months to help the id gain its ends), and superego (develops out of the ego at about age 3-5 years, includes the ego ideal and the conscience). Furthermore, Freud believed adult personality is established by about age five, following a more or less set course through a series of psychosexual stages: oral, anal, phallic, latency, and genital.

**109**

4. *Development of Maladaptive Behavior.* Symptoms of abnormality vary in the psychoanalytic thought depending upon the psychosexual stage in which conflicts and fixations first developed and the manner in which defense mechanisms are used to deal with the resulting anxiety. The fixation of excessive amounts of libido at pregenital stages generally results in various character patterns and psychopathology. Libido may also regress to a previous psychosexual stage or to an earlier object choice long since abandoned, usually one that was strongly fixated. Anxiety, operating largely at the unconscious level, is at the core of all psychopathology. The degree of anxiety depends on the leadership of the ego. A weekend ego spends excessive amounts of psychic energy wrestling with the id and superego, resulting in maladaptive behavior.

5. *Goals of Therapy.* The ultimate goal of psychoanalysis is not the removal of symptoms. Rather, it is the total reconstruction of personality through making the unconscious conscious. The person's ego is to be strengthened so that aggressive and sexual impulses can be brought under control. It is designed to reintegrate previously repressed experiences in the total personality structure.

6. *Function of the Therapist.* The analyst neither offers advice nor extends sympathy, but encourages clients to talk about whatever comes to mind, especially about childhood experiences. In classical psychoanalysis the analyst fosters a transference by allowing the client to project unresolved conflicts, feelings and experiences on to the analyst. This classical conception of the role of the psychoanalyst as an emotionally neutral figure, however, has been modified by modern psychoanalytic views that see the analyst as being more active.

7. *Major Methods and Techniques.* The most enduring therapeutic techniques of psychoanalysis are free association (the cardinal technique of allowing the client to say whatever comes to mind, no matter how illogical or trivial), dream analysis (interpreting the latent content of the dream primarily through the use of consistent symbols that signify the same thing for nearly everyone), analysis of transference (when the client responds to the analyst as a significant authority person from their life thus revealing the nature of childhood difficulties), and analysis of resistance (the unconscious resisting of efforts to help eliminate old behavior patterns, thereby impending any attempts to probe into the real sources of personality problems).

8. *Application.* Freud leaned heavily on case studies in the formulation of his theory. The case of "Dora" is one example that illustrated how Freud used resistance and transference to bring about psychological insight. Since the therapeutic goals are so high and difficult to obtain, and the self-defeating patterns so deeply established with the client, it is inevitable that psychoanalytic treatment be intensive and long-term. A modern-day excerpt from an analytic session was also depicted in the chapter.

9. *Critical Analysis.* Psychoanalysis has both devoted admirers and strong critics. Among its strengths are its comprehensive nature and its monumental value to spurring on other therapeutic theories. Among its shortcomings are methodological problems, an overemphasis on biological determinants of personality, relative vagueness of concepts, and male chauvinism.

10. *Current Status.* Contemporary analytic psychotherapies have evolved substantially beyond orthodox analytic thought. A major issue on which many contemporary analysts differ is the extent to which they adopt Freud's assumption that the infant (as well as the adult) is primarily motivated by pleasure seeking. Contemporary psychoanalytic thinking can be divided into Ego Psychology (present-oriented and reality-based, focusing on issues of identity, intimacy and integrity), Object-Relations Theories (focusing on early relations and rational drives), and Self Psychology (focusing on the construct of the self originating in infancy and its integrating function).

## GUIDED STUDY

These questions are meant to guide you through the major sections of the chapter. Write your answer in the space provided and then compare it with the marked section of the text.

1. Describe how Freud's formative years as a child may have impacted his theory.

_____

_____

_____

_____

2. In your own words, how would you describe the birth of psychoanalysis to someone who was not familiar with its history?

_____

_____

_____

_____

3. At the epicenter of Freud's theory is the unconscious. What is the unconscious and how does it work?

_____

_____

_____

_____

4. Using word pictures, how would you describe Freud's structure of personality (id, ego, and superego)?

_____

_____

_____

_____

5. Freud believed that personality develops through five stages of psychosexual development. What are these stages and how is each resolved?

_____

_____

_____

_____

6. Maladaptive behavior is universal and inevitable in Freud's model. Why is this so? Use the id, ego, and superego to describe how this happens.

_____

_____

_____

_____

7. What is the fundamental or overarching goal of psychoanalysis?

_____

_____

_____

_____

8. Freud consistently asserted that compassionate neutrality was the proper mind set for the analyst during the session. How does this view differ from more contemporary analytic therapists? Or does it?

_____

_____

_____

_____

9. Psychoanalysis introduced many treatment techniques. Describe analysis of transference and analysis of resistance.

_____

_____

_____

_____

10. What did you learn from Freud's treatment of "Dora"? Describe how he used psychoanalytic techniques in this case.

_____

_____

_____

_____

11. Psychoanalytic treatment has remained a controversial approach, being praised and criticized at the same time. What are its most noteworthy strengths and weaknesses?

_____

_____

_____

_____

12. While psychoanalytic purists do exist, several contemporary analytic psychotherapies have evolved. Describe the three most common of these.

_____

_____

_____

_____

# CHAPTER REVIEW

The following items will help you master the specific content of the chapter. Complete each of the following sentences by filling in the blanks.

## Biography

1. When Freud was three years old his father moved the family to _____, where Freud lived most of his life.

2. Freud and his wife had six children, three boys and three girls, the youngest of whom was _____.

3. Abandoning his long-time home to escape Nazi persecution, Freud moved to _____ where he died at the age of _____.

## Historical Development

1. The seeds of psychoanalysis were sown in the work surrounding Dr. Josef Breuer's patient, Bertha Pappenheim, or as she later came to be known, _____.

2. Dr. Breuer began describing his treatment of Bertha Pappenheim as the "_____."

3. On a sojourn to Paris, Freud met the famous French neurologist _____ from whom he learned about hypnosis.

## View of Human Nature

1. Freud believed a revelation of the _____ could explain all human thought, feeling, and action.

2. The _____ engages in primary process thinking, which is primitive and illogical.

3. The _____ spans the conscious, preconscious, and unconscious aspects of the mind, and id is capable of forming realistic plans of action.

4. The content of each person's superego results from _____, a process of incorporating the norms and standards of culture into personality by identifying with significant adults during childhood.

5. According to Freud, every human being experiences five sequential stages of psychosexual development: _____, _____, _____, _____, and _____.

## Development of Maladaptive Behavior

1. According to psychoanalytic thought, we are all "a little _____."

2. Operating largely at the unconscious level, _____ is at the core of all psychopathology.

3. The weak ego may be dominated by a stern _____ enforcing rigid defenses that deprive the person of pleasures most people consider socially acceptable.

## Goals of Therapy

1. Freud never promised that healing gained through psychoanalysis was _____ or irreversible.

2. The ultimate goal of psychoanalysis is not the removal of symptoms, but the total _____ of personality.

3. What Freud tried to accomplish in therapy was a general strengthening of a person's _____.

## Function of the Therapist

1. The analyst is a neutral _____ of the therapeutic process, intervening only occasionally to offer interpretations of the client's experiences.

2. In classical psychoanalysis the analyst fosters a _____ by allowing the client to project unresolved conflicts, feelings, and experiences on to the analyst.

3. Whereas a classic psychoanalyst is more concerned with lifting repressions of deeply unconscious material from the past, contemporary analytically oriented therapists may concentrate on conflicts in the _____.

## Major Methods and Techniques

1. The cardinal technique of psychoanalysis is _____, where the client is allowed to say anything and everything that comes to mind.

2. The analyst may discuss or interpret the meaning of dreams, which are said to contain surface material called the _____ content and then the deeper, hidden meaning called the _____ content.

3. A therapist must be keenly aware of a client's transference and not take it personally. When this occurs it is called _____.

4. Despite consciously desiring to change, a client may unconsciously _____ efforts to help eliminate old behavior patterns.

5. In the final stages of treatment, analysts encourage patients to convert their newly discovered insights into their everyday living experiences. This is sometimes called _____.

# Application

1. According to Freud, the case of Dora clearly revealed both _____ and _____.

# Critical Analysis

1. Much of psychoanalytic theory is presented in terms (e.g., life and death instincts) that do not lend themselves to _____ testing.

2. A major criticism of psychoanalytic thought emerges when it is applied to women. Quite bluntly, in Freud's view, women are _____ to men.

3. Since psychoanalysis focuses primarily on personality restructuring, not on solving immediate issues, this can present problems when it is applied to _____ counseling.

# Current Status

1. _____ psychology, sometimes dubbed the "American school," arose to give more attention to the conscious adaptive and controlling functions of the ego.

2. The "British school" has identified more clearly than strict Freudians how past childhood experience is reflected unconsciously in _____, a technical term roughly translated as "past interpersonal relationships."

3. Self-psychology was developed by Heinz _____ and it is based on the construct of the self integrating and developing incrementally to produce either healthy relationships or the opposite.

## KEY TERMS

Learning a theory depends, in large part, on mastering the vocabulary associated with that theory. The following key terms will help you do just that. You may want to use three-by-five cards to create your own flash card test from this list. Once you have studied this vocabulary, you will want to test your knowledge with the matching quiz which follows.

**Anal Stage** The second of Freud's psychosexual stages, during which gratification comes primarily from the elimination process.

**Anxiety** A feeling of fear and dread without an obvious cause.

**Castration Anxiety** A boy's fear during the Oedipal period that his penis will be cut off.

**Catharsis** The expression of emotions that is expected to lead to their reduction.

**Conscious** A component of the superego containing behaviors for which the child has been punished.

**Countertransference** The phenomenon of the therapist transferring feelings, fantasies, and behaviors from a previous relationship onto the client and thus creating an inappropriate therapeutic relationship.

**Defense Mechanisms** A strategy of distorting reality used by the ego to defend itself against the anxiety provoked by the conflicts of everyday life.

**Dream Analysis** A technique involving the interpretation of dreams to uncover unconscious conflicts.

**Ego** The rational aspect of the personality, responsible for directing and controlling instincts.

**Ego-Ideal** A component of the superego containing the moral or ideal behaviors for which a person should strive.

**Electra Complex** The unconscious desire of girls during the phallic stage of psychosexual development for their fathers, accompanied by a desire to replace or destroy their mothers.

**Fixation** The state in which a portion of the libido remains invested in one of the psychosexual stages because of excessive frustration or gratification.

**Free Association** A technique in which the client says whatever comes to mind; a kind of daydreaming out loud.

**Freudian Slip** A slip of the tongue, revealing unconscious material that has slipped out.

**Genital Stage** The fifth and final stage in Freud's psychosexual stages, during which a person learns socially appropriate channels for the expression of sexual impulses.

**Id** The aspect of personality operating according to the pleasure principle and allied with drives.

**Latent Content** The symbolic meaning of events in a dream.

**Latency Stage** The fourth stage of Freud's psychosexual stages, during which satisfaction is gained primarily through exploration of the environment and development of skills and interests.

**Libido** The form of psychic energy manifested by the life instincts that drive a person toward pleasurable behaviors and thoughts.

**Manifest Content** The actual events in a dream.

**Oedipus Complex** The unconscious desire of boys during the phallic stage of psychosexual development for their mothers, accompanied by a desire to replace or destroy their fathers.

**Oral Stage** The first and most primitive of Freud's psychosexual stages, during which the mouth region is the primary source of gratification.

**Penis Envy** The envy females feel toward males because they possess a penis, accompanied by a sense of loss because females do not have one.

**Phallic Stage** The third of Freud's psychosexual stages during which satisfaction is gained primarily through genital manipulation and exploration.

**Pleasure Principle** The id functions on this principle to avoid pain and to maximize pleasure.

**Preconscious Memory** Accessible to consciousness only after something calls one's attention to it.

**Primary Process** Childlike thinking by which the id attempts to satisfy the instinctual drives.

**Psychoanalysis** Sigmund Freud's system of therapy.

**Psychosexual Stages** The stages through which children pass and in which instinctual gratification depends on the stimulation of corresponding areas of the body.

**Reality Principle** The ego functions on this principle to provide appropriate constraints on the expression of the id instincts.

**Resistance** A blockage or refusal to disclose painful memories in free association.

**Secondary Process** Mature thought processes needed to deal rationally with the external world.

**Superego** The moral aspect of personality which has internalized parental and societal values and standards.

**Thanatos** The unconscious drive toward decay, destruction, and aggression.

**Transference** The phenomenon of clients placing their unconscious material onto the therapist and experiencing the therapist as if they were another previously encountered person.

**Unconscious** The domain of the psyche that stores repressed urges and primitive impulses.

**Womb Envy** The inferiority experienced by boys in discovering they cannot bear children.

# MATCHING ITEMS

## Terms

A. Latency Stage
B. Unconscious
C. Primary Process
D. Superego
E. Womb Envy
F. Conscious
G. Pleasure Principle
H. Thanatos
I. Anxiety
J. Anal Stage
K. Libido
L. Fixation
M. Penis Envy

N. Defense
　　Mechanisms
O. Catharsis
P. Transference
Q. Secondary Processes
R. Preconscious
S. Psychoanalysis
T. Countertransference
U. Dream Analysis
V. Oral Stage
W. Id
X. Oedipus Complex
Y. Resistance

Z. Castration Anxiety
AA. Electra Complex
BB. Reality Principle
CC. Phallic Stage
DD. Freudian Slip
EE. Manifest Content
FF. Ego
GG. Genital Stage
HH. Psychosexual Stages
II. Free Association
JJ. Ego Ideal
KK. Latent Content

## Description

_____ 1. The inferiority experienced by boys in discovering they cannot bear children.

_____ 2. The unconscious drive toward decay, destruction, and aggression.

_____ 3. The domain of the psyche that stores repressed urges and primitive impulses.

_____ 4. The second of Freud's psychosexual stages, during which gratification comes primarily from the elimination process.

_____ 5. A strategy of distorting reality used by the ego to defend itself against the anxiety provoked by the conflicts of everyday life.

_____ 6. Mature thought processes needed to deal rationally with the external world.

_____ 7. The id functions on this principle to avoid pain and to maximize pleasure.

_____ 8. Memory accessible to consciousness only after something calls one's attention to it.

_____ 9. A technique involving the interpretation of dreams to uncover unconscious conflicts.

_____10. The ego functions on this principle to provide appropriate constraints on the expression of id instincts.

_____11. A feeling of fear and dread without an obvious cause.

_____ 12. The phenomenon of clients placing their unconscious material onto the therapist and experiencing the therapist as if they were another previously encountered person.

_____ 13. A boy's fear during the Oedipal period that his penis will be cut off.

_____ 14. The moral aspect of personality which has internalized parental and societal values and standards.

_____ 15. The unconscious desire of girls during the phallic stage of psychosexual development for their fathers, accompanied by a desire to replace or destroy their mothers.

_____ 16. A blockage or refusal to disclose painful memories in free association.

_____ 17. The first and most primitive of Freud's psychosexual stages, during which the mouth region is the primary source of gratification.

_____ 18. A slip of the tongue, revealing unconscious material that has slipped out.

_____ 19. Childlike thinking by which the id attempts to satisfy the instinctual drives.

_____ 20. The third of Freud's psychosexual stages during which satisfaction is gained primarily through genital manipulation and exploration.

_____ 21. The actual events in a dream.

_____ 22. The fifth and final stage in Freud's psychosexual stages, during which a person learns socially appropriate channels for the expression of sexual impulses.

_____ 23. The expression of emotions that is expected to lead to their reduction.

_____ 24. A technique in which the client says whatever comes to mind; a kind of daydreaming out loud.

_____ 25. The aspect of personality operating according to the pleasure principle and allied with drives.

_____ 26. The symbolic meaning of events in a dream.

_____ 27. The rational aspect of the personality, responsible for directing and controlling instincts.

_____ 28. The fourth stage of Freud's psychosexual stages, during which satisfaction is gained primarily through exploration of the environment and development of skills and interests.

_____ 29. A component of the superego containing the moral or ideal behaviors for which a person should strive.

_____ 30. The stages through which children pass and in which instinctual gratification depends on the stimulation of corresponding areas of the body.

_____31. A component of the superego containing behaviors for which the child has been punished.

_____32. The state in which a portion of the libido remains invested in one of the psychosexual stages because of excessive frustration or gratification.

_____33. Sigmund Freud's system of therapy.

_____34. The unconscious desire of boys during the phallic stage of psychosexual development for their mothers, accompanied by a desire to replace or destroy their fathers.

_____35. The envy females feel toward males because they possess a penis, accompanied by a sense of loss because females do not have one.

_____36. The phenomenon of the therapist transferring feelings, fantasies, and behaviors from a previous relationship onto the client and thus creating an inappropriate therapeutic relationship.

_____37. The form of psychic energy manifested by the life instincts that drive a person toward pleasurable behaviors and thoughts.

## QUESTIONS FOR DISCUSSION
## AND PERSONAL REFLECTION

The following questions can be used in small group discussion for further exploration of the theory and/or personal reflection of how the theory applies to your own life.

1. How do you feel about the therapeutic value of remaining detached, objective and anonymous in the therapeutic process?

_____

_____

_____

_____

2. How do you view Freud's theory as applying to your own life? If you do not view it as having any applicability to your life, why?

_____

_____

_____

_____

3. If you could have a conversation with Freud, what questions would you have for him about his theory?

_____

_____

_____

_____

4. As you develop your own approach to therapeutic intervention, what will you take with you from psychoanalysis?

_____

_____

_____

_____

# ANSWERS TO CHAPTER REVIEW

## Biography

1. Vienna
2. Anna
3. London, 83

## Historical Development

1. Anna O.
2. talking cure
3. Jean Charcot

## View of Human Nature

1. unconscious
2. id
3. ego
4. introjection
5. oral, anal, phallic, latency, genital

## Development of Maladaptive Behavior

1. neurotic
2. anxiety
3. superego

## Goals of Therapy

1. permanent
2. reconstruction
3. ego

## Function of the Therapist

1. observer
2. transference
3. present

## Major Methods and Techniques

1. free association
2. manifest, latent
3. countertransference
4. resist
5. emotional reeducation

## Application

1. resistance, transference

## Critical Analysis

1. scientific
2. inferior
3. multicultural

## Current Status

1. Ego
2. object relations
3. Kohut

# ANSWERS TO MATCHING ITEMS

| | | |
|---|---|---|
| 1. E | 14. D | 26. KK |
| 2. H | 15. AA | 27. FF |
| 3. B | 16. Y | 28. A |
| 4. J | 17. V | 29. JJ |
| 5. N | 18. DD | 30. HH |
| 6. Q | 19. C | 31. F |
| 7. G | 20. CC | 32. L |
| 8. R | 21. EE | 33. S |
| 9. U | 22. GG | 34. X |
| 10. BB | 23. O | 35. M |
| 11. I | 24. II | 36. T |
| 12. P | 25. W | 37. K |
| 13. Z | | |

## CHAPTER 7

# Adlerian Therapy

## CHAPTER OVERVIEW

1. *Biography.* Adler (1870-1937) described his childhood as unhappy, growing up with physical and family setbacks. At age 25, he received his medical degree from the University of Vienna and soon worked in a neighborhood clinic. After the First World War, Adler established guidance clinics for the Vienna school system where he became convinced of the importance of child-rearing practices. In 1902 Adler was invited to join Freud's discussion group. Adler, however, never considered himself a disciple of Freud and the two men eventually drifted apart as Adler spoke openly about their differences. Adler, in fact, formed the Society for Individual Psychology and established his own theory of psychotherapy.

2. *Historical Development.* Adler's thinking was influenced greatly by Hans Vaihinger's "as if" principle. Janet also influenced his thinking on the power of inferiority, while Nietzsche's striving for perfection helped Adler shape his concept of the striving for superiority. And, of course, the greatest influence of Adler's thinking was Sigmund Freud, with whom he collaborated for nearly a decade (1902-1911).

3. *View of Human Nature.* Adler viewed people as irreducibly whole, thus the term *individual* psychology. Individuals, according to Adler, experience a sense of inferiority and strive to overcome it. This striving for superiority is what turns a deficiency into an advantage. Adler also believed that expectations and goals for the future motivate human activity and provide the capacity for social interest (an intrinsic concern for others), the most important goal toward which people strive.

4. *Development of Maladaptive Behavior.* According to Adler, maladaptive behavior results from discouraging or disappointing circumstances. When people lose the courage to face life's demands directly, they move from a sense of inferiority to an inferiority complex. Pathological behavior, while not always evident until later years, originates in childhood as a result of the family of origin relationships. Being pampered or neglected as a child, for example, contributes to maladaptive behavior because the child will compensate for either error by manifesting unrealistic striving for personal superiority.

5. *Function of the Therapist.* Adlerian therapists often function as educators who attempt to build on strengths the client already demonstrates. Encouragement is critical as the therapist works to establish and maintain an accepting, caring, cooperative relationship with the client. The work of therapy is viewed as collaborative, where the client and the counselor are partners, working toward mutually agreed-upon and clearly identified goals. In short, the Adlerian counselor's energy is invested, not in analysis, but encouragement.

6. *Goals of Therapy.* Adlerian therapy seeks to decrease a sense of inferiority in clients and help them encase their social interest. By helping people to contribute, by altering faulty motivations which underlie even acceptable behavior, by encouraging equality, Adlerians seek to change the lifestyles, the perceptions and goals of their clients.

7. *Major Methods and Techniques.* The most common therapeutic techniques of Adlerian therapy include investigating the client's life-style (basic orientation toward life). This is done systematically by exploring "three entrance gates to mental life." The first of these is birth order which pays attention to one's position within the family and the resulting expectations and roles that typically result from it. The second is early recollections which encapsulate one's present philosophy of life. And third is dreams which, in Adler's view, serve to rehearse how one might deal with problems in the future.

8. *Application.* Many of the most common Adlerian strategies can be seen clearly when working with children. The case of "Pablo," a nine-year-old middle child is such an example. Together with his teacher, the counselor worked to focus the counseling session on helping Pablo to belong to a peer group through improved social interactions and concern for others.

9. *Critical Analysis.* Adlerian therapy's versatility is evident. It has been proven to work with a wide variety of populations. Its impact on other counseling approaches is also very noteworthy. Its emphasis on equalitarian prosocial ideals is another plus. Few classical theorists have affirmed the importance of understanding diversity within the context of counseling more than Adler. However, Adlerian theory has been criticized for placing practice and teaching over definition and organization. As a result, a major difficulty with Adler's theory is the lack of systematization in his writings and the vagueness which clouds his constructs. Another limitation is its lack of a firm research base.

10. *Current Status.* While the number of "Adlerian" practitioners is not staggering, this approach to therapy is integrated to some degree or another into many of today's counseling approaches. Adler has had a tremendous impact on today's counselors, and specialized centers of learning continue to promote his methods and strategies with upcoming practitioners.

## GUIDED STUDY

These questions are meant to guide you through the major sections of the chapter. Write your answer in the space provided and then compare it with the marked section of the text.

1. Describe how Adler's formative years as a child may have impacted his theory.

   _____

   _____

   _____

   _____

2. In your own words, how should you describe the birth of individual psychology to someone who was not familiar with its history?

   _____

   _____

   _____

   _____

3. Central to Adler's theory is the premise that human beings are irreducibly whole. What does he mean by this and why is it emphasized?

   _____

   _____

   _____

   _____

4. How does Alder explain the role of physical abnormalities or personality deficits in their development of neurosis?

_____

_____

_____

_____

5. Whereas Freud believed that human behavior is pushed by the past, Adler believed it is pulled by the future. Explain this emphasis by using Adler's concept of "finalism."

_____

_____

_____

_____

6. One of the most important goals toward which people strive is social interest. What is it and why is it so important?

_____

_____

_____

_____

7. The seeds for pathological behavior, according to Adler, are planted early in life. Give some examples of how maladaptive behavior would develop from this Adlerian point of view.

_____

_____

_____

_____

8. Compare how the Adlerian therapist differs from the Freudian therapist in approach. What qualities and techniques are used?

_____

_____

_____

_____

9. What is the overarching goal of Adlerian therapy?

_____

_____

_____

_____

10. The life-style investigation is a major therapeutic technique in this approach. How is it conducted and what does it involve?

_____

_____

_____

_____

11. What did you learn from Adler's treatment of "Pablo"? Describe how he used Adlerian techniques in this case.

_____

_____

_____

_____

12. From a critical analysis, what are the most salient strengths and weaknesses of this approach?

_____

_____

_____

_____

## CHAPTER REVIEW

The following items will help you master the specific content of the chapter. Complete each of the following sentences by filling in the blanks.

## Biography

1. One of Adler's earliest memories was of sitting on a bench, bandaged and incapacitated by _____, while his athletic older brother played vigorously.

2. After the First World War, Adler was given the task of establishing
   _____ for the Vienna school system.

3. Early in 1911 Adler delivered to Viennese society three lectures which elaborated the differences that distinguished his work from _____.

## Historical Development

1. Among the influences on Adler's thinking was _____, who
   believed that a sense of inferiority is the general cause of neurosis.

2. Vaihinger's book, The Psychology of "_____," proposed that
   people live in accordance with fictional goals they set for themselves.

3. The greatest contemporary influence on Adler's Individual Psychology
   was _____, with whom Adler collaborated for almost a decade.

## View of Human Nature

1. Central to Adler's program is the premise that human beings are
   irreducibly _____.

2. All individual progress, growth, and development result from the
   attempt to _____ for our inferiorities, be they imagined or real.

3. Adlerian counseling assumes that individuals are motivated by a striving
   for _____.

4. Adler believed that people are inherently concerned with the welfare of
   others, a capacity that he labeled _____.

5. What is intriguing about personal goals, according to Adler, is that they
   do not exist as actualities but as _____.

## Development of Maladaptive Behavior

1. Unconsciously convinced of their _____, people develop
   abnormal behavior to divert attention from their troubles.

2. _____ robs children of their independence and initiative; it is
   the most serious of parental errors.

3. When parents fail to provide sufficient care for and attention to their
   children, they collapse into the error of _____, creating the
   impression that the world is cold and unsympathetic.

4. People may attempt to compensate for their sense of inferiority by
   developing what Adler called a _____, that is, by developing
   an exaggerated opinion of their own abilities and accomplishments.

## Goals of Therapy

1. In addition to fostering social interest, Adlerian therapy seeks to decrease a sense of _____ in clients.

2. Adlerian therapy seeks to develop _____ people who view a task or situation, not in terms of potential threats and dangers, but in terms of possible actions and solutions.

3. Cases are expected to show at least partial improvement by the _____ month of treatment.

## Function of the Therapist

1. Identifying and building on strengths the client already demonstrates, Adlerian therapists often function as _____.

2. While qualities of empathy, warmth and genuiness are important to Adlerian therapists, the focus is on _____-oriented behaviors such as interpretation, confrontation, and concreteness.

3. A therapist's _____ help clients to resolve apparent contradictions and realign mistaken goals.

## Major Methods and Techniques

1. _____ remains the bedrock of Adlerian intervention, especially in establishing a therapeutic relationship.

2. Every person develops a distinctive _____ — a basic orientation toward life, a psychological map that becomes a guide for action.

3. Adler found that _____ children are often oriented toward the past, locked in nostalgia, and pessimistic about the future.

4. To Adlerians, _____ encapsulate our present philosophy of life.

5. The so-called "_____" technique encourages clients to realize they have choices in responding to or reacting to stimuli in their lives. It teaches clients they can create desired feelings by choosing what to think about.

## Application

1. In the case of Pablo the focus in the counseling session was on helping him to belong to a peer group through improved social interactions and concern for _____.

## Critical Analysis

1. Adler placed emphasis on _____ and _____ instead of on theoretical definitions and organization.

2. While Adler's position on the individual's freedom to choose is clear, his explanation of the individual's _____ power that permits this freedom is not.

3. Adler's schema serves counselors who integrate _____ perspectives into a single compressive theoretical approach.

## Current Status

1. Freud's ideas may be the most remembered, but Adler's counseling techniques have been the most _____.

2. The question is no longer whether one is an Adlerian, but _____ _____ an Adlerian one is.

# KEY TERMS

Learning a theory depends, in large part, on mastering the vocabulary associated with that theory. The following key terms will help you do just that. You may want to use three-by-five cards to create your own flash card test from this list. Once you have studied this vocabulary, you will want to test your knowledge with the matching quiz which follows.

**Birth order** One's position in the family constellation (first-born, second-born, etc.) To Adler, it was a major factor in the development of personality.

**Compensation** A motivation to overcome real or imagined inferiority, to strive for higher levels of development through effort and practice.

**Creative power of the self** The ability of the individual to create an appropriate style of life.

**Early recollections** A therapeutic assessment technique in which a person's earliest memories are assumed to reveal the individual's primary interest in life.

**Fictional finalism** The idea that there is an imagined or potential goal that guides an individual's behavior because they act "as if" it were true.

**Individual psychology** The theory of counseling and method of diagnosis and treatment formulated by Alfred Adler.

**Inferiority complex** A condition that develops when an individual is unable to compensate for normal inferiority feelings. It is characterized by exaggerated feelings of weakness, including the belief that one cannot overcome one's difficulties through appropriate effort.

**Inferiority feelings** The source of human striving that is the normal condition of all people.

**Masculine protest** Behavior motivated by objections to the belief that society regards men as superior to women. It may occur in males or females.

**Neglect** Failing to give a child sufficient care and attention, thereby creating the belief that the world is a cold and unfriendly place.

**Organ inferiority** A significant physiological defect, usually of unknown cause, that can trigger strong feelings of inferiority.

**Pampering** Also known as "spoiling," it is giving a child excessive attention and protection, thereby preventing the development of initiative and independence and creating the impression that the world owes one a living.

**Social interest** The innate potential of all individuals to cooperate with other people to achieve personal and societal goals.

**Striving for Superiority** The urge toward perfection or completion, the ultimate goal that motivates the individual. Healthy strivings are guided by social interest, whereas pathological strivings ignore the welfare of others.

**Style of life** A unique character structure, or a pattern of personal behaviors and characteristics, by which an individual strives for perfection. Four basic styles of life are the dominant, getting, avoiding, and socially useful types.

**Superiority complex** A condition that develops when an individual overcompensates for normal inferiority feelings. It is a false feeling of power and security that invariably concerns an underlying inferiority complex.

**Teleological** From the Greek *tele*, meaning *far* or *distant*, an adjective indicating the goal-directness of human behavior.

# MATCHING ITEMS

## Terms

A. Style of Life
B. Early Recollections
C. Striving for Superiority
D. Organ Inferiority
E. Birth Order
F. Compensation

G. Social Interest
H. Individual Psychology
I. Teleological
J. Pampering
K. Neglect
L. Masculine Protest

M. Inferiority Feelings
N. Inferiority Complex
O. Creative Power of the Self
P. Fictional Finalism
Q. Superiority Complex

## Description

_____ 1. A therapeutic assessment technique in which a person's earliest memories are assumed to reveal the individual's primary interest in life.

_____ 2. The theory of counseling and method of diagnosis and treatment formulated by Alfred Adler.

_____ 3. Failing to give a child sufficient care and attention, thereby creating the belief that the world is a cold and unfriendly place.

_____ 4. One's position in the family constellation (first-born, second-born, etc.). To Adler, it was a major factor in the development of personality.

_____ 5. Also known as "spoiling," it is giving a child excessive attention and protection, thereby preventing the development of initiative and independence and creating the impression that the world owes one a living.

_____ 6. The urge toward perfection or completion, the ultimate goal that motivates the individual. Healthy strivings are guided by social interest, whereas pathological strivings ignore the welfare of others.

_____ 7. The ability of the individual to create an appropriate style of life.

_____ 8. A condition that develops when an individual overcompensates for normal inferiority feelings. It is a false feeling of power and security that invariably concerns an underlying inferiority complex.

_____ 9. The source of human striving that is the normal condition of all people.

_____ 10. From the Greek *tele*, meaning *far* or *distant*, an adjective indicating the goal-directness of human behavior.

_____ 11. A unique character structure, or a pattern of personal behaviors and characteristics, by which an individual strives for perfection. Four basic styles of life are the dominant, getting, avoiding, and socially useful types.

_____ 12. The innate potential of all individuals to cooperate with other people to achieve personal and societal goals.

_____ 13. A motivation to overcome real or imagined inferiority, to strive for higher levels of development through effort and practice.

_____ 14. A condition that develops when an individual is unable to compensate for normal inferiority feelings. It is characterized by exaggerated feelings of weakness, including the belief that one cannot overcome one's difficulties through appropriate effort.

_____ 15. The idea that there is an imagined or potential goal that guides an individual's behavior because they act "as if" it were true.

_____ 16. Behavior motivated by objections to the belief that society regards men as superior to women. It may occur in males or females.

_____ 17. A significant physiological defect, usually of unknown cause, that can trigger strong feelings of inferiority.

# QUESTIONS FOR DISCUSSION
# AND PERSONAL REFLECTION

The following questions can be used in small group discussion for further exploration of the theory and/or personal reflection of how the theory applies to your own life.

1. What is your general impression of Adler's theory? Do you agree that social interest is a primary goal toward which clients should strive? Why or why not?

_____

_____

_____

_____

2. How do you view Adler's theory as applying to your own life? If you do not view it as having any applicability to your life, why?

_____

_____

_____

_____

3. If you could have a conversation with Adler, what questions would you have for him about his theory?

_____

_____

_____

4. As you develop your own approach to therapeutic intervention, what will you take with you from individual psychology?

_____

_____

_____

_____

# ANSWERS TO CHAPTER REVIEW

## Biography

1. rickets
2. guidance clinics
3. Freud's

## Historical Development

1. Janet
2. "As If"
3. Sigmund Freud

## View of Human Nature

1. whole
2. compensate
3. superiority
4. social interest
5. potentialities

## Development of Maladaptive Behavior

1. inferiority
2. pampering
3. neglect
4. superiority complex

## Goals of Therapy

1. inferiority
2. courageous
3. third

## Function of the Therapist

1. educators (or tutors)
2. action
3. confrontations

## Major Methods and Techniques

1. encouragement
2. life-style

3. oldest (or first born)
4. early recollections
5. push button

## Application

1. others

## Critical Analysis

1. practice, teaching
2. creative
3. multicultural

## Current Status

1. practiced
2. how much

## ANSWERS TO MATCHING ITEMS

1. B
2. H
3. K
4. E
5. J
6. C
7. O
8. Q
9. M

10. I
11. A
12. G
13. F
14. N
15. P
16. L
17. D

## CHAPTER 8

# Existential Therapy

## CHAPTER OVERVIEW

1. *Biography.* May (1909-1994) grew up in the midwestern United States. He attended Michigan State and graduated from Oberlin College in Ohio with a B.A. in English. Shortly after graduation he taught in Salonika, Greece and spent two summers in Vienna where he enrolled in seminars conducted by Alfred Adler. After three years abroad, May returned to the US and enrolled in Union Theological Seminary in preparation for the ministry. After graduating, May's first two years as a pastor were disappointing and he soon enrolled in Columbia University to major in clinical psychology. His studies were cut short by a bout with tuberculosis but it was during this illness that he read Kierkegaard's works and became interested in existentialism. He eventually completed his Ph.D. and went on to write extensively on existential theory.

2. *Historical Development.* Existential psychotherapy is rooted in the philosophical writings of Kierkegaard and Nietzsche. They introduced existential thought to Western Europe and it was their work that established the footing for several influential philosophers, including Albert Camus, Jean-Paul Sartre, Martin Heidegger, and Martin Buber.

3. *View of Human Nature.* Existentialism is alternately religious, atheistic, and anti-religious. It emphasizes hope and optimism, as well as despair and nothingness. In short, existentialists do not agree on a basic view of human nature. Despite its diversity, however, all agree on the importance of existence, the phenomena which are inherent in the very nature of being alive. Existentialists believe that life is either fulfilled or constricted by a series of decisions that we make, with no way of knowing conclusively what the correct choices are. Existentialists emphasize experience as the primary

phenomenon in the study of human nature. Both theoretical explanations and overt behavior are secondary to experience itself and its meaning to the person.

4. *Development of Maladaptive Behavior.* If we fail to live in a state of awareness of our being, according to existential thought, we inevitably develop psychopathology. Of course, this state of being has the potential for great anxiety which can lead to self-deception and ever greater maladaptive behavior. The bottom line is that such maladaptive behavior is fundamentally the result of meaninglessness; maladaptive behavior is the result of not embracing our freedom and responsibility, or disregarding our true self, of forsaking genuine meaning in life.

5. *Goals of Therapy.* The overarching purpose of the existential approach is to help clients find purpose and meaning in life. More specifically, existentialism attempts to make clients more aware of their existence, elucidate their uniqueness, improve encounters with others, and to foster freedom and responsibility. The existential approach strives to help persons move in the direction of ever-increasing actualization and integration.

6. *Function of the Therapist.* The existential therapist is grounded in the immediate, subjective experience of encountering the client. In an effort to restore personal meaning in the life of a client, the existential therapist may use advocacy, empathy, concern, reflection, action, environmental modification, or support. They have a kind of intellectual flexibility that is not threatened by the ideas and beliefs of others and that does not adhere stubbornly to any one intellectual system, theory, or ideology.

7. *Major Methods and Techniques.* The methods used by existential counselors are varied. However, the typical course of therapy begins with the client's circumstances at the moment. Paradoxical intention, which requires clients to act against their anticipation of fear, is sometimes used. Dereflection, is an approach to treating excessive self-observation, obsession, or self-attention. It encourages clients to ignore the problem and direct awareness toward something favorable and pleasant. Modifying one's attitude, changing the way one thinks about a situation, is also commonly used existential method.

8. *Application.* The case of Mrs. Hutchens illustrates a number of principles Rollo May applied to counseling. This suburban woman in her mid-30s, suffered from a hysterical tenseness of the larynx. May found that the woman believed that if she spoke her mind to people, she would be rejected; it was safer to keep quiet. May also observed the patient's fainting spells and anxiety attacks and he interpreted them as attempts to kill her emerging consciousness. In the end, Mrs. Hutchens was left only to confront herself and the result was an opportunity for greater independence, positive growth, and the development of a healthier life.

9. *Critical Analysis*. Existential therapy must be commended for its breadth as well as its focus on issues other approaches have avoided. It is a position that has proved to be highly stimulating and rewarding. The existentialists' emphasis on our repressed fear of death and on our sense of alienation and meaninglessness has furthered our understanding of psychopathology and treatment. Existentialists have helped the professional community recognize that humans need and seek meaning. It is an approach that also lends itself to working with ethnic-minority clients. It provides cultural relativity by helping to understand one's own cultural heritage within the context of other perspectives. Still, existentialism pro vides no systematic presentation of procedure, methodology, or empirical validation of its therapeutic approach.

10. *Current Status*. While only a very small percentage of today's counselors label themselves primarily as existentialists, this approach has been a powerful force in changing the fact of contemporary psychotherapy. It has been incorporated in almost every major therapeutic tradition.

## GUIDED STUDY

These questions are meant to guide you through the major sections of the chapter. Write your answer in the space provided and then compare it with the marked section of the text.

1. Describe how Rollo May's formative years may have impacted the development of his theory.

_____

_____

_____

_____

2. In your own words, how would you describe the birth of existential therapy to someone who was not familiar with its history?

_____

_____

_____

_____

3. Central to existential theory is its emphasis on existence. Explain what this means and how the phenomena of being alive are related to it.

_____

_____

_____

_____

4. The existential therapist believes that if we fail to live in a state of awareness of our being, even at the risk of anxiety, we will inevitably fall into maladaptive behavior. How and why does this happen?

_____

_____

_____

_____

5. Existential therapy is not imposed. Neither are clients viewed as an object to be evaluated, assessed, or programmed. With this understanding, how would you describe the function of the existential therapist?

_____

_____

_____

_____

6. The ultimate goal of existential psychotherapy is to help the client become aware and make decisions which are responsible. Describe existential techniques to show how this is done.

_____

_____

_____

_____

7. Describe the typical course of existential therapy beginning with the initial session.

_____

_____

_____

_____

8. Explain Gendlin's technique of focusing and why it may be helpful.

_____

_____

_____

_____

9. In Victor Frankl's Logotherapy, he talks about the "Will to meaning." What is this and what relevance does it have to existential psychotherapy?

_____

_____

_____

_____

10. Compare how the existential approach compares to psychoanalysis and individual psychology.

_____

_____

_____

_____

11. What did you learn from May's treatment of Mrs. Hutchens? Describe how he used existential methods in this case.

_____

_____

_____

_____

12. From a critical analysis, what are the most important strengths and weaknesses of the existential approach?

_____

_____

_____

_____

# CHAPTER REVIEW

The following items will help you master the specific content of the chapter. Complete each of the following sentences by filling in the blanks.

## Biography

1. The existential approach to counseling is represented today by a number of different theorists, but it began with the work of Ludwig

   _____.

2. Returning to Union Theological Seminary in New York, Rollo May completed his studies under the German philosopher Paul _____, who strongly influenced May's thinking.

3. May's doctoral dissertation, _The Meaning of_ _____, was in many respects a prophetic work.

## Historical Development

1. As a philosophical movement, existentialism developed in continental _____ during the nineteenth century from the work of the philosophers Søren Kierkegaard and Friedrich Nietzsche.

2. Arguing that religious beliefs cannot be supported by rational argument, Kierkegaard believed that true faith is essentially irrational. At its heart, according to Kierkegaard, Christianity demands that the believer accept the "_____."

3. Nietzsche proclaimed, "God is _____," which became a popular theological slogan in the 1960s after an Episcopal bishop wrote a book by that title.

## View of Human Nature

1. The central focus of existentialism is on the essence of _____ — on the phenomena which are inherent in the very nature of being alive.

2. From the "here-and-now" or the _____ perspective, human choice is wholly subjective.

3. Only when individuals have learned to make choices and to live with the consequences, are they truly free. But because they freely choose, individuals are also fully _____ for their choices.

4. Death, or nonbeing, is significant to an existential understanding of human nature, for we live on two levels: in a state of _____ of being and in a state of _____ of being.

5. The existential therapist does not analyze human motivation in terms of past events. It is _____ that motivates us, that offers us possibilities that draw us forward.

## Development of Maladaptive Behavior

1. The existential therapist believes that if we fail to live in a state of _____, we will inevitably collapse into maladaptive behavior.

2. From the point of view of existential psychologists, psychopathology is not a difference in degree but in kind, and they consider traditional nomenclature, including _____ _____, to be alienating and depersonalizing.

3. For the existentialist, such maladaptive behavior is fundamentally the result of _____.

## Goals of Therapy

1. Because the goals of existential therapy emerge from the therapeutic process, they often seem _____.

2. Frankl emphasized _____ values over creative values and experiential values.

3. Clients have the capacity for change, which can occur on the twin axes of actualization and _____.

## Function of the Therapist

1. The existential therapist expects the therapeutic responsibility to rest squarely on the _____.

2. The existential therapist is grounded in the _____, subjective experience of encountering the client.

3. Only when clients embrace _____ can therapeutic change occur.

## Major Methods and Techniques

1. Perhaps more so than any other counselor, the existential therapist will rely on those techniques that are most compatible with his or her _____.

2. The initial therapy session begins with the client's circumstances at the _____ and moves on from there.

3. While not exclusively existential, Eugene Gendlin developed an approach known as _____, that is often used by existential counselors.

4. Victor Frankl first set forth his ideas of "_____," as a means of providing or experiencing healing through meaning.

5. Like Adler, Frankl found great value in "_____ _____," which requires clients to act against their anticipation of fear.

## Application

1. Rollo May interpreted Mrs. Hutchens fainting and attacks of anxiety as attempts to kill her emerging _____.

## Critical Analysis

1. With its particular focus on personal choice and freedom, existential therapy can be especially useful in helping _____ clients.

2. While rich in appreciation of the human condition, existentialism provides for no systematic presentation of _____.

3. While there may be some validity to the proposition that each existential practitioner is unique, it clearly prohibits the systematic _____ of the theory.

## Current Status

1. Although few, if any, counseling psychologists would advertise themselves as "Logotherapists" or "Existentialists," even fewer clients today enter therapy without exposing themselves to the assumptions and approaches of _____.

## KEY TERMS

Learning a theory depends, in large part, on mastering the vocabulary associated with that theory. The following key terms will help you do just that. You may want to use three-by-five cards to create your own flash card test from this list. Once you have studied this vocabulary, you will want to test your knowledge with the matching quiz which follows.

**Anxiety** Apprehension caused by a threat to some value deemed essential to the existence of one's personality. Since death is an absolute and inevitable aspect of existence, a certain amount of anxiety is a natural characteristic of being human.

**Daimonic** Innate benign and illicit forces capable of dominating one's entire personality, such as sex, passion and Eros, procreation, self-affirmation, destructiveness, rage, hostility, and the quest for power. Psychological health requires that the daimonic be accepted and integrated into consciousness.

**Dasein** A conscious and unconscious sense of oneself as a distinct, autonomous, and responsible entity existing in the world of physiological and physical surroundings (Umwelt), other people (Mitwelt), and one's own self (Eigenwelt). A strong Dasein is essential to the healthy personality.

**Daseinanalysis** A method of existential psychotherapy developed by Medard Boss which focuses on the individual's existence or his specific way of "being-in-the-world."

**Dereflection** A technique of counteracting obsessive ideation or hyper-reflection by helping the client stop thinking about the problem.

**Eigenwelt** The world of relationship to oneself, and to one's own potentials and values. One of the three simultaneous and interrelated modes of being-in-the-world.

**Focusing** A technique for introspection and change which identifies how a client talks about their experiencing.

**Guilt** Regret resulting from the impossibility of fulfilling all of one's innate potentials (a denial of Eigenwelt), of relating perfectly to others (a denial of Mitwelt), and of always recognizing our communion with nature (a denial of Umwelt).

**Intentionality** The capacity of human beings to have a conscious and unconscious sense of purpose, and behave teleologically.

**Logotherapy** An existential approach to psychotherapy developed by Victor Frankl shortly after World War II. It accents the capacity of each person to exercise the power of choice and experience healing through meaning.

**Love** A delight in the presence of another person and a readiness to affirm that person's values and development as much as one's own.

**Mitwelt** The world of relationship to other people. One of the three simultaneous and interrelated modes of being-in-the-world.

**Ontological characteristics** Those qualities that are distinctively and definitively human, including Dasein, anxiety, guilt, intentionality, love, and care.

**Ontology** The science of existence or being.

**Paradoxical intention** A technique for directing a client to do something contrary to one's actual instructions; the success of the directive is due to one not being able to force that which is involuntary.

**Phenomenological** An attitude of respect for the dignity and integrity of each person's experience and an approach or methodology for studying the personal meanings of experience.

**Teleology** The philosophical study of purpose, believing that natural processes are not determined by mechanism but rather by their utility in an overall natural design.

**Umwelt** The world of internal and external objects, which forms our physiological and physical environment. One of the three simultaneous and interrelated modes of being-in-the-world.

**Will** The conscious capacity to move toward one's self-selected goals. It is the more self-evident aspect of intentionality.

## MATCHING ITEMS

### Terms

A. Will
B. Diamonic
C. Mitwelt
D. Focusing
E. Dasein
F. Ontology
G. Love

H. Paradoxical
   Intention
I. Anxiety
J. Umwelt
K. Phenomenological
L. Guilt
M. Teleology

N. Ontological
   Characteristics
O. Dereflection
P. Intentionality
Q. Eigenwelt
R. Logotherapy
S. Daseinanalysis

### Description

_____ 1. A conscious and unconscious sense of oneself as a distinct, autonomous, and responsible entity existing in the world of physiological and physical surroundings (Umwelt), other people (Mitwelt), and one's own self (Eigenwelt). A strong Dasein is essential to the healthy personality.

_____ 2. A delight in the presence of another person and a readiness to affirm that person's values and development as much as one's own.

_____ 3. The world of relationship to other people. One of the three simultaneous and interrelated modes of being-in-the-world.

_____ 4. A technique of counteracting obsessive ideation or hyperreflection by helping the client stop thinking about the problem.

_____ 5. The science of existence or being.

_____ 6. An attitude of respect for the dignity and integrity of each person's experience and an approach or methodology for studying the personal meanings of experience.

_____ 7. Apprehension caused by a threat to some value deemed essential to the existence of one's personality. Since death is an absolute and inevitable aspect of existence, a certain amount of anxiety is a natural characteristic of being human.

_____ 8. The capacity of human beings to have a conscious and unconscious sense of purpose, and behave teleologically.

_____ 9. A technique for introspection and change which identifies how a client talks about their experiencing.

_____ 10. An existential approach to psychotherapy developed by Victor Frankl shortly after World War II. It accents the capacity of each person to exercise the power of choice and experience healing through meaning.

_____ 11. The philosophical study of purpose, believing that natural processes are not determined by mechanism but rather by their utility in an overall natural design.

_____ 12. The conscious capacity to move toward one's self-selected goals. It is the more self-evident aspect of intentionality.

_____ 13. The world of internal and external objects, which forms our physiological and physical environment. One of the three simultaneous and interrelated modes of being-in-the-world.

_____ 14. The world of relationship to oneself, and to one's own potentials and values. One of the three simultaneous and interrelated modes of being-in-the-world.

_____ 15. A method of existential psychotherapy developed by Medard Boss which focuses on the individual's existence or his specific way of "being-in-the-world."

_____ 16. A technique for directing a client to do something contrary to one's actual instructions; the success of the directive is due to one not being able to force that which is involuntary.

_____ 17. Those qualities that are distinctively and definitively human, including Dasein, anxiety, guilt, intentionality, love, and care.

_____ 18. Regret resulting from the impossibility of fulfilling all of one's innate potentials (a denial of Eigenwelt), of relating perfectly to others (a denial of Mitwelt), and of always recognizing our communion with nature (a denial of Umwelt).

_____ 19. Innate benign and illicit forces capable of dominating one's entire personality, such as sex, passion and Eros, procreation, self-affirmation, destructiveness, rage, hostility, and the quest for power. Psychological health requires that the daimonic be accepted and integrated into consciousness.

# QUESTIONS FOR DISCUSSION
# AND PERSONAL REFLECTION

The following questions can be used in small group discussion for further exploration of the theory and/or personal reflection of how the theory applies to your own life.

1. What is your general impression of existential psychotherapy? Do you agree that meaning is paramount in people's lives?

_____

_____

_____

_____

2. How do you view this theory applying to your own life? If you do not view it as having any applicability to your life, why?

_____

_____

_____

_____

3. If you could have a conversation with Rollo May or Victor Frankl, what questions would you have for either?

_____

_____

_____

_____

4. As you develop your own approach to therapeutic intervention, what will you take with you from existential counseling?

_____

_____

_____

_____

# ANSWERS TO CHAPTER REVIEW

## Biography

1. Binswanger
2. Tillich
3. Anxiety

## Historical Development

1. Europe
2. absurd
3. dead

## View of Human Nature

1. existence
2. phenomenological
3. responsible
4. forgetfulness, mindfulness
5. Dasein

## Development of Maladaptive Behavior

1. awareness
2. diagnostic labels
3. meaninglessness

## Goals of Therapy

1. vague (or obscure)
2. attitudinal
3. integration

## Function of the Therapist

1. clients
2. immediate
3. responsibility

## Major Methods and Techniques

1. personality
2. moment
3. focusing
4. Logotherapy
5. paradoxical intention

## Application

1. consciousness

## Critical Analysis

1. minority
2. procedure (or methodology)
3. teaching

## Current Status

1. existentialism

## ANSWERS TO MATCHING ITEMS

| | | | |
|---|---|---|---|
| 1. E | | 11. M | |
| 2. G | | 12. A | |
| 3. C | | 13. J | |
| 4. O | | 14. Q | |
| 5. F | | 15. S | |
| 6. K | | 16. H | |
| 7. I | | 17. N | |
| 8. P | | 18. L | |
| 9. D | | 19. B | |
| 10. R | | | |

## CHAPTER 9

# Person-Centered Therapy

## CHAPTER OVERVIEW

1. *Biography.* Rogers (1902-1987) grew up in a well-to-do, conservative, midwestern family. He read voraciously as a child and developed a precocious respect for the experimental method. Rogers majored in agriculture and history at the University of Wisconsin and as a sophomore he committed himself to Christian ministry. After Union Theological Seminary, he transferred to Columbia where he eventually earned his Ph.D. in clinical psychology. Rogers immersed himself in practical clinical work and after publishing his first book he was invited to teach at Ohio State University. Following professorships at the University of Chicago and then the University of Wisconsin, in 1968 he founded the Center for Studies of the Person in La Jolla, California, where he died at age 85.

2. *Historical Development.* The origins of person-centered therapy can be found in reaction to what Rogers often called "counselor-centered therapy," in which the therapist administers tests, asks questions, and suggests courses of action for the client. Rogers' revolutionary approach took on such subtle changes as using the term "client" instead of "patient," and it was he who first called his approach "nondirective counseling," later changing it to "person-centered counseling," as a means of emphasizing its positive focus on human capacities.

3. *View of Human Nature.* Rogers viewed people through an optimistic lens, seeing human nature as basically good. He emphasized an inherent tendency of people to grow and move in healthy directions. For Rogers, this *actualizing tendency* was the primary motivating force of every human being. It is guided by what he called the organismic valuing process, an inherent capacity to choose that which will enhance a person and reject

**153**

that which will not. The actualization drive creates the inner urge for fulfillment, and the *organismic valuing process* determines or reveals what will provide that inner fulfillment. Given the proper conditions, Rogers believed the capacities for normal growth and development could be released in every human being.

4. *Development of Maladaptive Behavior.* Distortions in the self-concept quickly warp the organismic valuing process and lead to maladaptive behavior. Rogers suggested that learned values, thoughts, feelings, and behaviors may differ so radically from the experiences approved by the person's own organismic valuing process, that an almost complete dissociation develops. The bottom line is that this leads to being more externally than internally oriented, and thus individuals contort feelings to match the expectations of others. It is this incongruity that gives birth to psychological pain and maladjustment.

5. *Goals of Therapy.* Person-centered therapy does not seek to solve problems, but to facilitate a process in which clients can know who they really are and become *fully functioning* human beings. It strives to eliminate the need for impressing others, lying to oneself, or distorting perceptions. Person-centered therapy tries to eliminate the unhealthy need to please others and to move toward increasingly trusting one's own experience.

6. *Function of the Therapist.* The role of the person-centered therapist is rooted, not in doing, but in being. The major task of the therapist is to provide a climate of safety and trust, which will encourage clients to reintegrate their self-actualizing and self-valuing processes. The therapist accomplishes this through accurate empathic understanding, congruence, and unconditional positive regard. Although these skills can be learned, to be effective, they must spring from the very being of the counselor. The person-centered therapist is nonauthoritarian, seldom, if ever, giving advice, making interpretations, or teaching their clients.

7. *Major Methods and Techniques.* Rogers' therapeutic work led him to identify three "necessary and sufficient" conditions for growth and change in personality: congruence (in which the therapist's inner experiences and their observable outward actions match), unconditional positive regard (the clients' worth is not dependent on other's expectations and approval), and empathic understanding (the therapist enters the place of the clients and understands the world from their perspective, adopting the clients' internal frame of reference).

8. *Application.* Rogers was the first to expose the practice of counseling to audio recording. He made great use of this technology and as a result developed thorough case studies during the formulation of his theory. The case of "Mrs. Oak" is one example that illustrates just how Rogers used the three essential ingredients to bring about a truer sense of one's self and greater autonomy. A comparison of Rogerian transcript with a more problem-solving approach reveals the stark difference between counselor-centered and client-centered approaches to therapy.

9. *Critical Analysis.* The respect of person-centered therapy for the individual and its reliance on the client is most admirable. Trusting clients to be
responsible has its advantages. However, this approach leads many to
ask how clients can supply accurate self-appraisals, and the underlying
philosophical assumption that people are fundamentally good raises
many questions among critics. Few can argue with the global impact and
contributions to cross-cultural counseling of person-centered therapy.
While it is not a complete answer to these circumstances (especially after
the initial facilitation processes), it certainly provides a foundation for
working with many ethnically diverse clients.

10. *Current Status.* Several generations of practitioners who have been trained
in Rogerian strategies report being strongly influenced by the person-
centered approach — especially eclectic counselors. Despite Rogers' significant influence, however, most psychologists do not claim person-
centered therapy as their primary theoretical orientation. One of their reasons for regarding the approach as necessary, rather than sufficient, may be
that Rogers opposed the formation of a person-centered "school" of counseling that would grant certificates and set standards for membership.

## GUIDED STUDY

These questions are meant to guide you through the major sections of the chapter. Write your answer in the space provided and then compare it with the
marked section of the text.

1. Describe how Rogers' formative years may have impacted the development of his theory.

_____

_____

_____

_____

2. In your own words, how would you describe the birth of person-
centered therapy to someone who was not familiar with its history?

_____

_____

_____

_____

3. Central to Rogers' theory is an optimistic view of human personality that focuses on present rather than past experience. Explain what the person-centered therapist means by this. Use the actualizing tendency as part of your answer.

_____

_____

_____

_____

4. Rogers talks about one's self-concept as playing a significant role in the development of maladaptive behavior. Explain more about how he views the development of maladaptive behavior.

_____

_____

_____

_____

5. The personhood of the therapist is paramount. This being so, how would you explain the primary function of the person-centered therapist?

_____

_____

_____

_____

6. What is the overarching goal of person-centered therapy and how does "moving away from the self one is not" factor into it?

_____

_____

_____

_____

7. Describe what Rogers means by "moving toward one's true self."

_____

_____

_____

_____

8. Rogers' therapeutic work led him to identify three "necessary and sufficient" conditions for growth and change in personality. Describe these conditions.

_____

_____

_____

_____

9. Explain the concept of congruence.

_____

_____

_____

_____

10. In person-centered therapy, the client's worth is not dependent on others' expectations. Why is this important?

_____

_____

_____

_____

11. What did you learn from Roger's treatment of Mrs. Oak? Describe how he used person-centered techniques in this case.

_____

_____

_____

_____

12. From a critical analysis, what are the most salient strengths and weaknesses of this approach?

_____

_____

_____

_____

# CHAPTER REVIEW

The following items will help you master the specific content of the chapter. Complete each of the following sentences by filling in the blanks.

## Biography

1. As an undergraduate, Rogers majored in _____ and _____ at the University of Wisconsin.

2. Although his father offered to pay all expenses if Rogers would go to Princeton, his son declared his independence and moved to the more liberal _____ Theological Seminary in New York, where he enrolled in the usual courses in scripture and theology.

3. In 1968 Rogers helped found the Center for Studies of the _____ in La Jolla, California, an experimental community in which social scientists and others undertook a variety of training, research, and social projects.

## Historical Development

1. Rogers' methods and perspective were a reaction to what he often labeled "_____-centered therapy."

2. Rogers used the term "client" instead of the traditional "_____," which seemed to him to indicate a "sick person who expects a cure from the doctor.

3. Initially termed "_____ counseling," Rogers' therapeutic approach was named "client-centered counseling" in 1951 as a means of emphasizing Rogers' positive focus on human capacities.

## View of Human Nature

1. Unlike the Freudian approach, person-centered therapy views people as basically _____.

2. Rogers emphasized an inherent tendency of people to grow and move in healthy directions, to develop their capacities to the fullest. He termed this directional leaning as a(n) _____ tendency.

3. Rogers recognized that human beings are capable of great evil, but he believed that these propensities are the result of negative "conditions of _____" imposed on children by family and society.

4. Given the proper _____, the capacities for normal growth and development can be released in every human being.

## Development of Maladaptive Behavior

1. Unpolluted by distortions caused by other persons' judgments, a _____ allows the organismic valuing process to continue to function as a trustworthy guide.

2. Children learn to falsify their _____ selves in order to maintain parental love and protection.

3. Maladaptive behavior results when persons become more _____ oriented than _____ oriented.

## Goals of Therapy

1. Person-centered therapy strives to create an environment safe enough to eliminate the need for _____.

2. Person-centered therapy initially strives to help clients relinquish _____.

3. The fully functioning person may do things to please others, but he or she will not _____ someone else just to please others.

4. As clients discard their emotional armor, they open themselves to others and the pleasures that come with being _____.

## Function of the Therapist

1. The major task of the therapist is to provide a climate of _____ and _____, which will encourage clients to reintegrate their self-actualizing and self valuing processes.

2. The so-called therapeutic triad includes: accurate _____ understanding, _____, and _____ positive regard.

3. Seldom, if ever, does the Rogerian counselor give _____ or teach the client.

## Major Methods and Techniques

1. Instead of explaining the causes of the client's problems or prescribing actions for him or her to take, Rogers discovered that the client improved when he simply _____ him or her as a valuable human being.

2. For a client to grow, a therapist must be genuine and transparent, a state of realness which Rogers called _____.

3. If a therapist is uncomfortable with some aspect of the client relationship but does not admit it, the discomfort acts as a shield against authenticity and creates _____.

4. In person-centered counseling, there are no _____ of worth that the client must meet to qualify for the therapist's acceptance.

5. The third ingredient of person-centered therapy is _____, the capacity to enter the place of another human being and understand the world from his or her perspective.

6. To facilitate empathic understanding, the person-centered therapist feeds back or "_____" to his or her clients, as accurately as possible, the feelings he or she is expressing.

## Application

1. In the case of Mrs. Oak progress was seen when she became less problem-oriented and better able to _____ herself.

## Critical Analysis

1. Perhaps Rogers' greatest strength is his unequivocal _____ for persons.

2. Critics say Rogers is naively _____ about human personality.

3. On a pragmatic and clinical level, many practitioners do not agree that it is preferable to dispense with _____ and rely wholly on genuiness, empathy, and unconditional positive regard.

## Current Status

1. Observing Rogers through filmed and video taped presentations has led practitioners to confuse _____ with substance.

2. Many counselors today regard person-centered therapy as _____ but not sufficient, treating it more as a _____ upon which they must build other therapeutic skills.

3. Since the person-centered approach takes a relatively short time to master and since it emphasizes _____ skills, it is the basis for much of today's counselor training.

# KEY TERMS

Learning a theory depends, in large part, on mastering the vocabulary associated with that theory. The following key terms will help you do just that. You may want to use three-by-five cards to create your own flash card test from this list. Once you have studied this vocabulary, you will want to test your knowledge with the matching quiz which follows.

**Actualizing Tendency** The inherent tendency of human beings to develop all of their potential, to become the best that their inherited natures will allow them to be.

**Conditional Positive Regard** Accepting another person only if that individual meets one's own standards.

**Congruence** A healthy state of unison between one's total organismic experience and a self-concept which is free of conditions of worth. It is one of the three basic conditions for therapeutic effectiveness.

**Empathy** The act of accurately understanding the client's world from the client's perspective. It is one of the three basic conditions for therapeutic effectiveness.

**Encounter Group** A small group of relatively well-adjusted individuals that, through intense interaction, allows individuals to discover more about themselves and how they relate to others.

**Experience** Everything, including thoughts, needs, perceptions, going on within the individual that is presently within awareness.

**Fully Functioning** Describes individuals who are using their capacities and talents, realizing their potential, and moving toward complete knowledge of themselves and their full range of experiences.

**Genuiness** Being truly oneself in relationship with others. It is one of the three basic conditions for therapeutic effectiveness.

**Ideal Self** The self-concept an individual would like to have (it includes aspirations, moral ideals, and values).

**Incongruence** A schism between one's total organismic experience and a self-concept burdened by conditions of worth, resulting in a state of inner tension and confusion.

**Internal Frame of Reference** The realm of experience that is available to the awareness of a person at a given moment.

**Introjection** Incorporating the standards of another person within one's own personality.

**Nondirective Therapy** Psychotherapy in which the client leads the way by expressing feelings, defining problems, and interpreting behavior, while the therapist cultivates a warm and accepting atmosphere in which the client can clarify his or her process rather than directing it.

**Organismic Valuing Process** The inherent capacity to choose that which will enhance our well-being and reject that which does not.

**Person-centered Approach** The phrase Rogers later used in place of "non-directive" because it more accurately reflected his approach.

**Phenomenology** An approach to understanding personality which emphasizes the importance of understanding the individual's subjective experiences, feelings, and private concepts.

**Positive Regard** Giving selective attention to the client's verbal and behavioral assets.

**Self-actualization** The tendency to actualize that portion of experience represented by the self-concept.

**Self-concept** A collection of learned perceptions about one's abilities and characteristics.

**Significant Other** An important source of positive regard, such as a parent.

**Unconditional Positive Regard** The acceptance of another person without conditions of worth. One of the three essential characteristics of the successful therapeutic relationship.

**Warmth** The primarily nonverbal (e.g., vocal tone, posture, facial expression, etc.) means of expressing care in a therapeutic relationship.

## MATCHING ITEMS

### Terms

A. Fully Functioning
B. Self-concept
C. Experience
D. Self-actualization
E. Person Centered Approach
F. Actualizing Tendency
G. Conditional Positive Regard

H. Phenomenology
I. Ideal Self
J. Introjection
K. Internal Frame of Reference
L. Congruence
M. Genuiness
N. Positive Regard
O. Encounter Group
P. Significant Other

Q. Empathy
R. Unconditional Positive Regard
S. Warmth
T. Incongruence
U. Organismic Valuing Process
V. Nondirective Therapy

### Description

_____ 1. An approach to understanding personality which emphasizes the importance of understanding the individual's subjective experiences, feelings, and private concepts.

_____ 2. A collection of learned perceptions about one's abilities and characteristics.

_____ 3. The realm of experience that is available to the awareness of a person at a given moment.

_____ 4. The inherent tendency of human beings to develop all of their potential, to become the best that their inherited natures will allow them to be.

_____ 5. The act of accurately understanding the client's world from the client's perspective. It is one of the three basic conditions for therapeutic effectiveness.

_____ 6. Being truly oneself in relationship with others. It is one of the three basic conditions for therapeutic effectiveness.

_____ 7. A schism between one's total organismic experience and a self-concept burdened by conditions of worth, resulting in a state of inner tension and confusion.

_____ 8. The tendency to actualize that portion of experience represented by the self-concept.

_____ 9. Incorporating the standards of another person within one's own personality.

_____ 10. A small group of relatively well-adjusted individuals that, through intense interaction, allows individuals to discover more about themselves and how they relate to others.

_____ 11. The primarily nonverbal (e.g., vocal tone, posture, facial expression, etc.) means of expressing care in a therapeutic relationship.

_____ 12. Accepting another person only if that individual meets one's own standards.

_____ 13. Psychotherapy in which the client leads the way by expressing feelings, defining problems, and interpreting behavior, while the therapist cultivates a warm and accepting atmosphere in which the client can clarify his or her process rather than directing it.

_____ 14. The acceptance of another person without conditions of worth. One of the three essential characteristics of the successful therapeutic relationship.

_____ 15. Describes individuals who are using their capacities and talents, realizing their potential, and moving toward complete knowledge of themselves and their full range of experiences.

_____ 16. The phrase Rogers later used in place of "nondirective" because it more accurately reflected his approach.

_____ 17. An important source of positive regard, such as a parent.

_____ 18. A healthy state of unison between one's total organismic experience and a self-concept which is free of conditions of worth. It is one of the three basic conditions for therapeutic effectiveness.

_____ 19. The self-concept an individual would like to have (it includes aspirations, moral ideals, and values).

_____ 20. Giving selective attention to the client's verbal and behavioral assets.

_____ 21. The inherent capacity to choose that which will enhance our well-being and reject that which does not.

_____ 22. Everything, including thoughts, needs, perceptions, going on within the individual that is presently within awareness.

## QUESTIONS FOR DISCUSSION AND PERSONAL REFLECTION

The following questions can be used in small group discussion for further exploration of the theory and/or personal reflection of how the theory applies to your own life.

1. What is your general impression of person-centered therapy? Do you agree with its optimistic view of human personality and its focus on the present rather than the past?

   _____

   _____

   _____

   _____

2. How do you view Roger's theory as applying to your own life? If you do not view it as having any applicability to your life, why?

   _____

   _____

   _____

   _____

3. If you could have a conversation with Rogers, what questions would you have for him about his theory?

   _____

   _____

   _____

   _____

4. As you develop your own approach to therapeutic intervention, what will you take with you from person-centered theory?

_____

_____

_____

_____

## ANSWERS TO CHAPTER REVIEW

## Biography

1. agriculture, history
2. Union
3. Person

## Historical Development

1. counselor
2. patient
3. nondirective

## View of Human Nature

1. good (or trustworthy)
2. actualizing
3. worth
4. conditions

## Development of Maladaptive Behavior

1. self-concept
2. falsify
3. externally, internally

## Goals of Therapy

1. facades
2. phoniness (or self-concealment)
3. become
4. authentic

## Function of the Therapist

1. safety, trust
2. empathic, congruence, unconditional
3. advice

## Major Methods and Techniques

1. accepted
2. congruence
3. incongruence
4. conditions
5. empathy
6. reflects

## Application

1. express

## Critical Analysis

1. respect
2. optimistic
3. interpretation

## Current Status

1. style
2. necessary, foundation
3. listening

## ANSWERS TO MATCHING ITEMS

| | | |
|---|---|---|
| 1. H | 9. J | 16. E |
| 2. B | 10. O | 17. P |
| 3. K | 11. S | 18. L |
| 4. F | 12. G | 19. I |
| 5. Q | 13. V | 20. N |
| 6. M | 14. R | 21. U |
| 7. T | 15. A | 22. C |
| 8. D | | |

## CHAPTER 10

# Gestalt Therapy

## CHAPTER OVERVIEW

1. *Biography.* Perls (1893-1970) grew up as the only son in a German family. He was an unruly child but loved to read and was an excellent student. He earned his M.D. degree from Frederick Wilhelm University and soon joined the German army as a medic. After World War I, Perls began psychoanalytic training and eventually took a position in Frankfort working with Kurt Goldstein, who taught him to view the human being as a complete entity, rather than the sum of its separate parts. During the 1930s Perls fled the Nazis, eventually emigrating to South Africa where he and his wife, Laura, built a strong practice. But it was after a meeting with Freud in 1936 that Perls moved to New York, where he founded the Institute for Gestalt Therapy and dedicated himself to proving Freud wrong.

2. *Historical Development.* The origins of Gestalt therapy are found in three Germans whom Perls studied: Wertheimer, Koffka, and Köhler. Perls saw an individual's perceptions in terms of the Gestalt dichotomy of figure-ground and established his theory on that premise. Another important historical influence on Gestalt therapy was the existential movement in philosophy and psychology.

3. *View of Human Nature.* Perls believed that people develop in relation to their environment, and he divided this development into the social, psychophysical, and spiritual stages. His existential and humanistic perspective viewed people as self-directed; he believed they must take responsibility for their own lives. Gestaltists believe that a healthy personality is the result of a person's experiences forming a meaningful whole (i.e., gestalt). This occurs when there is a smooth transition between those sets of experiences that are immediately in the focus of awareness and those that lie in the background.

4. *Development of Maladaptive Behavior.* In Gestalt theory people develop maladaptive behavior, characterized by a lack of awareness, self-responsibility, contact with environment, denial of needs, and so on, when they fail to utilize their own capacity for self-regulation and spend their energy on acting helpless, depending upon others, or manipulating the environment in countless ways. The result is an anxious state of temporal insecurity originating when the self is unable to determine the boundaries between the individual and the environment.

5. *Goals of Therapy.* Gestalt therapy tries to help individuals assume responsibility for themselves, rather than relying on others to make decisions for them. It tries to facilitate a process in which clients can become complete and integrated, functioning as a systematic whole which consists of feelings, perceptions, thoughts, and a physical body whose processes cannot be divorced from its more psychological components. This goal is often reached through an "Aha!" experience, in which we suddenly see and understand what had long eluded us.

6. *Function of the Therapist.* The role of the Gestalt therapist is to serve as a catalyst for change without assuming the responsibility for change within the clients. As a result, the Gestalt therapist plays an active role that often frustrates the clients' demands for support and help, forcing them to rely on their own resources. The Gestalt therapist also views change through a paradoxical lens, holding that change takes place, not when one tries to be what one is not, but when one becomes what one is. Thus, to be authentic, the Gestalt therapist must not try to be a better therapist, but to be who he or she is at the moment.

7. *Major Methods and Techniques.* Perls' work led him to identify many therapeutic techniques, all of which are experiential rather than verbal. Gestalt therapy is about doing rather than saying. After laying a foundation of general "rules" of therapy (e.g., communication is to be between equals in the present tense), a therapist may choose from a smorgasbord of methods: dream work, converting questions to statements, using personal pronouns, assuming responsibility, playing the projection, the empty chair, making the rounds, exaggeration, confrontation, and so on.

8. *Application.* Perls often demonstrated his therapeutic approach in open workshop settings. In his work *Gestalt Therapy Verbatim*, he provides many firsthand accounts of how Gestalt therapy can be applied to a variety of situations. The case of "Beverly" is one example that illustrates just how Perls probed a client to encourage her to externalize feelings, to center herself, and to get in touch with the games or gimmicks behind which she was hiding.

9. *Critical Analysis.* Gestalt therapy features a holistic emphasis on the integration of fragmented parts of the personality. More than any other theory, it stresses the unity of mind, body, and feelings. It has enormous

intuitive appeal, but its intended outcomes raise questions. With its strong emphasis on individuality, relationships are in danger of being relegated to a secondary status. The pre-eminent virtue is self-sufficiency. The Gestalt approach offers some benefits to cross-cultural counseling (e.g., its techniques can help dismantle some cross-cultural barriers) but also has many limitations (e.g., it can lead to resistance or greater shame). Nevertheless, in treating people with physical disabilities, Gestalt therapy has been found quite useful.

10. *Current Status.* As an experiential approach, Gestalt therapy has provided a provocative challenge to other theoretical approaches, but is it seldom recognized by academic psychology. In many respects, the Perls era of Gestalt therapy is over. Due in part to its lack of a research base, there are few Gestalt purists. Despite its waning popularity, however, the Gestalt approach continues to influence the field of counseling as its strategies are integrated into other approaches.

## GUIDED STUDY

These questions are meant to guide you through the major sections of the chapter. Write your answer in the space provided and then compare it with the marked section of the text.

1. Describe how Perls formative years may have impacted the development of his theory.

_____

_____

_____

_____

2. In your own words, how would you describe the birth of Gestalt therapy to someone who was not familiar with its history?

_____

_____

_____

_____

3. Describe the fundamental assumptions of Gestalt theory about human nature. Be sure to include the concepts of "organism-environment field, organismic self-regulation, psychological homeostasis, and awareness.

_____

_____

_____

_____

4. According to Gestalt theory, people develop psychological problems in several ways. Describe them.

_____

_____

_____

_____

5. Perls identified five layers of neurosis that potentially interfere with our being authentically in touch with ourselves. Describe each of these layers (phony, phobic, impasse, implosive, and explosive).

_____

_____

_____

_____

6. The role of the Gestalt therapist is an extremely active one. Explain why this is and what it involves.

_____

_____

_____

_____

7. One of the major goals of Gestalt therapy is helping individuals assume responsibility for themselves, rather than relying on others to make decisions for them. What other important goals are a part of this approach to counseling?

_____

_____

_____

_____

8. When it comes to the major methods and techniques of Gestalt therapy, an experiential, rather than a verbal approach is noticeable. Describe how this applies to the fourfold steps of this helping process.

_____

_____

_____

_____

9. Perls described dreams as "messages" that represent the person place at a certain time. How does this differ from the psychoanalytic theory of dream interpretation?

_____

_____

_____

_____

10. Describe how the "empty chair" technique is implemented by the Gestalt therapist.

_____

_____

_____

_____

11. What did you learn from Perls' treatment of Beverly? Describe how he used Gestalt techniques in this case.

_____

_____

_____

_____

12. From a critical analysis, what are the most salient strengths and weaknesses of this approach?

_____

_____

_____

_____

## CHAPTER REVIEW

The following items will help you master the specific content of the chapter. Complete each of the following sentences by filling in the blanks.

## Biography

1. After World War I, Perls began _____ training in Vienna and Berlin.

2. Anticipating the rising tide of Fascism in Europe, Perls fled Holland in 1934, barely ahead of the Nazis, and emigrated to _____ where he established an institute for psychoanalysis.

3. Eventually Perls became instrumental in the development of the _____ Institute in Big Sur, California.

## Historical Development

1. The distinguished roots of Gestalt therapy reach back into the _____ century, to the very beginning of psychology as a discipline.

2. Gestalt therapy seeks a smooth transition between those sets of experiences that are the _____, that are immediately in the focus of awareness, and those that form the _____ — the background.

3. In 1912 three young German psychologists, Max Wertheimer, Kurt _____, and Wolfgang Kohler, joined forces to found the Berlin Gestalt School.

## View of Human Nature

1. Perls believed that people develop in relation to their _____, and he distinguished three stages in this development.

2. The third stage, which Perls called the _____ stage, is reached by very few people.

3. What becomes foreground for an individual is based upon his or her current _____.

4. Just as living organisms seek a balance between salt and water or between acid and alkali, so are we regulated to maintain balance between ourselves and our environment. In Gestalt terms, this is called psychological _____.

5. _____ gives us a sense of direction and motivation to become more fully who we are.

## Development of Maladaptive Behavior

1. While Perls never developed a systematic theory of maladaptive behavior, he identified five layers of neurosis that potentially interfere with our being authentically in touch with ourselves. The first is the _____ layer.

2. At the phobic layer individuals attempt to avoid recognizing aspects of the _____ they would prefer to deny.

3. Personal conflicts are usually the result of an inability to bring together individual needs and _____ demands, so that people can be fully present in the now.

4. When one is completely incapable of determining the boundaries between one's self and the environment, the result is a(n) _____ state.

## Goals of Therapy

1. One of the most significant goals of Gestalt therapy is helping individuals assume _____ for themselves.

2. Gestalt therapy aims to challenge its clients to move from "environmental support" to "_____-support."

3. _____ means bringing together all of the parts of a person that have been disowned.

4. Another basic goal of Gestalt therapy is to help clients become aware the _____.

## Function of the Therapist

1. The role of the Gestalt therapist is extremely _____.

2. One of the major functions of the Gestalt therapist is to _____ the clients' demands for support and help, so they are forced to rely on their own resources.

3. Gestalt therapists do not make use of standardized _____.

## Major Methods and Techniques

1. Unlike psychoanalysts, Gestalt counselors do not _____ dreams.

2. Clients who experience repetitive dreams are encouraged to realize that _____ _____ is being brought into awareness and that they need to take care of the message.

3. The Gestalt therapist will often ask clients to turn their questions into _____ in order to help them take responsibility for their thoughts.

4. Clients are often encouraged to conclude all expression of feelings or beliefs with, "And I take _____ for it."

5. To help clients retrieve parts of themselves they are either unaware of or have denied, Gestalt therapists often give clients the opportunity to _____ _____ the way they would like to behave toward another person.

6. _____ helps heighten unwitting movements or gestures so that clients can become more aware of the inner meaning of their behaviors.

## Application

1. The case of "Beverly" is one of the best firsthand accounts of how Perls applied his theory in a "_____ work seminar."

## Critical Analysis

1. One of the most appealing features of Gestalt therapy is its _____ emphasis on the integration of fragmented parts of the personality.

2. A common concern over Gestalt therapy is not about the games played by clients, but about those played by _____ _____.

3. Gestalt techniques can be customized in ways that a client can perceive and interpret from a distinct _____ .

4. In treating clients with physical disabilities Gestalt therapy is particularly _____.

## Current Status

1. It can be said that while Gestalt therapy captured the zeitgeist, the spirit of the age, it failed to take _____.

2. Some argue that Gestalt therapy's decline in popularity is due, in part, to its lack of a _____ base.

3. There are more than _____ Gestalt therapy institutes throughout the world, and the *Gestalt Journal* is devoted to publishing articles on Gestalt therapy.

## KEY TERMS

Learning a theory depends, in large part, on mastering the vocabulary associated with that theory. The following key terms will help you do just that. You may want to use three-by-five cards to create your own flash card test from this list. Once you have studied this vocabulary, you will want to test your knowledge with the matching quiz which follows.

**Acknowledgment** Individuals discover themselves and develop a sense of self and appreciation through acknowledgment.

**Adaptation** In this process the individual discovers personal boundaries and differentiates self from nonself.

**Aggression** The organism's means of contacting its environment to satisfy its needs and of meeting resistance to the satisfaction of its needs. Its purpose is not destruction, but simply overcoming resistance.

**Approbation** A process through which people develop splits in their personalities and create a self-image (a notion of self based on external standards). Approbation interferes with the development of a sound and healthy notion of self.

**Awareness** The process of observing and attending to your thoughts, feelings, and actions, including body sensations as well as visual and auditory perceptions. It is seen as a flowing panorama that constitutes your "now" experience.

**Closure** The Gestalt concept that the mind synthesizes the missing parts of a perceived image and, in effect, closes the gap between the reality and the desired "picture."

**Figure** That which occupies the center of a person's attentive awareness; what the person is now paying attention to.

**Gestalt** German word meaning shape, figure, configuration, totality or whole.

**Gestalt Psychology** An approach that focuses on the dynamic organization of experience into patterns of configurations. This viewpoint came into prominence as a revolt against structuralism, which analyzed experience into static, atomistic sensations, and also against the equally atomistic approach of behaviorism, which dissected complex behavior into elementary conditioned reflexes.

**Ground** The part of the perceptual field that is not "figure" is identified as ground. Taken together, figure and ground constitute a gestalt.

**Here and Now** An emphasis on understanding present feelings as they occur in an ongoing treatment, with little or no emphasis on past experience.

**Homeostasis** The tendency for living organisms to find equilibrium or balance between themselves and their surrounding environment.

**Impasse** The situation in which progress in the treatment process has ceased, and failure in imminent. This situation occurs when further insight is not forthcoming, or when the process is blocked by extreme resistance.

**Introjection** The uncritical acceptance of other people's concepts, standards of behavior, and values. The person who habitually introjects does not develop his or her own personality.

**Organismic self-regulation** The process by which an individual, confronted by either an external demand or an internal need, strives to reduce tension by maintaining the organismic balance between demands and needs.

**Projection** The process by which the individual places in the outside world the parts of the personality that the organism refused (or is unable) to identify.

**Proximity** The Gestalt principle which states that objects or stimuli that are close together will be perceived as a unity. For example, a series of unconnected lines in a neon sign become a word or sentence.

**Retroflection** The process by which some function that was originally directed from the individual towards the world changes direction and is bent back towards the originator. The result is a split between the self as doer and the self as receiver.

**Self** The creative process that leads the person to actualizing behaviors by responding to emergent needs and environmental pressures. The fundamental characteristic of the self is the formation and distinction of gestures.

**Self-image** The part of the personality that hinders creative growth by imposing external standards.

**Similarity** When stimuli in the perceptual field causes us to group similar things together.

# MATCHING ITEMS

## Terms

| | | |
|---|---|---|
| A. Figure | I. Adaptation | O. Gestalt |
| B. Similarity | J. Organismic | P. Awareness |
| C. Aggression |    Self-regulation | Q. Projection |
| D. Self-image | K. Self | R. Proximity |
| E. Closure | L. Homeostasis | S. Approbation |
| F. Here and Now | M. Impasse | T. Acknowledgment |
| G. Introjection | N. Retroflection | U. Gestalt Psychology |
| H. Ground | | |

## Description

_____ 1. The process by which an individual, confronted by either an external demand or an internal need, strives to reduce tension by maintaining the organismic balance between demands and needs.

_____ 2. The organism's means of contacting its environment to satisfy its needs and of meeting resistance to the satisfaction of its needs. Its purpose is not destruction, but simply overcoming resistance.

_____ 3. The process by which some function that was originally directed from the individual towards the world changes direction and is bent back towards the originator. The result is a split between the self as doer and the self as receiver.

_____ 4. The Gestalt concept that the mind synthesizes the missing parts of a perceived image and, in effect, closes the gap between the reality and the desired "picture."

_____ 5. The process by which the individual places in the outside world the parts of the personality that the organism refused (or is unable) to identify.

_____ 6. A process through which people develop splits in their personalities and create a self-image (a notion of self based on external standards). Approbation interferes with the development of a sound and healthy notion of self.

_____ 7. When stimuli in the perceptual field causes us to group similar things together.

_____ 8. An approach that focuses on the dynamic organization of experience into patterns of configurations. This viewpoint came into prominence as a revolt against structuralism, which analyzed experience into static, atomistic sensations, and also against the equally atomistic approach of behaviorism, which dissected complex behavior into elementary conditioned reflexes.

_____ 9. The uncritical acceptance of other people's concepts, standards of behavior, and values. The person who habitually introjects does not develop his or her own personality.

_____ 10. Individuals discover themselves and develop a sense of self and appreciation through acknowledgment.

_____ 11. The creative process that leads the person to actualizing behaviors by responding to emergent needs and environmental pressures. The fundamental characteristic of the self is the formation and distinction of gestures.

_____ 12. The part of the perceptual field that is not "figure" is identified as ground. Taken together, figure and ground constitute a gestalt.

_____ 13. The process of observing and attending to your thoughts, feelings, and actions, including body sensations as well as visual and auditory perceptions. It is seen as a flowing panorama that constitutes your "now" experience.

_____ 14. The tendency for living organisms to find equilibrium or balance between themselves and their surrounding environment.

_____ 15. That which occupies the center of a person's attentive awareness; what the person is now paying attention to.

_____ 16. The Gestalt principle which states that objects or stimuli that are close together will be perceived as a unity. For example, a series of unconnected lines in a neon sign become a word or sentence.

_____ 17. In this process the individual discovers personal boundaries and differentiates self from nonself.

_____ 18. The part of the personality that hinders creative growth by imposing external standards.

_____ 19. German word meaning shape, figure, configuration, totality or whole.

_____ 20. An emphasis on understanding present feelings as they occur in an ongoing treatment, with little or no emphasis on past experience.

_____ 21. The situation in which progress in the treatment process has ceased, and failure in imminent. This situation occurs when further insight is not forthcoming, or when the process is blocked by extreme resistance.

## QUESTIONS FOR DISCUSSION
## AND PERSONAL REFLECTION

The following questions can be used in small group discussion for further exploration of the theory and/or personal reflection of how the theory applies to your own life.

1. What is your general impression of Gestalt therapy? Do you agree with its view of human personality and its focus on experience?

   _____

   _____

   _____

   _____

2. How do you view Perls' theory as applying to your own life? If you do not view it as having any applicability to your life, why?

   _____

   _____

   _____

   _____

3. If you could have a conversation with Perls, what questions would you have for him about his theory?

   _____

   _____

   _____

   _____

4. As you develop your own approach to therapeutic intervention, what will you take with you from person-centered theory?

   _____

   _____

   _____

   _____

# ANSWERS TO CHAPTER REVIEW

## Biography

1. psychoanalytic
2. South Africa
3. Esalen

## Historical Development

1. nineteenth
2. figure, ground
3. Koffka

## View of Human Nature

1. environment
2. spiritual
3. needs
4. homeostasis
5. awareness

## Development of Maladaptive Behavior

1. phony
2. self
3. environmental
4. anxious

## Goals of Therapy

1. responsibility
2. self
3. Integration
4. present

## Function of the Therapist

1. active
2. frustrate
3. assessments (or tests)

## Major Methods and Techniques

1. interpret
2. unfinished business
3. statements
4. responsibility
5. role play
6. Exaggeration

## Application

1. dream

## Critical Analysis

1. holistic
2. Gestalt therapists
3. culture
4. useful

## Current Status

1. hold
2. research
3. sixty

## ANSWERS TO MATCHING ITEMS

| | | |
|---|---|---|
| 1. J | 8. U | 15. A |
| 2. C | 9. G | 16. R |
| 3. N | 10. T | 17. I |
| 4. E | 11. K | 18. D |
| 5. Q | 12. H | 19. O |
| 6. S | 13. P | 20. F |
| 7. B | 14. L | 21. M |

## CHAPTER 11

# Transactional Analysis

## CHAPTER OVERVIEW

1. *Biography.* Born in Montreal, Canada, Berne (1910-1970) grew up admiring his father who was a physician devoted to his patients. After his father's early death, Berne entered medical school, became an American citizen, and soon entered the Army Medical Corps as a psychiatrist. After World War II, Berne moved to San Francisco and resumed psychoanalytic training under Eric Erikson. Never achieving official recognition by the psychoanalytic association, however, Bern developed his own orientation to psychotherapy: Transactional Analysis, a more "rational" approach. He wrote many papers and books, including *Games People Play.*

2. *Historical Development.* The origins of TA can be found in a wide variety of sources. Berne merged, mixed, and synthesized the approaches of Freud, Adler, and Rogers especially. From the beginning, Berne strove to make his theory accessible and he succeeded. The diagrams that Berne used to explain interactions between people have become increasingly common place in counseling offices, classrooms, and management seminars.

3. *View of Human Nature.* For Berne, people are motivated primarily by basic psychological hungers to transcend patterns of behavior that begin early in life: stimulus hunger (the need to be acknowledged or affirmed by others); structure hunger (how we use time to maximize the number of strokes we receive), and position hunger (the need to have our fundamental decisions about life validated and affirmed). Personality is composed of three conscious or preconscious ego states, each an organized psychological system of feelings, thoughts, and behaviors: the Parent, the Adult and the Child.

4. *Development of Maladaptive Behavior.* Psychopathology, according to Berne, is the result of confused ego states. This confusion occurs when a person vacillates between ego states without completing their transaction (i.e., blocking the free flowing interaction among ego states). In addition, maladaptive behavior can result from playing games, a recurring set of transactions with a concealed motivation. Games occur when persons turn to others for confirmation of their negative "not OK" position, and the result is the avoidance of intimacy.

5. *Goals of Therapy.* The fundamental goal of TA is to help clients achieve autonomy, that is, to assume responsibility for their own actions or feelings, to take control of their lives, and to plan and direct their own destiny, and to throw off any perceptions that are inappropriate for living here and now. In other words, TA helps to free one's Adult from the influence of the Child and Parent. Another goal of TA is the help clients analyze their relationships by discovering their predominant Life Positions (e.g., "I'm okay—you're okay").

6. *Function of the Therapist.* The TA counselor works at being a catalyst for enabling clients to mobilize their resources. Acting very much like a teacher, the therapist explains key concepts such as structural analysis, script analysis, and game analysis. In addition the therapist helps clients make full and effective use of all three ego states, to live game-free.

7. *Major Methods and Techniques.* TA typically begins with a contract between client and therapist, which includes statements about what the client hopes to achieve and what the counselor will do, as well as specific criteria for knowing when the goal has been achieved. Structural analysis is then employed to identify the client's ego states and to become aware of how they function. Functional analysis is a didactic method used to describe transactions to the client. Game analysis looks at the methods of game playing in which a client might be involved. And script analysis examines the person's life direction, which is usually set at an early age.

8. *Application.* TA does not provide an abundance of case material. Nonetheless, the case of "Mrs. Enatosky," a thirty-four-year-old who had previously been in TA, illustrates many of Berne's applications. Berne noted that she showed a special aptitude for TA and she soon began to exert social control over the games that occurred between herself and her husband and between herself and her son.

9. *Critical Analysis.* TA is conducive to short-term treatment and works well in a variety of settings. The use of TA and Gestalt therapy together has been especially helpful to many. It is one of the only approaches that illuminates interpersonal, as opposed to intrapsychic, reality. But while TA's language has made it accessible to a lay audience, it can be used to excess and the terminology threatens to create a barrier rather than a bridge. Cross-culturally, TA has shown some initiative in being sensitive to particular cultural needs and may lead to a greater sense of empowerment for minorities, but the TA jargon may also serve as a stumbling block for ethnic-minority groups.

10. *Current Status.* TA enjoyed a national ground swell of popularity in the 1960s and has been furthered by a body of data, a respected professional journal. Although it is often integrated into the work of a wide variety of therapists, few practitioners today would identify TA as their primary theoretical orientation. Nevertheless, its interventions continue to be used by many eclectic practitioners.

## GUIDED STUDY

These questions are meant to guide you through the major sections of the chapter. Write your answer in the space provided and then compare it with the marked section of the text.

1. Describe how Eric Berne's formative years may have impacted the development of his theory.

_____

_____

_____

_____

2. In your own words, how would you describe the birth of Transactional Analysis to someone who was not familiar with its history?

_____

_____

_____

_____

3. Berne believed that basic psychological hungers motivate people to transcend patterns of behavior that begin early in life. Expand on this fundamental assumption and explain Berne's view of human nature.

_____

_____

_____

_____

4. Berne describes three conscious or preconscious ego states. Identify and explain the characteristics of each one.

_____

_____

_____

_____

5. Maladaptive behavior, according to Berne, is the result of confused ego states. What does he mean by this and how do concepts such as blocking, contamination, exclusion and games play a part of maladaptive development?

_____

_____

_____

_____

6. Explain how injunctions can contribute to maladaptive behavior.

_____

_____

_____

_____

7. The TA therapist takes a significant amount of time to do both structural and Transaction Analysis. Explain how the TA therapist does this.

_____

_____

_____

_____

8. Describe how autonomy factors into the overarching goal of Transactional Analysis and incorporate the qualities of autonomy into your answer.

_____

_____

_____

_____

9. What is the difference between structural analysis, functional analysis, game analysis, and script analysis?

_____

_____

_____

_____

10. Summarize your understanding of Mary McClure Goulding's and Robert Goulding's "redecision school."

_____

_____

_____

_____

11. What did you learn from Berne's treatment of Mrs. Enatosky?

_____

_____

_____

_____

12. From a critical analysis, what are the most salient strengths and weaknesses of this approach?

_____

_____

_____

_____

## CHAPTER REVIEW

The following items will help you master the specific content of the chapter. Complete each of the following sentences by filling in the blanks.

## Biography

1. Inspired by the memory of his father, Eric followed his footsteps through medical school at _____ University, receiving his M.D. in 1935.

2. For more than fifteen years, Berne pursued credentialing as a _____ without ever achieving official recognition.

3. Most of his productive life Berne practiced in his two offices in Carmel and in _____.

## Historical Development

1. Berne's long association with _____ helped form the ideas which eventually became Transactional Analysis.

2. The roots of TA can be found at McGill University in the research conducted on the _____ by Dr. Wilder Penfield.

3. From the beginning, Berne strove to make his theory _____.

## View of Human Nature

1. Berne believed that basic psychological _____ motivate people to transcend patterns of behavior that begin early in life.

2. Berne described _____ as basic units of social interaction.

3. _____ hunger refers to how we maximize the number of strokes we receive.

4. _____ hunger is the need to have our fundamental decisions about life validated and affirmed.

5. According to Berne, personality is composed of three ego states: the _____, the _____, and the _____.

6. The _____ child strives for total freedom to do whatever it wants whenever it wants.

## Development of Maladaptive Behavior

1. The two major boundary problems in TA are Blocking and _____.

2. _____ takes place when one or two ego states dominate a personality.

3. Berne used the term _____ because it suggests the idea of a contest that involves players, rules, moves, and predictable outcomes.

4. As a means of convincing themselves that they are "not OK" and to justify their never taking risks with real intimacy, people often develop habitual ways of feeling which Berne called _____.

## Goals of Therapy

1. The fundamental goal of Transactional Analysis is the help clients achieve _____, which means assuming responsibility for one's own actions or feelings, taking control of one's life, planning and direction one's own destiny.

2. Another goal of TA is to help clients analyze their _____, that is, their transactions.

3. Life positions are acted out in _____, which are the dramas that tie together the games and transactions of our lives.

## Function of the Therapist

1. The TA counselor works at being a _____ for enabling clients to mobilize their resources.

2. Transactional Analysis is concerned with diagnosing _____ states that emerge in social interchange.

3. The most common crossed transaction occurs when an Adult-Adult transactional stimulus is coupled with a _____-Child response.

4. _____ transactions occur when more than two ego states operate simultaneously.

## Major Methods and Techniques

1. TA typically begins with the client and therapist initiating a _____, which includes a statement about what the client hopes to achieve in counseling, a statement about what the counselor will do to facilitate the process, and some specific criteria for knowing when the goal has been achieved.

2. One way of assessing how much energy exists in the five functional ego states of any person is through the use of an _____.

3. The preferred form of treatment for TA-based programs appears to be in _____.

4. The until script requires waiting until a certain time to do something before one can have a reward while the _____ script forbids one to do what one wants because the parent forbids it.

5. Claude Seiner talks about our need for emotional _____ as a rationale for changing past life scripts.

## Application

1. Berne's work with Mrs. Enatosky demonstrates the _____ aspect of Transactional Analysis.

## Critical Analysis

1. Since so much of our meaningful life experience is interpersonal, TA's major strength is that it illuminates interpersonal, as opposed to _____, reality.

2. The _____ used in the TA approach can serve as a means of preventing therapists from imposing their cultural values in a multicultural context.

3. The _____ of TA may often serve as a stumbling block, being foreign to many ethnic-minority groups and consequently cumbersome to implement.

## Current Status

1. In the 1960s the best selling book, _____ _____ _____, propelled TA into a huge ground swell of popularity that critics inevitably dismissed as a fad.

2. Today, TA is not nearly as popular as it once was, but it continues to be a part of the _____ repertoire of many practitioners.

## KEY TERMS

Learning a theory depends, in large part, on mastering the vocabulary associated with that theory. The following key terms will help you do just that. You may want to use three-by-five cards to create your own flash card test from this list. Once you have studied this vocabulary, you will want to test your knowledge with the matching quiz which follows.

**Activities** Any work or other goal-oriented behavior is an activity. In activity, the individual sets up a situation in which the accomplishment of the task brings the needed strokes.

**Adapted Child** The Adapted Child becomes more controlled by interacting with parents.

**Adult Ego State** Best characterized as being concerned with facts. It acts as an assimilator of information.

**Child Ego state** The Child ego state is composed of all the feelings and ways of behaving that were experienced during the early years of childhood.

**Complementary Transaction** Sometimes called a *parallel transaction*, it is one in which stimulus and response vectors are parallel so that only two ego states are involved, one from each person.

**Conditional Stroke** A stroke given for *doing* something.

**Contamination** One of two ego-state boundary problems. It occurs when the logical, clear thinking of the Adult is interfered with by the prejudicial or irrational ideas and attitudes of the Parent or by the archaic feelings of the Child.

**Contract** An agreement between counselor and client which specifies the goals, stages, and conditions of treatment. An agreement.

**Controlling Parent** Opinionated, powerful, strongly protective, principled, punitive, and demanding. Are in charge.

**Crossed Transaction** Occurs when the vectors are not parallel, or more than two ego states are involved. Crossed up.

**Discounting** Involves ignoring or distorting some aspect of internal or external experience. One may discount the existence of a problem, the significance of a problem, the change possibilities of a problem, or one's own personal abilities. Selling short.

**Drama Triangle** A triadic interaction in which one person acts as persecutor, another as rescuer, and the third as victim. Like love.

**Ego State** States of mind and their related patterns of behavior as they occur in nature.

**Exclusion** This boundary problem exists when one or more ego states are effectively prevented from operating. Kept outside.

**Filtered Stroke** A stroke that is distorted or containing nonrelevant information.

**Game** A series of "duplex transaction," which lead to a switch and a well-defined, predictable payoff that justifies a not-OK or discounted position.

**Injunction** A type of negative parenting behavior: edicts that require children to behave in certain prescribed ways. They are usually "don't" messages.

**Intimacy** A candid, game-free relationship with mutual, free giving and receiving without exploitation.

**Life Position** Early in life, people experience a need to take a position regarding their own intrinsic worth and that of others. There are four life positions: I'm OK, you're OK; I'm OK, you're not OK; I'm not OK, you're OK; I'm not OK, you're not OK.

**Little Professor** The part of the Child ego state that is the forerunner of Adult reasoning.

**Natural Child** This part of the Child ego state contains the young, impulsive, untrained, emotionally expressive child.

**Negative Stroke** A painful stroke carrying a "You're not OK" message, and resulting in unpleasant feelings for the receiver.

**Nurturing Parent** Caring, concerned, forgiving, reassuring, permissive, warmly protective, and worried.

**Parent Ego State** Consists of a collection of tapes from significant others who had some kind of power relationship with the person.

**Pass Time** A pastime is a semi-ritualized conversation in which people share opinions, thoughts, or feelings about relatively safe topics that don't require them to act.

**Position Hunger** The need to have one's basic decisions about life confirmed constantly—decisions about the "OKness" of oneself and the world.

**Positive Stroke** A pleasurable stroke carrying a "You're OK" message and resulting in good feelings for the receiver.

**Racket** An habitual process (usually of complementary transactions) by which a person interprets or manipulates the environment to justify a life position of not-OKness.

**Rituals** Highly stylized and predictable ways of exchanging low-involvement, low-risk strokes such as greetings.

**Script** A personal life plan, which each individual forms by a series of decisions early in life in reaction to his or her interpretation of the important things happening in his or her world.

**Stamps** Feelings or strokes collected to justify some later behavior.

**Stimulus Hunger** The universal need for stimulation or stroking.

**Stroke** A unit of attention providing stimulation to a person.

**Structure Hunger** People's need to use their time in ways that maximize the number of strokes they can receive.

**Symbiosis** Two or more individuals behave as though they form a whole person. Coming together.

**Transaction** An exchange of strokes between two persons, consisting of a stimulus and a response between specified ego states.

**Transactional Analysis** Psychotherapy which focuses on characteristic inter-actions that reveal internal "ego states" and the "games people play" in social situations.

**Ulterior Transaction** A transaction that contains both an overt (social) and a covert (psychological) message. They may be either angular or duplex. An angular transaction involves three ego states and occurs when mes-sages are sent simultaneously from one ego state of the initiator to two ego states of the respondent. A duplex transaction involves four ego states, two in each person. During the course of a duplex transaction, two sets of complementary transactions occur simultaneously, one on the social level and one on the psychological level.

**Unconditional Stroke** Given for *being,* this stroke pertains to conditions that occur naturally and do not require special effort.

**Withdrawal** The most limiting and least rewarding way of structuring time. People who structure time by withdrawing live on strokes stored from the past or fantasized in the future.

## MATCHING ITEMS

### Terms

| | | |
|---|---|---|
| A. Pass Time | O. Withdrawal | CC. Little Professor |
| B. Stamps | P. Intimacy | DD. Life Position |
| C. Filtered Stroke | Q. Discounting | EE. Racket |
| D. Contract | R. Structure Hunger | FF. Unconditional Stroke |
| E. Positive Stroke | S. Negative Stroke | GG. Child Ego State |
| F. Script | T. Adult Ego State | HH. Exclusion |
| G. Natural Child | U. Drama Triangle | II. Nurturing Parent |
| H. Activities | V. Parent Ego State | JJ. Transactional |
| I. Game | W. Contamination |  Analysis |
| J. Stroke | X. Crossed Transaction | KK. Ulterior Transaction |
| K. Adapted Child | Y. Ego State | LL. Stimulus Hunger |
| L. Rituals | Z. Injunction | MM. Conditioned Stroke |
| M. Transaction | AA. Symbiosis | NN. Complementary |
| N. Position Hunger | BB. Controlling Parent |  Transaction |

## Description

1. Any work or other goal-oriented behavior is an activity. In activity, the individual sets up a situation in which the accomplishment of the task brings the needed strokes.

_____ 2. States of mind and their related patterns of behavior as they occur in nature.

_____ 3. A candid, game-free relationship with mutual, free giving and receiving without exploitation.

_____ 4. Two or more individuals behave as though they form a whole person. Coming together.

_____ 5. An agreement between counselor and client which specifies the goals, stages, and conditions of treatment. An agreement.

_____ 6. Given for being, this stroke pertains to conditions that occur naturally and do not require special effort.

_____ 7. Involves ignoring or distorting some aspect of internal or external experience. One may discount the existence of a problem, the significance of a problem, the change possibilities of a problem, or one's own personal abilities. Selling short.

_____ 8. Psychotherapy which focuses on characteristic interactions that reveal internal "ego states" and the "games people play" in social situations.

_____ 9. This part of the Child ego state contains the young, impulsive, untrained, emotionally expressive child.

_____ 10. Sometimes called a *parallel transaction*, it is one in which stimulus and response vectors are parallel so that only two ego states are involved, one from each person.

_____ 11. Consists of a collection of tapes from significant others who had some kind of power relationship with the person.

_____ 12. A stroke that is distorted or containing nonrelevant information.

_____ 13. An habitual process (usually of complementary transactions) by which a person interprets or manipulates the environment to justify a life position of not-OKness.

_____ 14. One of two ego-state boundary problems. It occurs when the logical, clear thinking of the Adult is interfered with by the prejudicial or irrational ideas and attitudes of the Parent or by the archaic feelings of the Child.

_____ 15. A unit of attention providing stimulation to a person.

_____ 16. This boundary problem exists when one or more ego states are effectively prevented from operating. Kept outside.

_____ 17. People's need to use their time in ways that maximize the number of strokes they can receive.

_____ 18. A transaction that contains both an overt (social) and a covert (psychological) message. They may be either angular or duplex. An angular transaction involves three ego states and occurs when messages are sent simultaneously from one ego state of the initiator to two ego states of the respondent. A duplex transaction involves four ego states, two in each person. During the course of a duplex transaction, two sets of complementary transactions occur simultaneously, one on the social level and one on the psychological level.

_____ 19. The Adapted Child becomes more controlled by interacting with parents.

_____ 20. Caring, concerned, forgiving, reassuring, permissive, warmly protective, and worried.

_____ 21. A type of negative parenting behavior: edicts that require children to behave in certain prescribed ways. They are usually "don't" messages.

_____ 22. A pastime is a semi-ritualized conversation in which people share opinions, thoughts, or feelings about relatively safe topics that don't require them to act.

_____ 23. Opinionated, powerful, strongly protective, principled, punitive, and demanding. Are in charge.

_____ 24. The most limiting and least rewarding way of structuring time. People who structure time by withdrawing live on strokes stored from the past or fantasized in the future.

_____ 25. A painful stroke carrying a "You're not OK" message, and resulting in unpleasant feelings for the receiver.

_____ 26. A personal life plan, which each individual forms by a series of decisions early in life in reaction to his or her interpretation of the important things happening in his or her world.

_____ 27. The Child ego state is composed of all the feelings and ways of behaving that were experienced during the early years of childhood.

_____ 28. Highly stylized and predictable ways of exchanging low-involvement, low-risk strokes such as greetings.

_____ 29. Early in life, people experience a need to take a position regarding their own intrinsic worth and that of others. There are four life positions: I'm OK, you're OK; I'm OK, you're not OK; I'm not OK, you're OK; I'm not OK, you're not OK.

_____ 30. A triadic interaction in which one person acts as persecutor, another as rescuer, and the third as victim. Like love.

_____ 31. A pleasurable stroke carrying a "You're OK" message and resulting in good feelings for the receiver.

_____ 32. A series of "duplex transactions," which lead to a switch and a well-defined, predictable payoff that justifies a not-OK or discounted position.

_____ 33. A stroke given for _doing_ something.

_____ 34. An exchange of strokes between two persons, consisting of a stimulus and a response between specified ego states.

_____ 35. The universal need for stimulation or stroking.

_____ 36. Occurs when the vectors are not parallel, or more than two ego states are involved. Crossed up.

_____ 37. Feelings or strokes collected to justify some later behavior.

_____ 38. The part of the Child ego state that is the forerunner of Adult reasoning.

_____ 39. Best characterized as being concerned with facts. It acts as an assimilator of information, is mature.

_____ 40. The need to have one's basic decisions about life confirmed constantly — decisions about the "OKness" of oneself and the world.

# QUESTIONS FOR DISCUSSION
# AND PERSONAL REFLECTION

The following questions can be used in small group discussion for further exploration of the theory and/or personal reflection of how the theory applies to your own life.

1. What is your general impression of Transactional Analysis? Do you agree with its view of how human personality is structured?

_____

_____

_____

_____

2. How do you view Berne's theory as applying to your own life? If you do not view it as having any applicability to your life, why?

_____

_____

_____

_____

3. If you could have a conversation with Berne, what questions would you have for him about his theory?

_____

_____

_____

_____

4. As you develop your own approach to therapeutic intervention, what will you take with you from Transactional Analysis?

_____

_____

_____

_____

# ANSWERS TO CHAPTER REVIEW

## Biography

1. McGill
2. psychoanalyst
3. San Francisco

## Historical Development

1. psychoanalysis
2. brain
3. accessible

## View of Human Nature

1. hungers
2. strokes
3. structure
4. position
5. parent, adult, child
6. natural

## Development of Maladaptive Behavior

1. contamination
2. exclusion
3. game
4. rackets

## Goals of Therapy

1. autonomy
2. relationships
3. scripts

## Function of the Therapist

1. catalyst
2. ego
3. parent
4. ulterior

## Major Methods and Techniques

1. contract
2. egogram
3. groups
4. never
5. literacy

## Application

1. actionistic

## Critical Analysis

1. intrapsychic
2. contract
3. jargon (or language)

## Current Status

1. Games People Play
2. eclectic

## ANSWERS TO MATCHING ITEMS

| | | | |
|---|---|---|---|
| 1. H | 11. V | 21. Z | 31. E |
| 2. Y | 12. C | 22. A | 32. I |
| 3. P | 13. EE | 23. BB | 33. MM |
| 4. AA | 14. W | 24. O | 34. M |
| 5. D | 15. J | 25. S | 35. LL |
| 6. FF | 16. HH | 26. F | 36. X |
| 7. Q | 17. R | 27. GG | 37. B |
| 8. JJ | 18. KK | 28. L | 38. CC |
| 9. G | 19. K | 29. DD | 39. T |
| 10. NN | 20. II | 30. U | 40. N |

## CHAPTER 12

# Behavioral Therapy

## CHAPTER OVERVIEW

1. *Biography.* Skinner (1904-1990) spent most of his professional life at Harvard. He has been described as the most influential psychologist of this century and he certainly set the stage for the development of behavior therapy. Wolpe (1915-) received his medical degree in South Africa and after studying Pavlov, rebelled against his psychoanalytic training and devoted his career to an empirical approach to psychotherapy. He is best known for devising systematic desensitization. Bandura (1925-) has taught psychology his entire career at Stanford University where he has developed a broader perspective on behavior therapy by bringing in a social learning component.

2. *Historical Development.* The beginnings of behavior therapy can be found at the crossroads of the rise of behaviorism as a philosophical view (due in great part to John B. Watson) and empiricism as a growing method in psychology (due in great part to Pavlov and Skinner). With the advent of systematic desensitization in the 1950s, however, behavior therapy came into its own and grew quickly during the 1960s as an alternative to psychodynamic approaches.

3. *View of Human Nature.* Behavior therapists view humans as products of their experience. People are neither good nor bad. But the behavior therapist does view humans as hedonistic in nature, responding to requests to end or decrease personal suffering or to promote greater pleasure and enjoyment in life. Behavior therapists have no model of optimal human functioning toward which clients are led.

4. *Development of Maladaptive Behavior.* Psychopathology, from the behavioral perspective, is defined as behavior that is disadvantageous or dangerous to the individual and/or to other people. It can result from insufficient cues to predict consequences or from inadequate reinforcement. One of the most painful of all maladaptive behaviors stems from an overly severe set of self-standards, and the resulting excess of self-criticism.

5. *Goals of Therapy.* The goal of behavior therapy is to extinguish the client's identified maladaptive behavior and to introduce or strengthen adaptive behavior that can serve as a replacement and enable him or her to live a productive life. The key to reaching this goal is learning new behaviors. This relies on three paradigms that can stand alone but are often integrated in this approach: respondent learning, operant conditioning, and social modeling.

6. *Function of the Therapist.* The behavior therapist is generally very active in counseling. He or she serves as a consultant, a supporter, a resource, and a model. Functionally, the behavior therapist facilitates a process involving four major steps: accurately defining the problem, gathering a developmental history of the client, establishing specific goals, and determining the best methods for change.

7. *Major Methods and Techniques.* Since its task is to resolve client symptoms, there are literally dozens and dozens of behavior therapy techniques. Some of the most common methods include behavioral assessment (specifying an individualized treatment plan), positive reinforcement (reward for positive behavior), token economies (using tokens to be exchanged for desired objects or privileges), assertiveness training (enabling clients to more freely express thoughts and feelings), modeling (learning through observing the behavior of another), relaxation training (discriminating between tense and relaxed muscle groups to relax upon cue), systematic desensitization (pairing of a neutral stimulus with one that already elicits fear), flooding (maximizing the anxious state of a client for eventual extinction).

8. *Application.* Research has shown different forms of behavior therapy effective in treating anger, obsessive-compulsive disorders, phobias, depression, alcoholism, sexual dysfunctions, paraphilias, marital distress, and childhood disorders. It has been used successfully in a wide variety of settings. The case of "Mr. B" summarized by Joseph Wolpe illustrates the effectiveness of systematic desensitization and assertiveness training.

9. *Critical Analysis.* Behavior therapy provides a relatively coherent conceptual framework of psychotherapy. It is committed to systematization, objectivity, evaluation and a solid research base. It provides clients with an understanding of the treatment process and also supplies the practitioner with an abundance of effective techniques. Behavior therapy, however, is criticized for not dealing with the total person. Critics also point to the relatively little attention the behavioral approach has devoted to the therapeutic process. While behavior therapy offers some advantages to

multicultural counseling, it lacks relevance for the ethnic-minority client who is searching for a better sense of identity within a particular culture.

10. *Current Status.* After only a few decades, behavior therapy is now part of the professional therapeutic establishment. It is also much more sophisticated than its founders might have imagined, encompassing a broad spectrum of individual disorders and societal concerns. It is more diverse in its theory, techniques, and views. In spite of this newer broadening and diversity, approaches to therapy which integrate a behavioral perspective continue to grow.

# GUIDED STUDY

These questions are meant to guide you through the major sections of the chapter. Write your answer in the space provided and then compare it with the marked section of the text.

1. Describe how the formative years of the originators of behavior therapy may have impacted the development of this theory.

_____

_____

_____

_____

2. In your own words, how would you describe the birth of behavior therapy to someone who was not familiar with its history?

_____

_____

_____

3. From the behavioral perspective, the individual is seen as a product of his or her experience. Explain how this fundamental assumption colors the behavioral view of human nature.

_____

_____

_____

_____

4. One behavioral explanation of maladaptive behavior is the reliance on a single, self-defeating reinforcer. What other behavioral explanations of maladaptive behavior are there?

_____

_____

_____

_____

5. A behavioral counselor is typically very active. Describe the various functions of the behavioral therapist.

_____

_____

_____

_____

6. Discuss the major goals of behavioral psychotherapy (include the concepts of respondent learning, operant conditioning, and social modeling).

_____

_____

_____

_____

7. Explain how positive reinforcement is used by the behavioral therapist in treatment.

_____

_____

_____

_____

8. Modeling helps a client acquire desired responses or to extinguish fears through observing the behavior of another person. Explain how this happens and what forms it can take.

_____

_____

_____

_____

9. Apply systematic desensitization to the case of spider phobia. In other words, what would this technique look like in treating this problem?

_____

_____

_____

_____

10. How would you highlight several of the major distinctions between behavioral therapy and psychoanalysis and neoanalytic theories?

_____

_____

_____

_____

11. What did you learn from Joseph Wolpe's treatment of Mr. B?

_____

_____

_____

_____

12. From a critical analysis, what are the most important strengths and weaknesses of the behavioral approach?

_____

_____

_____

_____

## CHAPTER REVIEW

The following items will help you master the specific content of the chapter. Complete each of the following sentences by filling in the blanks.

## Biography

1. _____ has been described as the most influential psychologist of this century.

2. In 1966, _____, by then at Temple University School of Medicine in Philadelphia, launched a program of research and training in behavior therapy. The same year, a nonprofit clinic called the Behavior Therapy Institute headed by _____ opened in Sausalito, California.

3. Bandura is best known for helping us understand the role of _____ influences in personality development.

## Historical Development

1. The beginnings of behavior therapy can be found in two converging historical events: the rise of behaviorism and the development of the _____ method in psychology.

2. The leading figure in the behaviorism movement was _____, professor at Johns Hopkins University, who directly challenged the prevalent "intospectionist" theories.

3. The view known as logical _____, sees everything that exists as empirically verifiable.

4. Around the same time that Wilhelm Wundt was setting up the first psychological laboratory in Leipzig, Germany and Ivan Pavlov was demonstrating classical conditioning principles, E. L. Thorndike was developing his famous law of _____.

## View of Human Nature

1. The behavioral view of human nature is generally _____; that is, it gives serious consideration to both personal and environmental determinants of human behavior.

2. To behavior therapists, interpsychic views of personality underemphasize the pervasive effect which _____ events have upon persons. They believe instead that the behavior originates primarily from intrapsychic causes.

3. Most behavior therapists would argue that humans are basically _____ in nature.

## Development of Maladaptive Behavior

1. From the behavior therapy perspective psychopathology is defined as behavior that is _____ or _____ to the individual and/or to other people.

2. A cause of maladaptive behavior from the behavioral perspective is the reliance on a single, _____ reinforcer such as food, smoking, alcohol, or other addictive behaviors to cope with problems in life.

3. From a Skinnerian perspective, maladaptive behavior is often shaped through _____.

## Goals of Therapy

1. Essentially, the goal of behavior therapy is to _____ the client's identified maladaptive behavior and to introduce or strengthen adaptive behavior.

2. The key to reaching this goal has nothing to do with uncovering psychological conflicts and everything to do with helping the client _____ new behaviors.

3. _____ learning was discovered by Pavlov and it is evident when a stimulus that is _____ is paired with a stimulus that has an effect until the neutral stimulus begins to elicit the same effects as the primary stimulus.

4. _____ refers to aversive consequences of a response and is often followed by a decrease in that response.

## Function of the Therapist

1. A behavior therapist may take on one of several roles, depending on the client's goals, but generally a counselor who takes a behavioral approach is very _____ in counseling.

2. To begin with, the behavior therapist attempts to accurately and concretely _____ the problem.

3. The therapist must continually _____ the effectiveness of selected methods and modify ones that are not working or try new ones.

## Major Methods and Techniques

1. Perhaps the most widely used and most successful of all the behavioral modification techniques is _____.

2. _____ can be applied to shape behavior when approval and other intangible reinforcers do not work.

3. The major tenet of assertiveness training is that a person should be free to express thoughts and feelings appropriately without feeling undue _____ .

4. Live models are often the best form for _____ learning.

5. The most common form of relaxation training used by behavior therapists is called _____ relaxation or muscle relaxation.

6. While systematic desensitization seeks to minimize anxiety by pairing small doses of it with a deep relaxation, _____ maximizes the anxious state of the client.

## Application

1. The case of Mr. B by Joseph Wolpe illustrates systematic desensitization and _____ _____.

## Critical Analysis

1. The primary strength of behavior therapy has to do with its commitment to systematization and _____.

2. Another strength of behavioral therapy is its abundance of _____ and their applicability to a variety of settings.

3. On the negative side, behavior therapy does not deal with the total _____.

4. Although behavior therapists have been very productive in evaluating the efficacy of various techniques, relatively little attention has been devoted to the therapeutic _____.

5. When it comes to multicultural counseling, behavior therapy has some clear _____.

## Current Status

1. Behavioral principles have been assimilated into the mainstream of therapeutic counseling to the extent that even _____ counselors regularly use many of the techniques (e.g., goal setting, assertiveness training, relaxation).

2. Behavior therapy today is much more _____ than its original conception.

# KEY TERMS

Learning a theory depends, in large part, on mastering the vocabulary associated with that theory. The following key terms will help you do just that. You may want to use three-by-five cards to create your own flash card test from this list. Once you have studied this vocabulary, you will want to test your knowledge with the matching quiz which follows.

**Assertiveness training** is a semi-structured training approach that is characterized by its emphasis on acquiring assertiveness skills through practice. Assertiveness skills enable one to stand up for one's rights and beliefs more effectively.

**Aversive control (aversion therapy)** Using an aversive stimulus, such as an electric shock, to reduce the probability of pathological behaviors ( such as alcoholism). A relatively controversial form of behavior therapy.

**Behavior modification** A term referring specifically to Skinnerian methods for changing behavior, ones that need not necessarily involve psychopathology.

**Behavior rehearsal** is a therapeutic technique that consists of acting out short exchanges between client and counselor in settings from the client's life. The aim of such rehearsing is an effective preparation for the client to deal with a real "adversary," so that the anxiety that the latter evokes may be reciprocally inhibited.

**Behavior therapy** An approach to psychotherapy that seeks to change particular "target" behaviors and/or symptoms of the client, rather than trying to alter some unobservable or unconscious inner state.

**Behaviorism** An approach to psychology that regards only actual behavior as suitable to scientific study.

**Conditioned reinforcement** (secondary reinforcement) Reinforcement that is provided by a conditioned stimulus.

**Conditioned stimulus** A previously neutral stimulus that acquires positive or aversive properties through conditioning.

**Conditioning, aversive** This is a behavioral technique involving the association of the client's symptomatic behavior with a painful stimulus until the unwanted behavior is inhibited. The aversive stimulus is typically a mild electric shock or an emetic mixture, such as antabuse.

**Conditioning, classical (respondent conditioning)** A simple form of learning first demonstrated by Ivan Pavlov, wherein a conditioned stimulus (e.g., light) becomes capable of eliciting a particular conditioned response (salivation) by being repeatedly paired with an unconditioned stimulus (food).

**Conditioning, operant** Operant conditioning is a theory of learning derived from the work of B. F. Skinner. The essential difference between operant and classical conditioning is that in operant conditioning, the unconditional stimulus follows some predetermined behavior when that behavior occurs spontaneously. In this procedure, the unconditioned stimulus is called a reinforcer.

**Contingencies of reinforcement** The interrelationships between stimuli in the external environment, a particular response, and the reinforcement that follows that response.

**Continuous reinforcement** Reinforcement given after every correct response. The converse of intermittent reinforcement.

**Counterconditioning** is a technique in which the experimenter (or therapist) presents an unconditioned stimulus that elicits an unconditioned response that is incompatible with the conditioned response and thus inhibits the conditioned response. For example, relaxation (UR) is incompatible with fear (CR).

**Deprivation** Withholding a primary reinforcer (such as food or water) for some time, so that it may be used to reinforce and condition an operant.

**Desensitization** is a behavioral technique through which anxiety may be reduced by using relaxation as the counterconditioning agent. Graded anxiety-producing stimuli (in the anxiety hierarchy) are repetitively paired with a state of relaxation, until the connection between those stimuli and the response of anxiety is eliminated.

**Discrimination** (1) Reinforcing an organism for responding to some difference between two or more stimuli. (2) The resulting increase in the probability of responding to the reinforced stimulus.

**Extinction** is the process of removing an unwanted response by failing to reinforce it.

**Fixed-interval schedule (FI)** Reinforcing the first correct response that occurs after a specified interval of time, measured from the preceding reinforcement. A schedule of intermittent reinforcement.

**Fixed-ratio schedule (FR)** Reinforcing the last of a specified number of correct responses, counted from the preceding reinforcement. A schedule of intermittent reinforcement.

**Flooding** is a therapeutic technique in which repeated presentation of the conditioned stimulus without reinforcement brings about extinction of the conditioned response. It differs from desensitization in that no counterconditioning agent is used.

**Generalization** operates on the assumption that a reinforcement that accompanies a particular stimulus not only increases the probability of that stimulus eliciting a particular response, but also spreads the effect to other, similar stimuli. This process of generalization is extremely important, because no two stimuli or stimulus situations are exactly the same.

**Hierarchy** is a list of stimuli on a theme, ranked according to the amount of anxiety they produce. The hierarchy provides the therapist with a graded set of anxiety-producing stimuli to present to the client in conjunction with a counterconditioning agent in order to remove the anxiety attached to the stimuli.

**Imitative (social) learning** is a process whereby an observer learns a particular response by watching some other person (the model) in the environment perform the response.

**Intermittent reinforcement (partial reinforcement)** Reinforcement given after some correct responses, but not all. The converse of continuous reinforcement.

**Negative reinforcer** A stimulus that increases the probability of a response when removed following that response, such as an electric shock or disapproval.

**Neurotic behavior** is any persistent habit of unadaptive behavior acquired by learning in a physiologically normal organism. Anxiety is usually the central constituent of this behavior, being invariably present in the causal situation.

**Positive reinforcer** A stimulus that increases the probability of a response when presented following that response, such as food or approval.

**Programmed instruction** A Skinnerian approach to education wherein specific correct responses are reinforced, often by a teaching machine, in a sequence designed to produce optimal learning.

**Punishment** is an interactional behavior involving the application of an aversive event as a result of the individual's engaging in a particular behavior. Punishment, the converse of reinforcement, is applied only to those behaviors that are to be eliminated.

**Reciprocal inhibition** is the elimination or weakening of old responses by new ones. When a response is inhibited by an incompatible response and if a major drive-reduction follows, a significant amount of conditioned inhibition of the response will be developed.

**Reinforcement** is an specified event that strengthens the tendency for a response to be repeated.

**Reinforcement, negative** This is a form of conditioning involving the removal of an aversive event as a result of the appearance (or disappearance) of the target behavior.

**Reinforcement, positive** This is a form of conditioning in which the individual receives something pleasurable or desirable as a consequence of his behavior.

**Response** A single instance of an operant, such as one pack of the disk in a Skinner box.

**Response induction** A change in the probability of a response that has not itself been conditioned, because it is similar to one that has.

**Response shaping** is the process of moving from simple behaviors that are approximations of the final behavior to a final complex behavior. Through this process, certain behaviors that are close approximations of the desired behavior are reinforced, while other behaviors are not reinforced. At each stage of this process, a closer approximation of the desired behavior is required before reinforcement is given.

**Satiation** Decreasing the probability of an operant by providing reinforcement without requiring the correct response to be made.

**Schedules of reinforcement** Programs of continuous or (more frequently) intermittent reinforcement, including interval schedules, ratio schedules, and various combinations thereof.

**Spontaneous recovery** A temporary increase in the probability of an operant that is undergoing extinction, which occurs at the beginning of a new experimental session without an additional reinforcement.

**Systematic desensitization** A form of behavior therapy, devised by Joseph Wolpe, wherein the client imagines a hierarchical sequence of feared stimuli and inhibits the resulting anxiety by practicing previously taught techniques of muscular relaxation. Alternatively, *in vivo* desensitization may be used with clients who are unable to imagine the feared situations vividly enough to feel anxious.

**Token economy** A detailed and complicated form of behavior therapy, based on Skinnerian operant conditioning, wherein desirable behaviors are followed with conditioned positive reinforcers (such as plastic tokens) that can later be exchanged for more primary reinforcers chosen by the client.

**Unconditioned response** An automatic, unlearned response elicited by an unconditioned stimulus.

**Unconditioned stimulus** A stimulus that automatically elicits a particular (unconditioned) response, without any learning or conditioning being necessary.

**Variable-interval schedule (VI)** Reinforcing the first correct response that occurs after a varying interval of time, measured from the preceding reinforcement, with the series of intervals having a specified mean. A schedule of intermittent reinforcement.

**Variable-ratio schedule (VR)** Reinforcing the last of a varying number of correct responses, counted from the preceding reinforcement, with the series of ratios having a specified mean. A schedule of intermittent reinforcement.

# MATCHING ITEMS

## Terms

A. Extinction
B. Response
C. Hierarchy
D. Desensitization
E. Neurotic Behavior
F. Unconditioned Response
G. Schedules of Reinforcement
H. Conditioning, aversive
I. Token Economy
J. Response Shaping
K. Flooding
L. Behavior Therapy
M. Generalization
N. Conditioned Stimulus
O. Aversion Therapy
P. Discrimination
Q. Variable Ratio Schedule
R. Conditioning, classical

S. Punishment
T. Programmed Instruction
U. Reciprocal Inhibition
V. Contingencies of Reinforcement
W. Spontaneous Recovery
X. Reinforcement, negative
Y. Imitative (social) learning
Z. Counterconditioning
AA. Systematic Desensitization
BB. Behavior Modification
CC. Reinforcement, positive
DD. Behavior Rehearsal
EE. Reinforcement
FF. Positive Reinforcement

GG. Variable Interval Schedule
HH. Conditioning, operant
II. Intermittent Reinforcement
JJ. Behaviorism
KK. Response Induction
LL. Continuous Reinforcement
MM. Deprivation
NN. Fixed Interval Schedule
OO. Unconditioned Stimulus
PP. Assertiveness Training
QQ. Negative Reinforcer
RR. Satiation
SS. Fixed Ratio Schedule
TT. Conditioned Reinforcement

## Description

_____ 1. A form of behavior therapy, devised by Joseph Wolpe, wherein the client imagines a hierarchical sequence of feared stimuli and inhibits the resulting anxiety by practicing previously taught techniques of muscular relaxation. Alternatively, *in vivo* desensitization may be used with clients who are unable to imagine the feared situations vividly enough to feel anxious.

_____ 2. This is a behavioral technique involving the association of the client's symptomatic behavior with a painful stimulus until the unwanted behavior is inhibited. The aversive stimulus is typically a mild electric shock or an emetic mixture, such as antabuse.

_____ 3. (1) Reinforcing an organism for responding to some difference between two or more stimuli. (2) The resulting increase in the probability of responding to the reinforced stimulus.

_____ 4. A Skinnerian approach to education wherein specific correct responses are reinforced, often by a teaching machine, in a sequence designed to produce optimal learning.

_____ 5. Is the elimination or weakening of old responses by new ones. When a response is inhibited by an incompatible response and if a major drive-reduction follows, a significant amount of conditioned inhibition of the response will be developed.

_____ 6. An approach to psychotherapy that seeks to change particular "target" behaviors and/or symptoms of the client, rather than trying to alter some unobservable or unconscious inner state.

_____ 7. Is an specified event that strengthens the tendency for a response to be repeated.

_____ 8. Is a process whereby an observer learns a particular response by watching some other person (the model) in the environment perform the response.

_____ 9. Operant conditioning is a theory of learning derived from the work of B. F. Skinner. The essential difference between operant and classical conditioning is that in operant conditioning, the unconditional stimulus follows some predetermined behavior when that behavior occurs spontaneously. In this procedure, the unconditioned stimulus is called a reinforcer.

_____ 10. Is any persistent habit of unadaptive behavior acquired by learning in a physiologically normal organism. Anxiety is usually the central constituent of this behavior, being invariably present in the causal situation.

_____ 11. Reinforcement given after some correct responses, but not all. The converse of continuous reinforcement.

_____ 12. Is a technique in which the experimenter (or therapist) presents an unconditioned stimulus that elicits an unconditioned response that is incompatible with the conditioned response and thus inhibits the conditioned response. For example, relaxation (UR) is incompatible with fear (CR).

_____ 13. A stimulus that automatically elicits a particular (unconditioned) response, without any learning or conditioning being necessary.

_____ 14. Using an aversive stimulus, such as an electric shock, to reduce the probability of pathological behaviors (such as alcoholism). A relatively controversial form of behavior therapy.

_____ 15. Decreasing the probability of an operant by providing reinforcement without requiring the correct response to be made.

_____ 16. Is the process of removing an unwanted response by failing to reinforce it.

_____ 17. Is an interactional behavior involving the application of an aversive event as a result of the individual's engaging in a particular behavior. Punishment, the converse of reinforcement, is applied only to those behaviors that are to be eliminated.

_____ 18. Reinforcement given after every correct response. The converse of intermittent reinforcement.

_____ 19. Is the process of moving from simple behaviors that are approximations of the final behavior to a final complex behavior. Through this process, certain behaviors that are close approximations of the desired behavior are reinforced, while other behaviors are not reinforced. At each stage of this process, a closer approximation of the desired behavior is required before reinforcement is given.

_____ 20. Withholding a primary reinforcer (such as food or water) for some time, so that it may be used to reinforce and condition an operant.

_____ 21. This is a form of conditioning involving the removal of an aversive event as a result of the appearance (or disappearance) of the target behavior.

_____ 22. A term referring specifically to Skinnerian methods for changing behavior, ones that need not necessarily involve psychopathology.

_____ 23. Programs of continuous or (more frequently) intermittent reinforcement, including interval schedules, ratio schedules, and various combinations thereof.

_____ 24. Is a behavioral technique through which anxiety may be reduced by using relaxation as the counterconditioning agent. Graded anxiety-producing stimuli (in the anxiety hierarchy) are repetitively paired with a state of relaxation, until the connection between those stimuli and the response of anxiety is eliminated.

_____ 25. This is a form of conditioning in which the individual receives something pleasurable or desirable as a consequence of his behavior.

_____ 26. A previously neutral stimulus that acquires positive or aversive properties through conditioning.

_____ 27. A stimulus that increases the probability of a response when presented following that response, such as food or approval.

_____ 28. The interrelationships between stimuli in the external environment, a particular response, and the reinforcement that follows that response.

_____ 29. A change in the probability of a response that has not itself been conditioned, because it is similar to one that has.

_____ 30. Is a therapeutic technique in which repeated presentation of the conditioned stimulus without reinforcement brings about extinction of the conditioned response. It differs from desensitization in that no counterconditioning agent is used.

_____ 31. Is a semi-structured training approach that is characterized by its emphasis on acquiring assertiveness skills through practice. Assertiveness skills enable one to stand up for one's rights and beliefs more effectively.

_____ 32. Reinforcing the last of a varying number of correct responses, counted from the preceding reinforcement, with the series of ratios having a specified mean. A schedule of intermittent reinforcement.

_____ 33. Reinforcing the last of a specified number of correct responses, counted from the preceding reinforcement. A schedule of intermittent reinforcement.

_____ 34. An automatic, unlearned response elicited by an unconditioned stimulus.

_____ 35. Reinforcement that is provided by a conditioned stimulus.

_____ 36. A temporary increase in the probability of an operant that is undergoing extinction, which occurs at the beginning of a new experimental session without an additional reinforcement.

_____ 37. Reinforcing the first correct response that occurs after a specified interval of time, measured from the preceding reinforcement. A schedule of intermittent reinforcement.

_____ 38. A detailed and complicated form of behavior therapy, based on Skinnerian operant conditioning, wherein desirable behaviors are followed with conditioned positive reinforcers (such as plastic tokens) that can later be exchanged for more primary reinforcers chosen by the client.

_____ 39. An approach to psychology that regards only actual behavior as suitable to scientific study.

_____ 40. Operates on the assumption that a reinforcement that accompanies a particular stimulus not only increases the probability of that stimulus eliciting a particular response, but also spreads the effect to other, similar stimuli. This process of generalization is extremely important, because no two stimuli or stimulus situations are exactly the same.

_____ 41. A stimulus that increases the probability of a response when removed following that response, such as an electric shock or disapproval.

_____ 42. A simple form of learning first demonstrated by Ivan Pavlov, wherein a conditioned stimulus (e.g., light) becomes capable of eliciting a particular conditioned response (salivation) by being repeatedly paired with an unconditioned stimulus (food).

_____ 43. Reinforcing the first correct response that occurs after a varying interval of time, measured from the preceding reinforcement, with the series of intervals having a specified mean. A schedule of intermittent reinforcement.

_____ 44. A single instance of an operant, such as one pack of the disk in a Skinner box.

_____ 45. Is a therapeutic technique that consists of acting out short exchanges between client and counselor in settings from the client's life. The aim of such rehearsing is an effective preparation for the client to deal with a real "adversary," so that the anxiety that the latter evokes may be reciprocally inhibited.

_____ 46. Is a list of stimuli on a theme, ranked according to the amount of anxiety they produce. The hierarchy provides the therapist with a graded set of anxiety-producing stimuli to present to the client in conjunction with a counterconditioning agent in order to remove the anxiety attached to the stimuli.

## QUESTIONS FOR DISCUSSION
## AND PERSONAL REFLECTION

The following questions can be used in small group discussion for further exploration of the theory and/or personal reflection of how the theory applies to your own life.

1. What is your general impression of behavioral therapy? Do you agree with its view of how human personality is influenced by the environment?

_____

_____

_____

_____

2. How do you view behavioral theory as applying to your own life? If you do not view it as having any applicability to your life, why?

_____

_____

_____

_____

3. If you could have a conversation with B.F. Skinner, Joseph Wolpe, or Albert Bandura, what questions would you have for any of them about this theory?

_____

_____

_____

_____

4. As you develop your own approach to therapeutic intervention, what will you take with you from behavioral therapy?

_____

_____

_____

_____

## ANSWERS TO CHAPTER REVIEW

### Biography

1. Skinner
2. Joseph Wolpe, Arnold Lazarus
3. modeling

### Historical Development

1. experimental
2. John B. Watson
3. positivism
4. effect

## View of Human Nature

1. interactional
2. external
3. hedonistic

## Development of Maladaptive Behavior

1. disadvantageous, dangerous
2. self-defeating
3. reinforcement

## Goals of Therapy

1. extinguish
2. learn
3. respondent, neutral
4. punishment

## Function of the Therapist

1. active
2. define
3. assess (or measure)

## Major Methods and Techniques

1. positive reinforcement
2. token economies
3. anxiety
4. vicarious
5. progressive
6. flooding

## Application

1. assertiveness training

## Critical Analysis

1. objectivity (or evaluation, good research base)
2. techniques
3. person
4. process
5. advantages

## Current Status

1. insight-oriented
2. broad (or diverse)

## ANSWERS TO MATCHING ITEMS

| | | | |
|---|---|---|---|
| 1. AA | 13. OO | 25. CC | 36. W |
| 2. H | 14. O | 26. N | 37. NN |
| 3. P | 15. RR | 27. FF | 38. I |
| 4. T | 16. A | 28. V | 39. JJ |
| 5. U | 17. S | 29. KK | 40. M |
| 6. L | 18. LL | 30. K | 41. QQ |
| 7. EE | 19. J | 31. PP | 42. R |
| 8. Y | 20. MM | 32. Q | 43. GG |
| 9. HH | 21. X | 33. SS | 44. B |
| 10. E | 22. BB | 34. F | 45. DD |
| 11. II | 23. G | 35. TT | 46. C |
| 12. Z | 24. D | | |

## CHAPTER 13

# Rational Emotive & Other Cognitive Therapies

## CHAPTER OVERVIEW

1. *Biography.* Ellis (1913-) grew up in New York, where as a young adolescent he dreamed of becoming a novelist. In 1934 he graduated from City College of New York with a BA in business administration. In his spare time, Ellis wrote fiction, but his literary efforts did not pay off. After eight of his novels were rejected by publishers, Ellis decided to study psychology and eventually earned his Ph.D. in clinical psychology from Columbia University. Ellis began practicing psychoanalysis but eventually became more active and directive with his patients, gradually developing his own approach to therapy.

2. *Historical Development.* Although the origins of RET can be traced as far back as ancient Greece, the approach more recently stems from cognitive learning theory. Despite Ellis's original training and practice of psychoanalysis, he remained dissatisfied with this approach and hypothesized that his patients' behaviors were influenced by their attitudes and perceptions. This hypothesis motivated Ellis to work diligently toward a rational approach to psychotherapy.

3. *View of Human Nature.* Ellis holds that human nature has the potential to control much of the pleasure and pain that seemingly results from life's circumstances. According to Ellis, the human psyche is intricately entwined with thoughts and feelings. Ellis's view of human nature can be summarized in his formulation of the A-B-C theory, which suggests that people come to therapy because of a disturbing consequence (C), which is attributed to an activating event (A), as if there were a causal relationship. According to Ellis, however, people are not disturbed by events themselves, but by the beliefs (B) they hold about those events.

4. *Development of Maladaptive Behavior.* Because humans are self-conscious creatures, they observe their disturbance and then make themselves disturbed all over again about being disturbed. Maladaptive behavior, therefore, results from a number of illogical ideas (e.g., Being loved and approved by everyone is necessary for happiness) that are held and perpetuated until a new way of thinking is learned. These illogical ideas result in feelings of worthlessness, depression, rage, anxiety, mania, or self-pity. Although we are born with the potential to be rational, we become illogical because of distortions during childhood and the contemporary reinforcement of those distortions.

5. *Goals of Therapy.* The ultimate goal of RET is to "teach" clients to analyze and correct their distortions of reality. It aims to help clients separate their rational from their irrational beliefs. Then the identified irrational beliefs are challenged; that is, the client is brought to a point of disputing irrational emotional beliefs. RET aims to eliminate the irrational beliefs and substitute them with a new, more rational philosophy. If this disputation is effective, it will be apparent in the diminished emotional distress, and it will result in clients assuming more responsibility for their own lives.

6. *Function of the Therapist.* In RET the therapist is unequivocally verbal and directive, intentionally attempting to lead the patient to a healthier perspective. By using persuasion and debate to attack self-defeating patterns, the therapist works as quickly as possible to help clients face their illogical thinking. Exploring the details of the past is only a smoke screen, hiding the real issue of irrational thinking. The process for the RET therapist, then, centers on showing clients how and when they are irrational.

7. *Major Methods and Techniques.* RET consists of three general phases. In the "cognitive" phase the therapist presents the rationale for therapy to the clients. The "emotive" phase is devoted to helping clients become aware of their thoughts. During the "behavioristic" phase clients are trained to verbalize alternative cognitions and to change their behavior. During each of these phases, techniques such as disputation, countering, and action homework may be used.

8. *Application.* A transcript cannot completely capture the role that Ellis's personality plays in how he applies RET, but the case of a 26-year-old male commercial artist who is homophobic portrays much of its dramatic momentum. In this case, Ellis quickly taps into the client's irrational, illogical thinking and through disputation quickly attempts to dismantle it. After eight sessions, the client's obsession is relieved.

9. *Other Cognitively Based Theories.* While RET is the most widely known cognitive approach, it is not the only one. Aaron Beck also developed a highly effective cognitive theory based on the rationale that the way people feel and behave is determined by how they structure their experience. Emphasizing "dysfunctional" thinking, he tries to help clients become more realistic in their interpretation of events by projecting less often. Donald Meichenbaum has inaugurated a "cognitive-behavioral" approach,

which emphasizes that clients need to become aware of how they think, feel, and behave in order to interrupt the scripted nature of their behavior so that they can evaluate their behavior in various situations.

10. *Critical Analysis.* The cognitive approach to therapy is a proven short-term strategy for preventing clients from seriously passing judgment on themselves based on some inconsequential aspect of their behavior. But it has been criticized for simplifying the complexity of human experience and for trying to implement a truly "valueless" approach to therapy. Concerning multicultural counseling, the cognitive approach is capable of transcending many cultural barriers but runs the risk of misconstruing as "irrational" the values of ethnic minority clients that are related to their particular world view.

11. *Current Status.* In recent years RET and other cognitive approaches have come to enjoy wide acceptance. Much of its following and support can be attributed to the empirical evidence which undergirds its efforts. Also, Ellis's two nonprofit institutes, with headquarters in New York City, promote RET in many areas. Thousands of practitioners subscribe to a form of cognitive therapy today, making it one of the most popular modes of psychotherapy.

## GUIDED STUDY

These questions are meant to guide you through the major sections of the chapter. Write your answer in the space provided and then compare it with the marked section of the text.

1. Describe how the formative years of Albert Ellis may have impacted the development of his theory.

   _____

   _____

   _____

   _____

2. In your own words, how would you describe the birth of rational-emotive therapy to someone who was not familiar with its history?

   _____

   _____

   _____

   _____

3. When it comes to human nature, Ellis does not maintain that we are victims of our environment. Explain why this is fundamental to the rational-emotive understanding of human personality.

_____

_____

_____

_____

4. Describe how emotions occur from a rational point of view. Be sure to use the A-B-C theory in your explanation.

_____

_____

_____

_____

5. How would you describe the cognitive approach to psychopathology? In other words, how does maladaptive behavior develop in this framework?

_____

_____

_____

_____

6. "To be worthwhile, one should be thoroughly adequate" is a common irrational thought. What are some of the other most commonly occurring irrational beliefs which typically lead to emotional disturbance?

_____

_____

_____

_____

7. The rational-emotive therapist is unequivocally directive. Discuss how this plays out in the function of the rational-emotive therapist.

_____

_____

_____

_____

8. What is the overarching goal of RET and how is it accomplished?

_____

_____

_____

_____

9. How does the rational-emotive therapist go about identifying client's beliefs?

_____

_____

_____

_____

10. Explain how rational analysis would take place for a person who is afraid to ask someone on a date?

_____

_____

_____

_____

11. What did you learn from Ellis's treatment of the 26-year-old commercial artist who was homophobic?

_____

_____

_____

_____

12. From a critical analysis, what are the most important strengths and weaknesses of the cognitive approach?

_____

_____

_____

_____

# CHAPTER REVIEW

The following items will help you master the specific content of the chapter. Complete each of the following sentences by filling in the blanks.

## Biography

1. As a young adolescent in junior high school, Ellis dreamed of becoming a _____.

2. Ellis was hard-pressed to find the training he desired in psychoanalysis and finally succeeded in obtaining personal analysis for three years from the _____ group.

3. Today Ellis lives in New York City, where he sees as many as _____ clients each week and supervises up to eight group sessions.

## Historical Development

1. The origins of rational-emotive therapy can be traced to the philosophy of _____ in ancient Greece, which distinguished an act from its interpretation.

2. Ellis's contemporary theory has flourished within the context of what is sometimes called the _____ revolution, a scientific revolution that has assembled research in physiology, philosophy, linguistics, computer science, medicine, and various other areas of psychology.

3. Ellis attributes some of the beginnings of his theory to a decision he made to force himself out of his shyness. His self-designed treatment involved talking to unfamiliar _____.

## View of Human Nature

1. Ellis claims that we have final _____ over much of the pleasure and pain which come from circumstances beyond our control.

2. Ellis often summarized his view of human nature by means of a so-called _____ theory of our behavior.

3. Although human nature is determined to some extent by biological and social pressures, the fact remains clear from the cognitive approach that we do have _____ _____ and can create our own worlds.

4. One of the strongest human, innate tendencies is to be influenced by _____ and by _____.

## Development of Maladaptive Behavior

1. This theory is based on the premise that maladaptive behavior results from a number of major _____ ideas that are held and perpetuated until a new way of thinking is learned.

2. A common irrational belief is: "_____ is caused externally; therefore people have little or no ability to control their sorrows and disturbances."

3. Another irrational belief is: "It is easier to avoid _____ than to face them."

4. The most common irrational beliefs involve _____ from others and _____.

## Goals of Therapy

1. The goal of RET is to _____ clients to analyze and to correct their distortions of reality.

2. _____ requires clients to challenge their irrational beliefs, aims to eliminate those beliefs and substitute them with a new, more rational philosophy.

3. RET urges clients to assume _____ for their lives and work out their own problems.

4. Healthy clients are logical and objective and thus generally _____ minded.

## Function of the Therapist

1. Intentionally attempting to _____ patients to a healthier perspective, the rational-emotive therapist is unequivocally directive.

2. To help clients face their illogical thinking as quickly as possible, the therapist will use _____ in attacking clients' self-defeating patterns even at the outset of counseling.

3. _____ beliefs are consistent with reality and can be supported with hard evidence.

## Major Methods and Techniques

1. RET consist of three general modes or phases, the _____, the _____, and the _____, each accompanied by its own set of techniques.

2. Themes that RET therapists look for include magnification, self-blame and _____ reasoning, where one assumes that negative emotions reflect the way things really are.

3. The cognitive practitioner will often ask clients to engage in rational _____-analysis, which allows them to apply the A-B-C theory to their situations and which helps them to actively dispute their own irrational beliefs.

4. The RET therapist can help clients become more aware of the _____ of the A-B-C-D-E model through the use of numerical ratings and self-recording.

5. Because the RET practitioner believes clients' problems stem from an exaggerated sense of the significance of unfortunate events, he or she will sometimes use _____ to show clients how to "lighten up" and view their difficulties in the light of day.

## Application

1. The case of the 26-year-old commercial artist who is homophobic demonstrates Ellis's ability to _____ in on the irrational, illogical thinking that has led to the client's obsession.

## Other Cognitively Based Theories

1. About the same time that Albert Ellis was perfecting his therapeutic techniques, _____ _____, a Philadelphia psychiatrist, developed a cognitive theory based on the rationale that the way people feel and behave is determined by how they structure their experience.

2. Another method, commonly referred to as "cognitive-behavioral therapy," has emerged from the work of _____ social learning and self-efficacy theory and Donald Meichenbaum's cognitive behavior modification or stress-_____ training.

## Critical Analysis

1. Since the cognitive approach fits instinctually with the rational aspect of human beings, it has generated a significant amount of bibliotherapeutic material and positive _____ findings.

2. One criticism of RET is that it attempts to implement a truly
_____ approach to therapy.

3. The cognitive approach can be easily misconstrued as "irrational" the
values of ethnic-minority clients what are relation to their particular
_____  _____.

## Current Status

1. Today, a great deal of _____ on RET routinely appears in the
*Journal of Rational Emotive and Cognitive-Behavior Therapy.*

## KEY TERMS

Learning a theory depends, in large part, on mastering the vocabulary associated with that theory. The following key terms will help you do just that. You may want to use three-by-five cards to create your own flash card test from this list. Once you have studied this vocabulary, you will want to test your knowledge with the matching quiz which follows.

**Action Homework** Assignments designed to encourage clients to dispute their irrational ideas behaviorally. These assignments nearly always involve some degree of risk since clients are often asked to do the very thing they fear most.

**All-or-nothing thinking** Seeing things in black-or-white, yes or no, for me or against me, categories. If a conversation is anything less than perfect, is it seen as a total failure. Example: A student who receives a C on a single exam thinks he or she is a total academic failure.

**Cognitive** Characteristic of putting importance on purpose, knowing, understanding, thinking, and reasoning in behavior.

**Countering** A technique whereby clients are asked to identify "counters" for each of their significant irrational beliefs and then to argue against these beliefs. In other words, countering involves arguing in a very assertive fashion and convincing oneself of the falsity of a belief.

**Discounting** Rejecting positive experiences by insisting they "don't count." Example: Earning high marks in a class are discounted by saying, "anyone could have done it."

**Emotion-control Card** A wallet-sized card containing four emotionally debilitating categories (anger, self-criticism, anxiety, and depression) and a list of inappropriate feelings and a parallel list of appropriate feelings. It is used in practicing rational-emotive imaging.

**Emotional Reasoning** Assuming that negative emotions reflect the way things really are. Example: "I feel guilty so I must be guilty."

**Emotive** Having to do with emotion-provoking stimuli.

**Insight Number 1** What Ellis calls showing clients how and when they are irrational.

**Insight Number 2** What Ellis calls convincing clients that they maintain their own emotional disturbance by reindoctrinating themselves with the same repetitious irrational ideas.

**Insight Number 3** What Ellis calls leading clients to a full acknowledgment that ridding themselves of their disturbances depends on their willingness to join in challenging their beliefs and in developing new ways of thinking.

**Irrational** Characterized by being influenced or guided by "crooked" thinking.

**Magnification** Exaggerating the importance of problems and shortcomings. Example: "With my IQ I can never get a really good job."

**Mind Reading** Making inferences about how people feel and think. Example: "The president doesn't like people; no one can get in to see him because he tells the secret service to keep them away."

**Overgeneralization** Seeing a single event as a never-ending pattern of defeat by using the words "always" or "never" when thinking about it. Example: "I am always in the wrong place at the wrong time."

**Rational** Characterized by being influenced or guided by reason.

**Self-blame** Taking personal responsibility for events that are beyond one's control. Example: "If I had not asked to go shopping he never would have been in the wreck."

**Self-efficacy** A comprehensive sense of one's own capability, effectiveness, strength, or power to attain desired results.

**Social learning** A modified form of behaviorism that stresses the importance of cognitive processes as causal agents in behavior. Albert Bandura is the leading contemporary exponent of this point of view.

## MATCHING ITEMS

### Terms

| | | |
|---|---|---|
| A. Discounting | H. Self-blame | O. Social Learning |
| B. Rational | I. Countering | P. All or Nothing |
| C. Self-efficacy | J. Cognitive | Thinking |
| D. Emotion-control | K. Mind Reading | Q. Overgeneralization |
| Card | L. Magnification | R. Emotional |
| E. Insight Number 1 | M. Emotive | Reasoning |
| F. Irrational | N. Insight Number 2 | S. Insight Number 3 |
| G. Action Homework | | |

# Description

_____ 1. Characterized by being influenced or guided by "crooked" thinking.

_____ 2. Making inferences about how people feel and think. Example: "The president doesn't like people; no one can get in to see him because he tells the secret service to keep them away."

_____ 3. Seeing things in black-or-white, yes or no, for me or against me, categories. If a conversation is anything less than perfect, is it seen as a total failure. Example: A student who receives a C on a single exam thinks he or she is a total academic failure.

_____ 4. Characterized by being influenced or guided by reason.

_____ 5. Having to do with emotion-provoking stimuli.

_____ 6. A technique whereby clients are asked to identify "counters" for each of their significant irrational beliefs and then to argue against these beliefs. In other words, countering involves arguing in a very assertive fashion and convincing oneself of the falsity of a belief.

_____ 7. What Ellis calls leading clients to a full acknowledgment that ridding themselves of their disturbances depends on their willingness to join in challenging their beliefs and in developing new ways of thinking.

_____ 8. A wallet-sized card containing four emotionally debilitating categories (anger, self-criticism, anxiety, and depression) and a list of inappropriate feelings and a parallel list of appropriate feelings. It is used in practicing rational-emotive imaging.

_____ 9. Exaggerating the importance of problems and shortcomings. Example: "With my IQ I can never get a really good job."

_____ 10. Assignments designed to encourage clients to dispute their irrational ideas behaviorally. These assignments nearly always involve some degree of risk since clients are often asked to do the very thing they fear most.

_____ 11. What Ellis calls convincing clients that they maintain their own emotional disturbance by reindoctrinating themselves with the same repetitious irrational ideas.

_____ 12. Rejecting positive experiences by insisting they "don't count." Example: Earning high marks in a class are discounted by saying, "anyone could have done it."

_____ 13. Seeing a single event as a never-ending pattern of defeat by using the words "always" or "never" when thinking about it. Example: "I am always in the wrong place at the wrong time."

_____ 14. Characteristic of putting importance on purpose, knowing, understanding, thinking, and reasoning in behavior.

_____ 15. What Ellis calls showing clients how and when they are irrational.

_____ 16. Assuming that negative emotions reflect the way things really are. Example: "I feel guilty so I must be guilty."

_____ 17. Taking personal responsibility for events that are beyond one's control. Example: "If I had not asked to go shopping he never would have been in the wreck."

_____ 18. A comprehensive sense of one's own capability, effectiveness, strength, or power to attain desired results.

## QUESTIONS FOR DISCUSSION
## AND PERSONAL REFLECTION

The following questions can be used in small group discussion for further exploration of the theory and/or personal reflection of how the theory applies to your own life.

1. What is your general impression of rational emotive therapy? Do you agree with its view of how human personality is structured?

_____

_____

_____

_____

2. How do you view cognitive theories as applying to your own life? If you do not view aspects of these theories as having any applicability to your life, why?

_____

_____

_____

_____

3. If you could have a conversation with Albert Ellis, what questions would you have for him about his theory?

_____

_____

_____

_____

4. As you develop your own approach to therapeutic intervention, what will you take with you from the cognitive theories?

_____

_____

_____

_____

## ANSWERS TO CHAPTER REVIEW

## Biography

1. novelist
2. Karen Horney
3. eighty

## Historical Development

1. Stoicism
2. cognitive
3. women

## View of Human Nature

1. dominion
2. A-B-C
3. free will
4. family, culture

## Development of Maladaptive Behavior

1. illogical
2. unhappiness
3. difficulties (or responsibilities)
4. approval, perfection

## Goals of Therapy

1. teach
2. disputation
3. responsibility
4. open

## Function of the Therapist

1. lead
2. persuasion (or debate)
3. rational

## Major Methods and Techniques

1. cognitive, emotive, behavioristic
2. emotional
3. self
4. effects
5. humor

## Application

1. zero (or target)

## Other Cognitively Based Theories

1. Aaron Beck
2. Albert Bandura, inoculation

## Critical Analysis

1. research
2. valueless
3. world view

## Current Status

1. research

## ANSWERS TO MATCHING ITEMS

| | |
|---|---|
| 1. F | 11. N |
| 2. K | 12. A |
| 3. P | 13. Q |
| 4. B | 14. J |
| 5. M | 15. E |
| 6. I | 16. R |
| 7. S | 17. H |
| 8. D | 10. C |
| 9. L | |
| 10. G | |

## CHAPTER 14

# Reality Therapy

## CHAPTER OVERVIEW

1. *Biography.* Glasser (1925-) was born in Cleveland, Ohio, and his early years were characterized by a happy childhood in a loving family. He majored in chemical engineering and after graduation pursued a Ph.D. in clinical psychology. However, when Glasser's advisers rejected his dissertation, he gained admission to medical school and received his M.D. degree from Western Reserve University in 1953 and completed a psychiatric residency at UCLA in 1957. During this time, Glasser became disillusioned with the efficacy of traditional psychoanalytic procedures and began experimenting with alternative methods of treatment.

2. *Historical Development.* The origins of reality therapy are found in Glasser's basic dislike of the psychoanalytic approach, which focuses primarily on neurosis and mental illness. Glasser rejected the medical model of mental illness and argued that the patient is weak, not ill. It was Glasser's teacher, however, G. L. Harrington, who spurred him on in his unorthodox beliefs and his rejection of the medical model. Eventually taking a position as head psychiatrist at a youth facility for female delinquents run by the state of California, Glasser was finally free to practice his treatment strategies without hindrance. After he cut recidivism dramatically in the institution, he began writing about his unique approach.

3. *View of Human Nature.* Reality therapy assumes everyone wants to be different and has an intrinsic and inherited need to feel somehow separate and distinct from every other living being. Glasser defines two kinds of identity — positive and negative — which he views through behavior, testing it against reality. Individuals function either in consonance or dissonance with reality.

4. *Development of Maladaptive Behavior.* According to Glasser, a person chooses mental illness. He ignores biology as a factor in mental illness and instead views maladaptive functioning as the consequence of irresponsibility. According to Glasser, individuals must maintain a satisfactory standard of behavior if they are to have a "success identity," feel worthwhile, and avoid forms of maladaptive behavior.

5. *Goals of Therapy.* The primary goal of reality therapy is to help clients identify and change self-defeating behavior, to help them make appropriate choices, and to develop a sense of responsibility. Reality therapy strives to help clients clarify what they want in life and then examine obstacles that stand in the way of their reaching what they want.

6. *Function of the Therapist.* Viewing responsibility as a foundational value, the therapist attempts to help clients change irresponsible behavior. To do so the therapist works to build a solid emotional relationship with the client by being tough, interested, warm, understanding, sensitive, and genuine. The bottom line is that the reality therapist must be an excellent example of responsible behavior.

7. *Major Methods and Techniques.* Glasser outlines eight general procedures that therapists can apply in helping their clients face reality and become more responsible: establishing a caring rapport, focusing on behavior (not feelings), focusing on the present (not the past), making a specific plan, getting a commitment, accepting no excuses, eliminating punishment, and never giving up. In addition, the reality therapist may employ a variety of techniques such as writing a contract with the client, role playing, finding "positive addictions," and so on.

8. *Application.* Reality therapy has been applied to a wide variety of clinical issues, but the essentials of Glasser's approach can be illustrated in the case of "Pat," a wealthy, young, overindulged, satisfactorily married mother of two. It is a typical case in that it begins with Glasser investing in Pat and then helping her become responsible for what she wants, weight reduction. The therapy continued slowly as Pat was unable to make Glasser assume a role she could reject. This helped her develop some respect and trust in the process and eventually come to accept that only she could make herself responsible. After almost a year, Glasser could point out Pat's irresponsibilities and truly encourage her to take a chance and change. Pat felt a keener sense of achievement and she lost fifty pounds.

9. *Critical Analysis.* Reality therapy has great versatility with applications to different populations and in a variety of settings. It is also goal-specific, allowing for accessible monitoring of progress. Another strength is that it provides a refreshing alternative to pathology-centered approaches. On the other hand, reality therapy does not validate other valuable concepts like personal history and the unconscious as well as biological factors contributing to mental illness. However, when reality therapy turns to ethnic-minority clients, it offers an approach that is free from jargon and relatively inviting. Since the approach leaves it to the client to determine what he or

she wants, it allows ethnic-minority clients to retain their ethnic identity and values while integrating other desired values and practices.

10. *Current Status.* Glasser's thinking on reality therapy continues to expand and is being undergirded more firmly by control theory. The research base continues to grow with a steady stream of doctoral dissertations being written on reality therapy. The Institute for Reality Therapy offers seminars that lead to certification for its practitioners, and there is a journal devoted to publishing articles on reality therapy. Today Glasser's approach is being successfully applied in schools, correctional institutions, hospitals, clinics, and social service settings while Dr. Glasser continues to be active in writing about his unique approach to counseling.

## GUIDED STUDY

These questions are meant to guide you through the major sections of the chapter. Write your answer in the space provided and then compare it with the marked section of the text.

1. Describe how what little is known of William Glasser's background and training may have impacted the development of his theory.

   _____

   _____

   _____

2. In your own words, how would you describe the birth of reality therapy to someone who was not familiar with its history?

   _____

   _____

   _____

   _____

3. Everyone wants to be different according to reality therapy. How else would you describe this perspective on human nature?

   _____

   _____

   _____

4. Reality therapists reject the medical model of how maladaptive behavior develops. In other words, it is not like a case of the measles. How then do reality therapists see dysfunctional behavior developing?

_____

_____

_____

_____

5. The focus of the reality therapist is clearly on changing irresponsible behavior. Describe the function the therapist serves beyond this.

_____

_____

_____

_____

6. Describe the fundamental goals of reality therapy, including Glasser's criteria for behavior that is suitable and healthy.

_____

_____

_____

_____

7. Why is getting a commitment from the client so crucial to effective reality therapy?

_____

_____

_____

_____

_____

_____

_____

8. How do reality therapists help clients structure their expectations?

_____

_____

_____

_____

9. Confrontation is inevitable in reality therapy. Why and how is it used constructively?

_____

_____

_____

_____

10. What is meant by "positive addictions"?

_____

_____

_____

_____

11. What did you learn from Glasser's treatment of Pat?

_____

_____

_____

_____

12. From a critical analysis, what are the most important strengths and weaknesses of reality therapy?

_____

_____

_____

_____

## CHAPTER REVIEW

The following items will help you master the specific content of the chapter. Complete each of the following sentences by filling in the blanks.

## Biography

1. William Glasser was born in _____, _____, in 1925.

2. While in his residency, Glasser became increasingly pained over the disjunction between the _____ methods he had studied and approaches that truly seemed to help the patient.

3. In 1962 Glasser joined the staff of an institute for adolescent girls in Ventura, California and three years later he published _____ _____, which made ample use of his experiences at the school in order to illuminate the details of his therapeutic approach.

## Historical Development

1. The presupposition that justifies reality therapy is an earlier account of brain functioning called _____ theory.

2. Glasser believes in the potential for each individual to choose their own direction. The roots of this thinking can be found in Ralph Waldo Emerson's concept of _____.

3. The ever-practical Glasser arrived at his treatment theory at least in part because he was not optimistic about starting a _____ _____.

4. So successful were Dr. Glasser's efforts in _____, that he soon began lecturing extensively on reality therapy throughout the United States and Canada.

## View of Human Nature

1. Reality therapy assumes that every person wants to be _____ and it underscores this desire by identifying the unique needs of the individual.

2. According to Glasser, during the first six years of our lives we develop either a negative or positive _____.

3. Unlike behavioristic theory that focuses on a stimulus-response paradigm, reality therapy measures behavior against the objective standard of _____, with which individuals are either in consonance or dissonance.

## Development of Maladaptive Behavior

1. Despite heavy criticism, Glasser ignores _____ as a factor in mental illness and instead views maladaptive functioning as the consequence of irresponsibility.

2. When some people refuse to accept or ignore that responsibility, the price they pay is the emergence of a _____ identity.

3. In his model of maladaptive behavior, Glasser posits individuals who _____ behaviors.

## Goals of Therapy

1. Glasser believes that clients have more control over their _____ than over their thinking or feeling responses.

2. Without rejecting the client, the counselor rejects their _____ behavior.

3. Only when clients assume _____ for their personal behavior can it be said that they have made progress toward reaching their goals.

## Function of the Therapist

1. The reality therapist attaches direct values to _____, measuring clients' success or failure in treatment against their ability to meet these values.

2. Because the reality therapist believes that a change in behavior must precede a change in _____, the focus is on changing irresponsible, self-defeating behavior.

3. In order to provide clients with examples of responsible behavior, the therapist must fulfill his or her own _____ and be willing to talk about personal struggles.

## Major Methods and Techniques

1. A treatment plan is not worthwhile unless the therapist manages to get a _____ from the client to carry it out.

2. Reality therapists are interested in the future and maintain an attitude of no _____.

3. Reality therapists help clients to _____ their expectations.

4. At the outset of therapy clients will be immediately _____ with present reality.

5. A _____ is an ongoing reminder of the specific sequence and schedule in the clients' plans.

6. A major intervention in reality therapy centers on the question: "Does your present _____ enable you to get what you want now, and will it take you in the direction you want to go?"

7. _____ helps clients "presentize" their behavior and it allows them to rehearse events that cause their anxiety.

## Application

1. In treating "Pat," Glasser demonstrates how his approach can bring a person to a place of greater _____.

## Critical Analysis

1. One strength of reality therapy is that it has successfully challenged the medical model of psychotherapy, providing a refreshing alternative to _____-centered approaches to counseling.

2. Reality therapy has been criticized for exaggerating _____ behavior traits, while ignoring other valuable concepts like the unconscious.

3. Reality therapy makes little allowance for the needs of some clients to resolve _____ events.

4. Since reality therapy's focus is on acting and thinking rather than on identifying and exploring feelings, and since it is not burdened with a great deal of technical jargon, many _____ clients can find this approach relatively inviting.

## Current Status

1. Since 1965 reality therapy has achieved a substantial following, especially among _____ and youth guidance counselors.

2. Never content to allow his approach to remain without constant scrutiny, additions, and changes, Dr. Glasser continues to be a quite active student, especially of _____ systems.

## QUESTIONS FOR DISCUSSION AND PERSONAL REFLECTION

The following questions can be used in small group discussion for further exploration of the theory and/or personal reflection of how the theory applies to your own life.

1. What is your general impression of reality therapy? Do you agree with its view of how human personality is structured?

_____

_____

_____

_____

2. How do you view Glasser's theory as applying to your own life? If you do not view it as having any applicability to your life, why?

_____

_____

_____

_____

3. If you could have a conversation with William Glasser, what questions would you have for him about his theory?

_____

_____

_____

_____

4. As you develop your own approach to therapeutic intervention, what will you take with you from reality therapy?

_____

_____

_____

_____

## ANSWERS TO CHAPTER REVIEW

## Biography

1. Cleveland, Ohio
2. Freudian
3. Reality Therapy

## Historical Development

1. control
2. self-reliance
3. private practice
4. education

## View of Human Nature

1. different
2. identity
3. reality

## Development of Maladaptive Behavior

1. biology
2. failure
3. create

## Goals of Therapy

1. behavior
2. unrealistic (or irresponsible)
3. responsibility

## Function of the Therapist

1. behavior
2. identity
3. needs

## Major Methods and Techniques

1. commitment
2. excuses
3. structure
4. confronted
5. contract
6. behavior
7. role playing

## Application

1. responsibility

## Critical Analysis

1. pathology
2. observable
3. past
4. ethnic-minority

## Current Status

1. teachers
2. educational

## CHAPTER 15

# Conclusion: Comparing the Major Therapeutic Theories

In this final exercise on major therapeutic theories, take a moment to review your answer to question number two in the Introduction to Major Therapeutic Theories. Under this item you described your personal theory of counseling in very elementary terms. Now that you have studied the major theories, how would you revise your own theory? Comparing your own views to Freud, Adler, May, and all the rest, how would you describe your unique approach to counseling? Use the following outline to summarize your perspective.

**View of Human Nature**

_____
_____
_____
_____
_____
_____
_____
_____
_____
_____
_____

## Development of Maladaptive Behavior

_____

_____

_____

_____

_____

_____

_____

_____

_____

_____

## Goals of Therapy

_____

_____

_____

_____

_____

_____

_____

_____

_____

_____

_____

# Function of the Therapist

_____

_____

_____

_____

_____

_____

_____

_____

_____

_____

_____

_____

_____

# Major Methods and Techniques

_____

_____

_____

_____

_____

_____

_____

_____

_____

_____

_____

_____

# PART II

# Exercises for Practicing Skills

# Psychoanalytic Therapy

Psychoanalysts and other contemporary psychoanalytically oriented therapists have introduced several treatment variations of the early psychoanalytic techniques first developed by Sigmund Freud. The four major methods or techniques of psychoanalytic therapy that still endure are: *free association* (the cardinal technique of allowing the client to say whatever comes to mind, no matter how trivial or irrational), *dream analysis* (interpreting the latent content of the dream primarily through the use of consistent symbols that signify the same thing for almost everyone), *analysis of transference* (when the client responds to the analyst as a significant authority person from their life thus revealing the nature of their childhood conflicts), and *analysis of resistance* (the unconscious resisting of efforts to help eliminate old behavior patterns, thereby blocking attempts to probe into the real sources of personality problems).

In this Activity Unit, we will cover two psychoanalytic therapy techniques that are often used: *free association* and *dream analysis*. You will be presented with a typical counseling problem or issue and then asked to respond as if you were a Psychoanalytic Therapist. If your answer is correct, we will explain why it is correct and then you will be directed to the next exchange or dialogue between therapist and client. If your answer is incorrect, we will explain why it is wrong and ask you to reconsider it and select another answer. It is important that you do not move on to the next exchange or dialogue until you have successfully completed each step in the programmed approach to learning effective therapeutic interviewing skills. This approach covers one skill at a time, based partially on the microcounseling concept of teaching single skills (see Evans, Hearn, Uhlemann, & Ivey, 1984).

# 1. FREE ASSOCIATION

---

**1.1**             *Client:*    *I feel kind of down and lousy today . . . like I often feel . . . but I'm not sure why . . .*

Choose the most appropriate response:
*Therapist:*   *(Remains quiet and waits)* (Go to 1.2)
*Therapist:*   *Sounds like you're feeling pretty depressed without knowing why* (Go to 1.3)
*Therapist:*   Oh you shouldn't be feeling so down, without any valid reasons, especially since you've been doing well academically! (Go to 1.4)

---

**1.2**   *Your Answer:*   *(Remains quiet and waits)*

Correct. The Psychoanalytic Therapist usually waits and allows the client to continue, whether with pauses, tears, silence, further talking, or some other response, giving the client enough time to *free associate* and open up more. Proceed to 1.5

---

**1.3**   *Your Answer:*   *Sounds like you're feeling pretty depressed without knowing why.*

This would be a good Person-Centered or Rogerian Therapy response but not the most appropriate one for a Psychoanalytic Therapist who is trying to facilitate *free association* by the client. Return to 1.1 and try again.

---

**1.4**   *Your Answer:*   *Oh, you shouldn't be feeling so down, without any valid reasons, especially since you've been doing well academically!*

This is not a helpful response, because it does not reflect empathy or understanding but some judgment and poor advice-giving. It is definitely not an appropriate response for a Psychoanalytic Therapist trying to encourage *free association* by the client! Return to 1.1 and try again.

---

**1.5**             *Client:*    *. . . It's hard for me to cope with these feelings of depression when I don't know why I have them . . . or where they're coming from . . . (pause for a few seconds)*

Choose the most appropriate response:
*Therapist:*   *It doesn't matter if you know or don't know why you are depressed or not. You should embrace your feelings fully, even if they are emotionally painful like depression.* (Go to 1.6)

|  |  |  |
|---|---|---|
| | *Therapist:* | *It must be painful and difficult for you to feel down with no obvious reasons.* (Go to 1.7) |
| | *Therapist:* | *What else comes to mind?* (Go to 1.8) |

---

**1.6**   *Your Answer:*   *It doesn't matter if you know or don't know why you are depressed. You should embrace your feelings fully, even if they are emotionally painful like depression.*

This is not an appropriate response for a Psychoanalytic Therapist to make in order to encourage *free association*. It is also generally not a helpful response, reflecting a lack of empathy and poor and premature advice-giving. It also tends to shut the client down because he or she may feel judged. Return to 1.5 and try again.

---

**1.7**   *Your Answer:*   *It must be painful and difficult for you to feel down with no obvious reasons.*

This is a good Person-Centered or Rogerian Therapy response that reflects empathy, but it is not the most appropriate response for a Psychoanalytic Therapist to make to facilitate *free association*. Return to 1.5 and try again.

---

**1.8**   *Your Answer:*   *What else comes to mind?*

Correct. After waiting for the client who pauses for a few seconds and doesn't say anything else, the Psychoanalytic Therapist will often ask such a question to encourage the client to *free associate* or speak whatever else comes to mind without censure. Proceed to 1.9

---

**1.9**   *Client:*   *. . . When I feel lousy like this, I often feel like a little child all alone . . . and . . . abandoned . . . like where's mummy? . . . (sobs for a few seconds, and pauses quietly) . . .*

Choose the most appropriate response:

*Therapist:*   *Your feelings of depression remind you of feeling abandoned by your mother and being all by yourself . . .kind of painful and scary?* (Go to 1.10)

*Therapist:*   *Tell me more about what you're thinking at this moment, what other thoughts come to mind.* (Go to 1.11)

*Therapist:*   *This seems to be a significant recollection, feeling abandoned by your mother. Let's pause here and use an imagery technique to help you to describe the details of what happened then more vividly.* (Go to 1.12)

---

**1.10**     *Your Answer:*     *Your feelings of depression remind you of feeling abandoned by your mother and being all by yourself . . . kind of painful and scary?*

This response is a good Person-Centered or Rogerian response that reflects empathy. It is not the most appropriate response however for a Psychoanalytic Therapist trying to facilitate *free association*. Return to 1.9 and try again.

---

**1.11**     *Your Answer:*     *Tell me more about what you're thinking at this moment, what other thoughts come to mind.*

Correct. This is another typical response of a Psychoanalytic Therapist trying to encourage the client to *free associate* and say more about whatever comes to mind. Proceed to 1.13.

---

**1.12**     *Your Answer:*     *This seems to be a significant recollection, feeling abandoned by your mother. Let's pause here and use an imagery technique to help you to describe the details of what happened then more vividly.*

This is not an appropriate response for a Psychoanalytic Therapist to make to facilitate *free association*. It is too directive and action-oriented, and is more typical of cognitive and behavioral therapists who often use directive interventions such as imagery techniques. Return to 1.9 and try again.

---

**1.13**          *Client:*     *. . . I can recall a particularly painful memory when I was a child . . . about 7 years old . . . and my mother and I were at Disneyland and it was very crowded . . . suddenly I could not find her . . . and I felt terrified and so alone and . . . and abandoned by her! "Where are you mummy?" I cried over and over again . . .*

Choose the most appropriate response:

*Therapist:*     *As a small child, that must have felt like the end of the world, being lost and not being able to find mummy, in a large place like Disneyland.* (Go to 1.14)

*Therapist:*     *Let's pause here and do some brief relaxation exercises so you can calm down and not hyperventilate, and then tell me more about what happened.* (Go to 1.15)

*Therapist:*     *Uhmhmm . . . what else comes to mind now?* (Go to 1.16)

---

**1.14**   *Your Answer:*   *As a small child, that must have felt like the end of the world, being lost and not being able to find mummy, in a huge place like Disneyland.*

This is a good response for reflecting empathy that a Person-Centered or Rogerian therapist might use. However, it is not the most appropriate response for a Psychoanalytic Therapist to use for encouraging further *free association*. Return to 1.13 and try again.

---

**1.15**   *Your Answer:*   *Let's pause here and do some relaxation exercises so you can calm down and not hyperventilate, and then tell me more about what happened.*

This is not an appropriate response for a Psychoanalytic Therapist to make to facilitate *free association*. It is too directive and action-oriented. The use of relaxation exercises is more typical of cognitive and behavioral therapists. They may however not choose to use relaxation exercises at this particular point of the therapeutic dialogue because it may not be the right timing. It is probably better to let the client go on talking. Return to 1.13 and try again.

---

**1.16**   *Your Answer:*   *Uhmhmm . . . what else comes to mind now?*

Correct. Again a Psychoanalytic Therapist will often use such a question or response to encourage further *free association* by the client. The therapist could also simply remain silent and pause until the client talks again and continues the dialogue. When the client has given enough material by way of *free association* and self-disclosure, the Psychoanalytic Therapist will then offer occasionally an *interpretation* of what seems to be happening, focusing especially on *unconscious* processes such as *transference* and other unresolved conflicts from childhood, often involving sexual and aggressive themes. Another major intervention used by Psychoanalytic Therapists is *dream analysis*, which also often employs *free association* in the interpretation of dreams. Dreams were seen by Sigmund Freud as "the royal road to the unconscious."

# 2. DREAM ANALYSIS

2.1          Client:     *. . . I had a dream last night . . . I can't remember all the details*
                         *. . but I do remember it was about me riding a motorcycle and*
                         *going way too fast . . . and I was just about to crash into a wall*
                         *when I suddenly awoke, with a cold sweat and my heart beat-*
                         *ing really fast! It was a scary and bad dream!*

             Therapist:  Choose the most appropriate response:
                         *How often do you have dreams like this, dreams that are very*
                         *vivid and real to you, making you awaken with a strong emo-*
                         *tional response like fear?* (Go to 2.2)
             Therapist:  *Your dream seems to be warning you that you are going too*
                         *fast in your life and life-style, and need to really slow down, or*
                         *else you'll crash and burn out!* (Go to 2.3)
             Therapist:  *What comes to mind as you're relating the dream to me? What*
                         *other thoughts and feelings?* (Go to 2.4)

2.2   Your Answer:   *How often do you have dreams like this, dreams that are very*
                     *vivid and real to you, making you awaken with a strong emo-*
                     *tional response like fear?*

                     This response is a good one for eliciting more factual
                     information about the frequency and type of dreams the
                     client may be having. However, the Psychoanalytic
                     Therapist is more interested in helping the client *free asso-*
                     *ciate* in order to get to the deeper, latent meaning of his or
                     her dream, and not get stuck on factual information
                     regarding the client's dreams. This is therefore not the
                     most appropriate response for psychoanalytic *dream*
                     *analysis*. Return to 2.1 and try again.

2.3   Your Answer:   *Your dream seems to be warning you that you are going too*
                     *fast in your life and life-style, and need to really slow down, or*
                     *else you'll crash and burn out!*

                     This is *not* the most appropriate response for a Psycho-
                     analytic Therapist to make who is trying to help the client
                     *free associate* first in order to do *dream analysis* at a deeper,
                     more latent level of meaning of the dream. This response is
                     actually a premature attempt at *dream analysis*, without first
                     obtaining more dream material as well as *free associations* to
                     the material. Some psychoanalysts will call this response
                     an example of "wild analysis" that is premature and usu-
                     ally inaccurate. Return to 2.1 and try again.

**2.4**   *Your Answer:*   *What comes to mind as you're relating the dream to me? What thoughts and feelings?*

Correct. This is an example of what a Psychoanalytic Therapist might say in response to an initial description of a dream by a client. This response or question encourages the client to *free associate* to the dream material or bring out more dream material so that the Psychoanalytic Therapist can eventually have enough material to help interpret or analyze the dream not only in terms of its obvious *manifest* content, but more importantly in terms of its *deeper unconscious or latent content and meanings.* Sexual and aggressive themes or meanings often emerge. Proceed to 2.5.

---

**2.5**         *Client:*   *. . . I do think of the dream as a warning to me, because I know that I've been living too hectic a life and been too busy with work, often working 14-16 hours a day, even on weekends. I've been feeling very tired and somewhat depressed, and at times that I will crash or be crushed . . . yet I also have an urge periodically to just throw all my self-discipline and workaholism to the wind, and have a fling . . . and do something wild or fun for a change.*

Choose the most appropriate response:

*Therapist:*   *You feel the dream has some meaning, that it's telling you something . . . what else comes to mind in association with the fling or doing something wild? (Go to 2.6)*

*Therapist:*   *I believe you are right, that the dream is possibly warning you to slow down and change your life-style. What are some significant problem areas you're facing right now? What do you think may need changing and how? (Go to 2.7)*

*Therapist:*   *You feel that the dream is revealing that you need to slow down and change your life-style, but that you also have a deep wish inside to take a risk and do something more fun or wild for a change. (Go to 2.8)*

---

**2.6**   *Your Answer:*   *You feel the dream has some meaning, that it's telling you something . . . what else comes to mind in association with the fling or doing something wild?*

Correct. This is another example of what a Psychoanalytic Therapist might say to help the client *free associate* more to particular parts of a dream or to previous *free associations* with the dream. Such *free associations* bring up more material for the therapist to work on, so that the *dream analysis* or interpretation will be based on sufficient material brought out by the client, instead of on "wild analysis" that is premature and preconceived by the therapist. Proceed to 2.9.

---

**2.7** *Your Answer:* *I believe you are right, that the dream is possibly warning you to slow down and change your life-style. What are some significant problem areas you're facing right now? What do you think may need changing and how?*

This is not an appropriate response for a Psychoanalytic Therapist to make in *dream analysis* with the client. It is rather a more direct and problem-solving intervention that steers the client away from further *free association* and analysis of the dream, and leads the client to engage in problem-solving of his or her struggles with too hectic and workaholic a life-style. Return to 2.5 and try again.

---

**2.8** *Your Answer:* *You feel that the dream is revealing that you need to slow down and change your life-style, but that you also have a deep wish inside to take a risk and do something more fun or wild for a change.*

This is not a bad response per se: in fact it is a good response for showing empathy and understanding to the client. It is often used by a Rogerian or Person-Centered therapist. However, it stops short of encouraging the client to do further *free association* and reflection on the dream or previous *free associations* with it regarding having a fling or doing something wild. It is therefore *not* the most appropriate response to facilitate psychoanalytic *dream analysis*. Return to 2.5 and try again.

---

**2.9** *Client:* *I'm not sure what I really desire to do that is fun or wild or a fling . . . but I believe that riding a motorcycle really fast, even risking crashing into a wall represents the part of me that has been repressed and wants to be free. I have never ridden on a motorcycle before . . .*

Choose the most appropriate response:

*Therapist:* *You feel that the dream about riding a motorcycle really fast reflects your deep desire to be more free and spontaneous in your life, to do things that are fun, even risky. Perhaps you're feeling too constricted, too hemmed in, by demands from others and yourself to perform, to be productive, to be almost perfect.* (Go to 2.10)

*Therapist:* *Go on . . . what might the motorcycle itself mean to you or represent to you?* (Go to 2.11)

*Therapist:* *Well, let's brainstorm some of the things you think you might want to try or do, to feel more free and spontaneous.* (Go to 2.12)

---

**2.10** *Your Answer:* *You feel that the dream about riding on a motorcycle really fast reflects your deep desire to be more free and spontaneous in your life, to do things that are fun, even risky. Perhaps you're* *feeling too constricted, too hemmed in, by demands from others and yourself, to perform, to be productive, to be almost perfect.*

This is a response that reflects deeper empathy and also offers some interpretation of how the client might be actually feeling, beyond what he or she has said so far. However, it is *not* the most appropriate response to help the client focus on the dream and further *free associations* with the dream in order to facilitate deeper psychoanalytic *dream analysis*. Return to 2.9 and try again.

---

**2.11**   *Your Answer:*   *Go on . . . what might the motorcycle itself mean to you or represent to you?*

Correct. This response is often used by the Psychoanalytic Therapist to help the client focus on a particular part or element of the dream and to *free associate* with it or reflect on its possible meanings for the client. The danger here is that the client can end up intellectualizing the different possible meanings of the motorcycle, but he or she can also give a "gut response" or spontaneous, uncensored free association that might help the client and therapist get at the deeper meaning of the dream. Proceed to 2.13.

---

**2.12**   *Your Answer:*   *Well, let's brainstorm some of the things you think you might want to try or do, to feel more free and spontaneous.*

This is *not* an appropriate response for a Psychoanalytic Therapist to make in *dream analysis.* It does not encourage further *free association* or reflections on the dream. Instead, it is a direct, problem-solving intervention often used by cognitive and behavior therapists. Return to 2.9 and try again.

---

**2.13**          *Client:*   *The motorcycle . . . makes me think actually . . . of something powerful and exciting . . . almost sexual . . . riding it gives me the feeling of sensual power and pleasure. . . . I'm almost embarrassed by what I'm saying but I guess my sex life has been nonexistent for quite a while . . . perhaps I deeply desire to have a sexual fling but I'm afraid I'll crash and hurt myself very badly . . .*

Choose the most appropriate response:

*Therapist:*   *So, it seems the motorcycle represents something sexual and very powerful for you, but you are afraid of it as well. What other thoughts or feelings come to mind as you* free associate *more to having a sexual fling or to sex per se in your life? (Go to 2.14)*

Therapist: *You seem to be in conflict over your sexual desires . . . you want to express them but you are afraid you'll end up seriously hurting yourself.* (Go to 2.15)

Therapist: *Let's talk about why your sex life has been non-existent for awhile. What's holding your back? What are some of the problems or blocks?* (Go to 2.16)

---

**2.14** *Your Answer:* *So, it seems the motorcycle represents something sexual and very powerful for you, but you are afraid of it as well. What other thoughts or feelings come to mind as you free associate more to having a sexual fling or to sex per se in your life?*

Correct. The Psychoanalytic Therapist will often use such a response to encourage the client to reflect or *free associate* even more deeply to the sexual theme that has come up so far in the *dream analysis,* so that eventually a deeper interpretation of the dream's latent, unconscious meanings will result.

---

**2.15** *Your Answer:* *You seem to be in conflict over your sexual desires . . . you want to express them but you are afraid you'll end up seriously hurting yourself.*

This is a response that reflects empathy for the client, and is a good summary of what he or she may be partially experiencing. However, it is *not* the most appropriate response to help the client continue with *free association* and psychoanalytic *dream analysis* because the focus on the dream and especially the motorcycle in the dream, is not being kept. Return to 2.13 and try again.

---

**2.16** *Your Answer:* *Let's talk about why your sex life has been non-existent for awhile. What's holding your back? What are some of the problems or blocks?*

This response is *not* an appropriate one for psychoanalytic *dream analysis.* The focus on the dream or a significant element in it (i.e., the motorcycle) is lost, and instead the therapist here engages in a direct, problem-solving intervention that is more characteristic of other action-oriented therapies such as cognitive and behavior therapies. Return to 2.13 and try again.

---

# Reference

Evans, D. R., Hearn, M. T., Uhlemann, M. R., & Ivey, A. E. (1984). *Essential interviewing: A programmed approach to effective communication* (2nd ed.). Monterey, CA: Brooks/Cole Publishing.

# ROLE PLAY FOR PSYCHOANALYTIC THERAPY

Find two others who have also completed this activity unit. Role play brief interviews (anywhere from five to fifteen minutes each) alternating the client, counselor, and observer roles. Record each brief interview on audio- or video-tape for later review and evaluation.

- The *counselor* in this role play should practice the techniques of free association and dream analysis.

- The *client* should provide sufficient information (based on reality) for the counselor to practice free association and dream analysis.

- The *observer* should note the counselor's attempts to practice these techniques, taking detailed notes on each exchange between counselor and client in the space provided below.

   Observer's notes on you as the counselor:

_____

_____

_____

_____

   At the conclusion of the brief interview, participants should discuss the performance of the counselor, learning from each other how these specific techniques are properly used. Focusing on positive as well as less effective responses can improve the performance and understanding of these techniques for each participant.

## On Your Own

Once you have completed the above role play, listen to the tape of the interview (on your own) with you as the counselor. Enter your remarks, verbatim, in the spaces provided. Then consider ways in which you could have more accurately demonstrated the techniques (based on the theory) and write these improved responses in the space following each original response.

Original response 1 _____

_____

_____

_____

Improved response _____

_____

_____

_____


Original response 2 _____

_____

_____

_____


Improved response _____

_____

_____

_____


Original response 3 _____

_____

_____

_____


Improved response _____

_____

_____

_____


Original response 4 _____

_____

_____

_____


Improved response _____

_____

_____

_____

Original response 5 _____

_____

_____

_____

Improved response_____

_____

_____

_____

Original response 6 _____

_____

_____

_____

Improved response_____

_____

_____

_____

# *Adlerian Therapy*

Adlerian therapy developed by Alfred Adler and originally called individual psychology by him, has a number of therapeutic techniques that are used not only by Adlerian Therapists but oftentimes by other psychotherapists as well! The most common Adlerian therapeutic techniques include *investigating the client's life-style or basic orientation toward life*. This is usually done by *exploring "three entrance gates to mental life": birth order, early recollections* (which encapsulate one's present philosophy of life) and *dreams* (which Adler viewed as means of rehearsing how one might deal with problems in the future). More specific Adlerian interventions include *asking "The Question"* ("What would be different if you were well?") to help clients determine how they want to change, *acting "as if"* to try out new behaviors, *paradoxical intention* or encouraging clients to exaggerate or do the very behaviors they are trying to avoid or overcome, and *the "push button" technique* in which clients realize they can push particular mental buttons or thoughts to feel better or worse.

In this Activity Unit, we will cover two Adlerian therapy techniques that are often used: *early recollections* (e.g., *by saying, "Think as far back as you can and tell me your earliest memory from your childhood years."*) and asking *"The Question"* (*"What would be different if you were well?"*). The same programmed approach to learning effective therapeutic interviewing skills, covering one skill at a time, will be used.

## 1. EARLY RECOLLECTIONS

| | | |
|---|---|---|
| **1.1** | *Client:* | *I feel anxious and fearful often but don't really understand why because there is no reason for me to feel this way.* |

Choose the most appropriate response:

*Therapist:*   *Let's explore what may specifically make you anxious even though you may not be fully aware of it. When you last felt very anxious or fearful, what was happening around you and what were you thinking about? (Go to 1.2)*

*Therapist:*   *You have frequent fears or anxieties but don't know why. (Go to 1.3)*

*Therapist:*   *As we explore your anxieties or fears more, it may be helpful for you to think as far back as you can and tell me your earliest memory from your childhood years. (Go to 1.4)*

---

**1.2**   *Your Answer:*   *Let's explore what may specifically make you anxious even if you may not be fully aware of it. When you last felt very anxious or fearful, what was happening around you and what were you thinking about?*

This is a common question often asked by cognitive and behavior therapists to try to determine the specific stimuli and thoughts that may be causing the client to feel anxious. It is not the most appropriate response for an Adlerian Therapist who is trying to help the client with *early recollections*. Return to 1.1 and try again.

---

**1.3**   *Your Answer:*   *You have frequent fears and anxieties but don't know why.*

This is a good summary response to show empathy for the client but it is not the most appropriate response to encourage the client to explore *early recollections*. Return to 1.1 and try again.

---

**1.4**   *Your Answer:*   *As we explore your anxieties and fears more, it may be helpful for you to think as far back as you can and tell me your earliest memory from your childhood years.*

Correct. This is a response often used by the Adlerian Therapist to help the client think back to the past and come up with *early recollections*. They need to be *specific* and *not* general or vague memories. Proceed to 1.5

**1.5**            Client:    *Well . . . I can recall going to the beach often in the summer when I was a young child . . .*

Choose the most appropriate response.

Therapist:    *(Remains quiet and waits)* (Go to 1.6)
Therapist:    *Can you remember a more specific event of what happened when you were a young child at the beach?* (Go to 1.7)
Therapist:    *What else comes to mind, as you recall this?* (Go to 1.8)

---

**1.6**    Your Answer:    *(Remains quiet and waits)*

This response is more typical of a psychoanalytic therapist. The Adlerian Therapist is more encouraging, and will ask for more specific memories in helping the client with *early recollections.* Return to 1.5 and try again.

---

**1.7**    Your Answer:    *Can you remember a more specific event or memory of what happened when you were a young child at the beach?*

Correct. The Adlerian Therapist would usually ask such a question to elicit a more specific memory or *early recollection* rather than stop at a general memory such as going to the beach often. Proceed to 1.9

---

**1.8**    Your Answer:    *What else comes to mind, as you recall this?*

This is a response that is more typical of a psychoanalytic therapist interested in facilitating free association by the client. It is not the most appropriate response for the Adlerian Therapist to use to encourage more specific *early recollections.* Return to 1.5 and try again.

---

**1.9**            Client:    *Hmmm . . . well, I can kind of remember that I was about 5 years old and my father and I were with a few other friends playing on the beach and building sandcastles . . . and he embarrassed me by saying what a lousy and ugly-looking sandcastle I had made compared to the others . . .*

Choose the most appropriate response:

Therapist:    *Sounds like your father put you down in front of your friends and you felt hurt and humiliated.* (Go to 1.10)
Therapist:    *(Remains quiet and waits)* (Go to 1.11)
Therapist:    *That's a good recollection of a specific early memory . . . go on and tell me more about it.* (Go to 1.12)

1.10   *Your Answer:*   *Sounds like your father put you down in front of your friends and you felt hurt and humiliated.*

This is a good response to show empathy to the client but it is not the most appropriate response for an Adlerian Therapist to use to encourage the client to go on describing the *early recollection* in more specific detail. Return to 1.9 and try again.

---

1.11   *Your Answer:*   *(Remains quiet and waits.)*

Again, this response is more characteristic of a psychoanalytic therapist. It is not the most appropriate response for eliciting more detail of a specific memory in the Adlerian technique of *early recollections*. Return to 1.9 and try again.

---

1.12   *Your Answer:*   *That's a good recollection of a specific early memory . . . go on and tell me more about it.*

Correct. The Adlerian Therapist would make such a comment to *encourage* the client (*encouragement* is the bedrock of Adlerian intervention, especially for establishing a good therapeutic relationship with the client) as well as to facilitate more detailed recollection of a specific early memory. Proceed to 1.13.

---

1.13            *Client:*   *. . . I felt hurt and also a strong sense of fear and inferiority came over me . . . and I guess since then I've always felt anxious and unsure of myself or inferior, as if I'll never be good enough in comparison to others no matter how hard I try or what I do . . . my father always had such high standards for me . . .*

Choose the most appropriate response:

*Therapist:*   *That embarrassing experience with your father at the beach seems to have made you feel afraid and inferior in general ever since.* (Go to 1.14)

*Therapist:*   *Since that early experience you seem to approach life feeling that you need to compare yourself with others, and yet always feeling you'll never measure up, thus making you feel anxious and inferior a lot.* (Go to 1.15)

*Therapist:*   *When you feel anxious or inferior, what do you do to cope with such painful feelings?* (Go to 1.16)

**1.14**   *Your Answer:*   *That embarrassing experience with your father at the beach seems to have made you feel afraid and inferior in general ever since.*

This is a good summary response to reflect empathy to the client. However, it is more typical of a Person-Centered or Rogerian therapist. The Adlerian Therapist would say more about how this *early recollection* has influenced the client's present philosophy of life or approach to life. Return to 1.13 and try again.

---

**1.15**   *Your Answer:*   *Since that early experience you seem to approach life feeling that you need to compare yourself with others, yet always feeling you'll never measure up, thus making you feel anxious and inferior a lot.*

Correct. The Adlerian Therapist will make a response such as this is in order to point out to the client how an *early recollection* has affected his or her whole approach to or philosophy of life. The theme of inferiority often comes up.

---

**1.16**   *Your Answer:*   *When you feel anxious or inferior, what do you do to cope with such painful feelings?*

This is more of a problem-solving intervention, often used by behavior and cognitive therapists to help the client come up with effective coping strategies to deal with anxiety or thoughts of inferiority. It is not the most appropriate response for an Adlerian Therapist to use to help the client see how a specific *early recollection* has influenced his or her present philosophy of life. Return to 1.13 and try again.

---

## 2. ASKING "THE QUESTION" ("WHAT WOULD BE DIFFERENT IF YOU WERE WELL?")

---

**2.1**          *Client:*   *My feeling anxious or fearful often really gets in the way of my getting things done in my life, and my enjoying life.*

Choose the most appropriate response:

*Therapist:*   *You find you can't really enjoy life or accomplish what you want because you feel anxious so often. (Go to 2.2)*

Therapist:  *I wonder if your frequent experiences of anxiety may be telling you something, may mean something deeper or significant to you.* (Go to 2.3)

Therapist:  *Your anxiety gets in the way of what you want to accomplish in your life, as well as prevents you from enjoying life. What would be different if you were well?* (Go to 2.4)

---

**2.2**    Your Answer:  *You find you can't really enjoy life or accomplish what you want because you feel anxious often.*

This is a summary response reflecting empathy to the client. It is not the most appropriate response for an Adlerian Therapist to use in order to ask "The Question" and get at the heart of how the client may want to change. Return to 2.1 and try again.

---

**2.3**    Your Answer:  *I wonder if your frequent experiences of anxiety may be telling you something, may mean something deeper or significant to you.*

This response encourages the client to explore the deeper meanings of his or her anxiety experiences, but it is more typical of an Existential therapist or even a Cognitive therapist. The Adlerian Therapist interested in getting at the heart of the client's motivation for change will go on and ask "The Question." Return to 2.1 and try again.

---

**2.4**    Your Answer:  *Your anxiety gets in the way of what you want to accomplish in your life, as well as prevents you from enjoying life. What would be different if you were well?*

Correct. The Adlerian Therapist, after empathically summarizing what the client has just expressed, proceeds to ask *"The Question"* to help the client deal with how he or she wants to change. Proceed to 2.5

---

**2.5**         Client:  *If I were well and if I did not have anxiety so often, I would be a happier and more confident person . . . I would go on to graduate school and finish an M.B.A., perhaps even start my own business . . .*

Choose the most appropriate response:

Therapist:  *If you could overcome your anxiety, you feel you'll be happier and more sure of yourself, even going to graduate school or starting your own business.* (Go to 2.6)

|  |  |  |
|---|---|---|
| | *Therapist:* | *What else comes to mind? (Go to 2.7)* |
| | *Therapist:* | *So if you were well you would do an M.B.A. and even possibly start your own business. What else would be different if you were well without so much anxiety? (Go to 2.8)* |

---

**2.6**   *Your Answer:*   *If you could overcome your anxiety, you feel you'll be happier and more sure of yourself, even going to graduate school or starting your own business.*

This is a summary response to show empathy to the client but it is not the best response for the Adlerian Therapist to use to encourage the client to further explore how he or she may want to change. Return to 2.5 and try again.

---

**2.7**   *Your Answer:*   *What else comes to mind?*

This is a response often used by the psychoanalytic therapist to facilitate more free association by the client. It is not the most appropriate response for the Adlerian Therapist to make to encourage the client to focus on how he or she wants to change. Return to 2.5 and try again.

---

**2.8**   *Your Answer:*   *So if you were well you would do an M.B.A. and even possibly start your own business. What else would be different if you were well without so much anxiety?*

Correct. This response is more typical of an Adlerian Therapist who wants to encourage the client with empathy as well as to further ask "The Question" to focus on change. Proceed to 2.9

---

**2.9**   *Client:*   *Hmmm . . . if I were well, I would also be more outgoing and sociable . . . I would love to go to parties more often, and go hiking or camping or do some other outdoor adventure thing . . . right now I'm so house-bound and afraid to do almost anything, so I stay home a lot and feel anxious and miserable.*

Choose the most appropriate response:

*Therapist:*   *Sounds like you feel pretty lonely and isolated because you stay home a lot due to your anxiety. You would really like to be with people more and do more adventurous outdoor activities. (Go to 2.10)*

*Therapist:*   *If you were well, you sound excited about doing more social things with people such as parties, hiking, camping, etc. You feel miserable in your present situation. Sounds like you really want to change! Do you? (Go to 2.11)*

| | Therapist: | *You should just ignore your anxiety and go out and just do it! Whatever you really want to do, such as going to parties or hiking or camping. Let's do some planning now.* (Go to 2.12) |

**2.10** Your Answer: *Sounds like you feel pretty lonely and isolated because you stay home a lot due to your anxiety. You would really like to be with people more and do more adventurous outdoor activities.*

This is a summary response reflecting empathy to the client. It is not the best response for the Adlerian Therapist to use to encourage the client to focus more on how he or she wants to change. Return to 2.9 and try again.

**2.11** Your Answer: *If you were well, you sound excited about doing more social things with people such as parties, hiking, camping, etc. You feel miserable in your present situation. Sounds like you really want to change! Do you?*

Correct. The Adlerian Therapist uses this response to empathically summarize what the client is experiencing, and then encourages the client to focus on his or her desire to change. This can lead to some specific ideas or strategies for change later. Proceed to 2.13

**2.12** Your Answer: *You should just ignore your anxiety and go out and just do it! Whatever you really want to do, such as going to parties or hiking or camping. Let's do some planning now.*

This is not the most appropriate response because it lacks empathy and jumps too quickly to problem-solving and planning before addressing the client's motivation or commitment to change, an important process for the Adlerian Therapist. Return to 2.9 and try again.

**2.13** Client: *I guess . . . I kind of feel excited about what I can or want to do if I were well . . . but I am not well and have all this anxiety . . . I wish I could get rid of it and do what I really want to do . . . Yes I do want to be well . . . I'm sick and tired of this anxiety that has dogged me for so long!*

Choose the most appropriate response:

Therapist: *You really seem committed to changing and wanting to be well! I believe that you are capable of changing. Let's discuss how you think you can go about changing, being less anxious and more sociable and active. We may need to focus particularly on your feeling inferior.* (Go to 2.14)

*Therapist:*   *Sounds like you really want to get well and be rid of the anxiety you've had almost all your life.* (Go to 2.15)

*Therapist:*   *Well, good! Let's begin by making up a list of things that tend to make you anxious - an anxiety or fear hierarchy, after which I'll teach you some relaxation techniques to help you overcome or control the anxiety.* (Go to 2.16)

---

**2.14**   *Your Answer:*   *You really seem committed to changing and wanting to be well! I believe that you are capable of changing. Let's discuss how you think you can go about changing, being less anxious and more sociable and active. We may need to focus particularly on your feeling inferior.*

Correct. While this is a fairly long response, it is a good summary of what the Adlerian Therapist believes needs to be expressed to encourage the client to go on and begin to make changes. The "inferiority complex" that Adler is so well-known for, also needs to be dealt with as a special focus.

---

**2.15**   *Your Answer:*   *Sounds like you really want to get well and be rid of the anxiety you've had all your life.*

This is a good response for reflecting empathy but it is not the most appropriate response to encourage the client to go on and begin to make changes as the Adlerian Therapist is interested in doing. Return to 2.13 and try again.

---

**2.16**   *Your Answer:*   *Well, good! Let's begin by making up a list of things that tend to make you anxious - an anxiety or fear hierarchy, after which I'll teach you some relaxation techniques to help you overcome or control the anxiety.*

This response is more typical of a behavior or cognitive therapist about to begin a systematic desensitization, stress-inoculation or coping skills intervention for anxiety management. It is a bit premature at this time, although it could be a helpful intervention later. The Adlerian Therapist will focus more on the client's motivation for change and discuss how the client wants to change before moving on to specific methods of change. Return to 2.13 and try again.

---

# ROLE PLAY FOR ADLERIAN THERAPY

Find two others who have also completed this activity unit. Role play brief interviews (anywhere from five to fifteen minutes each) alternating the client, counselor, and observer roles. Record each brief interview on audio- or video-tape for later review and evaluation.

- The *counselor* in this role play should practice the techniques of exploring early recollections and asking "The Question."

- The *client* should provide sufficient information (based on reality) for the counselor to practice exploring early recollections and asking "The Question."

- The *observer* should note the counselor's attempts to practice these techniques, taking detailed notes on each exchange between counselor and client in the space provided below.

    Observer's notes on you as the counselor:

_____

_____

_____

_____

At the conclusion of the brief interview, participants should discuss the performance of the counselor, learning from each other how these specific techniques are properly used. Focusing on positive as well as less effective responses can improve the performance and understanding of these techniques for each participant.

## On Your Own

Once you have completed the above role play, listen to the tape of the interview (on your own) with you as the counselor. Enter your remarks, verbatim, in the spaces provided. Then consider ways in which you could have more accurately demonstrated the techniques (based on the theory) and write these improved responses in the space following each original response.

    Original response 1 _____

_____

_____

_____

Improved response _____

_____

_____

_____

Original response 2 _____

_____

_____

_____

Improved response _____

_____

_____

_____

Original response 3 _____

_____

_____

_____

Improved response _____

_____

_____

_____

Original response 4 _____

_____

_____

_____

Improved response _____

_____

_____

_____

Original response 5 _____

_____

_____

_____

Improved response _____

_____

_____

_____

Original response 6 _____

_____

_____

_____

Improved response _____

_____

_____

_____

# Existential Therapy

Existential therapy is associated with a number of therapists such as the late Rollo May, and Victor Frankl, the founder of Logotherapy. Its main focus is to help clients *experience* their *existence* in as real, authentic, and responsible a way as possible, and to learn to freely choose or make decisions in their lives, particularly to create *meaning* for themselves. Existential therapy emphasizes the importance of the therapeutic relationship and the encounter between the client and therapist. It therefore does not provide a systematic presentation of procedure, method or empirical validation of its therapeutic approach. Nevertheless, there are a few techniques that are well-known, especially from Frankl's Logotherapy school of existential therapy. They include: *paradoxical intention* which requires the client to act against his or her anticipation of fear by doing or even exaggerating the very act he or she is afraid of doing (this is also an Adlerian intervention, and has been adapted and adopted in other therapies as well); *dereflection* which encourages the client to ignore the problem and direct awareness or attention toward something else more positive or pleasant; and *modifying the client's attitudes or thinking*, especially regarding the past which cannot be changed, so that more meaningful and hopeful or optimistic ways of looking at things can emerge.

In this Activity Unit, we will cover two existential therapy or logotherapy techniques: *paradoxical intention* and *dereflection*. The same programmed approach to learning effective therapeutic interviewing skills, covering one skill or technique at a time, will be used.

# 1. PARADOXICAL INTENTION

1.1              *Client:*     *I get anxious whenever I have to talk to my boss at work . . . and when I feel anxious I tend to have sweaty palms . . . which makes me even more anxious because I don't want to get embarrassed when he shakes my hand and it's all sweaty . . . I don't know what to do! So I try to avoid my boss as much as possible . . . even thinking about it makes me anxious . . .*

                                     Choose the most appropriate response:

        *Therapist:*     *What do you think about when you feel anxious like that in front of your boss?* (Go to 1.2)

        *Therapist:*     *You'll need some techniques to help you cope with your anxiety. Let's begin with some simple relaxation exercises like taking slow deep breaths, telling yourself to relax and calm down, and imagining pleasant scenes . . .* (Go to 1.3)

        *Therapist:*     *So, even when you think about talking to your boss you get anxious, with sweaty palms. You therefore do your best to avoid meeting with him . . . I'm going to ask you to do something that may sound crazy to you but it may actually help you. Can you try your best to make your palms sweat even more while either thinking of talking with your boss or actually meeting with him?* (Go to 1.4)

---

1.2    *Your Answer:*    *What do you think about when you feel anxious like that in front of your boss?*

This response is more typical of a cognitive therapist interested in identifying the thoughts that may trigger anxiety. It is not the most appropriate response for an Existential Therapist to make in conducting *paradoxical intention*. Return to 1.1 and try again.

---

1.3    *Your Answer:*    *You'll need some techniques to help you cope with your anxiety. Let's begin with some simple relaxation exercises like taking slow deep breaths, telling yourself to relax and calm down, and imagining pleasant scenes . . .*

This response is more typical of behavior or cognitive therapists interested in teaching the client directly some specific anxiety management or relaxation skills. It is not the most appropriate response for an Existential Therapist to use in order to conduct *paradoxical intention*. Return to 1.1 and try again.

**1.4**   *Your Answer:*   *So, even when you think about talking to your boss you get anxious, with sweaty palms. You therefore do your best to avoid meeting with him . . . I'm going to ask you to do something that may sound crazy to you but it may actually help you. Can you try your best to make your palms sweat even more while either thinking of talking with your boss or actually meeting with him?*

Correct. The Existential Therapist will first respond with some empathic comments and then proceed to suggest to the client to do more of the very behavior he or she is afraid of, in this case, having sweaty palms, in conducting *paradoxical intention* with the client. Proceed to 1.5.

---

**1.5**   *Client:*   *I'm really afraid to have sweaty palms . . . the more sweaty they are the worse I feel . . . I'm afraid I may even drip drops of sweat and my boss will notice how anxious I am . . . and especially if he shakes my hand . . . he'll feel the sweat and know I'm all nervous and fearful!*

Choose the most appropriate response:

*Therapist:*   *You are afraid of your fear and sweaty palms, and your boss noticing, especially if he shakes your hand. It seems especially terrible if he finds out . . . Again, I want you now to close your eyes and imagine that you are having a meeting with him . . . now do your best and try your hardest to sweat as much as possible in your palms . . . do the very thing you are afraid will happen . . .* (Go to 1.6)

*Therapist:*   *You seem to be afraid of your own fear and sweaty palms, and especially your boss finding out . . .* (Go to 1.7)

*Therapist:*   *What does it mean to you if your boss does notice or find out that you are anxious and nervous with sweaty palms?* (Go to 1.8)

---

**1.6**   *Your Answer:*   *You are afraid of your fear and sweaty palms, and your boss noticing, especially if he shakes your hand. It seems especially terrible if he finds out . . . Again, I want you now to close your eyes and imagine that you are having a meeting with him . . . now do your best and try your hardest to sweat as much as possible in your palms . . . do the very thing you are afraid will happen . . .*

Correct. The Existential Therapist or Logotherapist will make a few empathic statements to relate deeply with the client and his or her experience, and then proceed to use *paradoxical intention* by giving the client specific instructions to do the very thing he or she fears, in imagery first. Proceed to 1.9.

---

**1.7**   *Your Answer:*   *You seem to be afraid of your own fear and sweaty palms, and especially your boss finding out . . .*

This is a response that reflects empathy for the client, typical of what a Person-Centered or Rogerian therapist may say. While an Existential Therapist may also use such a response to show empathy, it is not a sufficient response to demonstrate the use of *paradoxical intention*. Return to 1.5 and try again.

---

**1.8**   *Your Answer:*   *What does it mean to you if your boss does notice or find out that you are anxious and nervous with sweaty palms?*

This is a question often asked by cognitive therapists to get at the thinking of the client that may trigger anxiety. While an Existential Therapist may use a similar question to deal with meaning issues, this is not the most appropriate response for him or her to use in order to conduct *paradoxical intention* with the client. Return to 1.5 and try again.

---

**1.9**   *Client:*   *. . . It's hard for me to even think or imagine myself with really sweaty palms before my boss . . . in fact, my heart is now pounding so hard and I feel so anxious that I'm afraid I might have a heart attack or something . . .*

Choose the most appropriate response:

*Therapist:*   *Now calm down, take a really slow deep breath, hold it for a few moments . . . and relax and release the tension . . . good . . .* (Go to 1.10)

*Therapist:*   *You're really feeling anxious as you think of having really sweaty palms . . . in fact you're feeling so bad now that you're actually fearful of having a heart attack . . .* (Go to 1.11)

*Therapist:*   *You're feeling even more anxious as you think of having really sweaty palms . . . but continue to try your hardest to sweat even more till you're dripping drops of sweat, and imagine yourself feeling so anxious with your heart pounding so badly that you are actually having a heart attack! Go on and have a heart attack now!* (Go to 1.12)

---

**1.10**   *Your Answer:*   *Now calm down, take a really slow deep breath, hold it for a few moments . . . and relax and release the tension . . . good . . .*

This response is more typical of cognitive or behavior therapists who tend to use direct techniques of relaxation to calm clients down when necessary. It is not the most appropriate response for the Existential Therapist to use to facilitate *paradoxical intention*. Return to 1.9 and try again.

---

**1.11**   *Your Answer:*   *You're really feeling anxious as you think of having really sweaty palms . . . in fact you're feeling so bad now that you're actually fearful of having a heart attack . . .*

This is a response showing empathy for the client, that is more typical for a Person-Centered therapist to make. It is not a sufficient response for the Existential Therapist to use to facilitate further *paradoxical intention*. Return to 1.9 and try again.

---

**1.12**   *Your Answer:*   *You're feeling even more anxious as you think of having really sweaty palms . . . but continue to try your hardest to sweat even more till you're dripping drops of sweat, and imagine yourself feeling so anxious with your heart pounding so badly that you are actually having a heart attack! Go on and have a heart attack now!*

Correct. The Existential Therapist, after making a brief empathic response, goes on and furthers the process of *paradoxical intention* by asking the client not only to sweat more but also to have a heart attack immediately! The exaggeration here introduces an element of humor and impossibility which helps the client eventually to relax more and even laugh at himself or herself. Proceed to 1.13.

---

**1.13**        *Client:*   *Well . . . I . . . I just can't go ahead and simply have a heart attack now . . . or sweat more! In fact, the harder I try, the less I feel I can . . . and it's so silly . . . and . . . funny! (Laughs a little) . . .*

Choose the most appropriate response:
*Therapist:*   *You're beginning to see how silly or funny all of this can be . . . especially when you really try to do what you are afraid will happen! This technique of "paradoxical intention" can help you, and therefore I suggest you use it repeatedly at home in imagination first, and then at the office the next time your boss talks to you, okay? (Go to 1.14)*
*Therapist:*   *Sounds like you're able now to see the lighter side of things, and you don't feel as anxious anymore . . . (Go to 1.15)*
*Therapist:*   *What else comes to mind? . . . (Go to 1.16)*

---

**1.14**   *Your Answer:*   *You're beginning to see how silly or funny all of this can be . . . especially when you really try to do what you are afraid will happen! This technique of "paradoxical intention" can help you, and therefore I suggest you use it repeatedly at home in imagination first, and then at the office the next time your boss talks to you, okay?*

Correct. The Existential Therapist will make a brief summary statement reflecting empathy to the client, and then proceed to reinforce the positive effects of *paradoxical intention,* and prescribe it for homework practice and actual application in the real-life or in vivo situation with the boss.

---

**1.15**   *Your Answer:*   *Sounds like you're able now to see the lighter side of things, and you don't feel as anxious anymore . . .*

This is a good response to reflect empathy to the client and summarize what he or she is experiencing. However, it is not the best or most appropriate response for the Existential Therapist to make in using *paradoxical intention* and wrapping up the use of it. Return to 1.13 and try again.

---

**1.16**   *Your Answer:*   *What else comes to mind? . . .*

This response is more typical of a psychoanalytic therapist wanting to facilitate free association by the client, or of a cognitive therapist interested in identifying further the thoughts of the client. It is not the most appropriate response for the Existential Therapist to make in wrapping up the use of *paradoxical intention.* Return to 1.13 and try again.

---

## 2. DEREFLECTION

---

**2.1**        *Client:*   *I can't stop ruminating over the missed opportunity last week for scoring the winning goal for my soccer team at college! I go over and over again how I missed by an inch or so and kicked the ball just over the goal-post bar. I feel really badly for letting my team down and I am still depressed over this!*

Choose the appropriate response:

*Therapist:*   *. . . what else comes to mind? (Go to 2.2)*

*Therapist:*   *You did your best, so you can't blame yourself! It was just bad luck that you missed by an inch or so! I'm sure your team appreciated your efforts. (Go to 2.3)*

*Therapist:*   *I know you feel really badly and depressed over missing your shot at goal . . . but I wonder what else about the game you can describe that went well . . . some of the highlights, you know . . . (Go to 2.4)*

---

**2.2**   *Your Answer:*   *. . . what else comes to mind?*

This response is more typical of a psychoanalytic thera-pist trying to facilitate free association by the client. It is not the most appropriate response by the Existential Therapist trying to encourage *dereflection* to something more pleasant or favorable. Return to 2.1 and try again.

---

**2.3**   *Your Answer:*   *You did your best, so you can't blame yourself! It was just bad luck that you missed by an inch or so! I'm sure your team appreciated your efforts.*

This response is generally not a helpful one. It contains too many opinions and judgments made by the thera-pist, and lacks empathy and understanding for the client. The Existential Therapist will be more empathic initially. This response is also not the most appropriate one for conducting *dereflection*. Return to 2.1 and try again.

---

**2.4**   *Your Answer:*   *I know you feel really badly and depressed over missing your shot at goal . . . but I wonder what else about the game you can describe that went well . . . some of the highlights, you know . . .*

Correct. This response is characteristic of what the Existential Therapist will say, to reflect some empathy, and then to encourage the client to dereflect from his or her preoccupation with missing the shot at goal and to refocus on some of the more pleasant highlights of the game for him or her. Proceed to 2.5

---

**2.5**        *Client:*   *It's hard for me not to continue to think of that missed goal! But, I guess if I try to forget that . . . and think of the highlights of the game . . . well, I did have several good moves, including assisting my teammate to score the equalizer for our team . . .*

Choose the most appropriate response:
*Therapist:*   *It's hard for you to forget that missed goal but you do recall some good moments in the game for you.* (Go to 2.6)
*Therapist:*   *How do you feel as you think about assisting your teammate score the equalizer for your team?* (Go to 2.7)
*Therapist:*   *Good . . . so you do recall some highlights in the game for you, including helping your teammate score the equalizer! What other special moments in the game can you remember?* (Go to 2.8)

**2.6**  *Your Answer:*  *It's hard for you to forget that missed goal but you do recall some good moments in the game for you.*

This response conveys empathy to the client, but it is not the best response to facilitate further *dereflection* on the part of the client. Return to 2.5 and try again.

**2.7**  *Your Answer:*  *How do you feel as you think about assisting your teammate score the equalizer for your team?*

This response is more characteristic of a cognitive therapist interested in helping the client to connect feelings with thoughts, or of another therapist wanting to explore further the client's feelings. It is not the best response for the Existential Therapist wanting to encourage *dereflection* on the part of the client. Return to 2.5 and try again.

**2.8**  *Your Answer:*  *Good . . . so you do recall some highlights of the game for you, including helping your teammate score the equalizer! What other special moments in the game can you remember?*

Correct. The Existential Therapist encourages the client and expresses empathy before proceeding to help the client to focus on more special moments or highlights of the game for him or her, thus facilitating further *dereflection*. Proceed to 2.9

**2.9**  *Client:*  *I do feel good, thinking of helping my teammate score the equalizer . . . also I helped to break up a dangerous attack by the other team . . .*

Choose the most appropriate response:

*Therapist:*  *Sounds like you actually played a really good game, helping to score a goal and helping to stop the other team from scoring! More highlights or special moments of the game for you?* (Go to 2.10)

*Therapist:*  *(Remains quiet and waits)* (Go to 2.11)

*Therapist:*  *See . . . you did well! There is no need at all to feel badly that you missed that shot at goal. So stop thinking about it, okay?* (Go to 2.12)

**2.10**  *Your Answer:*    *Sounds like you actually played a really good game, helping to score a goal and helping to stop the other team from scoring! More highlights or special moments of the game for you?*

Correct. The Existential Therapist encourages the client with an empathic and positive statement, and then proceeds to help the client to dereflect even more by asking for other highlights of the game for him or her. Proceed to 2.13

---

**2.11**  *Your Answer:*    *(Remains quiet and waits)*

This response of silence and waiting is more characteristic of a psychoanalytic therapist who is trying to facilitate further free association by the client. It is not the best response for encouraging further *dereflection* by the client. Return to 2.9 and try again.

---

**2.12**  *Your Answer:*    *See . . . you did well! There is no need at all to feel badly that you missed that shot at goal. So stop thinking about it, okay?*

This is not a good or helpful response in general. It contains opinionated advice-giving and lacks empathy for the client. It does not encourage further *dereflection* by the client. Return to 2.9 and try again.

---

**2.13**  *Client:*    *Come to think of it . . . I also headed off a dangerously high ball from a corner kick by the other team! I guess I did play well . . . and playing well perhaps is the most important thing rather than winning . . . I feel better already.*

Choose the most appropriate response:
*Therapist:*    *I'm glad you're feeling better as you've engaged in thinking more positively . . . you see how your thoughts affect your feelings . . . (Go to 2.14)*
*Therapist:*    *Sounds like you definitely played a good game . . . refocusing your attention on the highlights has helped you to stop ruminating on that missed goal. Even more significant, you seem to have a deeper insight or meaning that playing well is more important than always winning the game . . . an insight that applies to life! (Go to 2.15)*
*Therapist:*    *What else comes to mind, what other thoughts or feelings? (Go to 2.16)*

**2.14**   *Your Answer:*   *I'm glad you're feeling better as you've engaged in thinking more positively . . . you see how your thoughts affect your feelings . . .*

This is a good summary response, but it is more typical of a cognitive therapist who is helping the client learn how thoughts affect feelings. It is not the most appropriate response for an Existential Therapists to make, who is wrapping up the use of *dereflection* and also always helping the client to gain insight or deeper meaning in his or her life. Return to 2.13 and try again.

---

**2.15**   *Your Answer:*   *Sounds like you definitely played a good game . . . refocusing your attention on the highlights has helped you to stop ruminating on that missed goal. Even more significant, you seem to have a deeper insight or meaning that playing well is more important than always winning the game . . . an insight that applies to life!*

Correct. The Existential Therapist summarizes the usefulness of *dereflection* and then interprets the insight or meaning the client came up with, and extends it to all of life.

---

**2.16**   *Your Answer:*   *What else comes to mind, what other thoughts or feelings?*

This is a response more typical of a psychoanalytic therapist trying to facilitate further free association by the client. It is not the most appropriate response for the Existential Therapist to make to wrap up the use of *dereflection* and help the client gain further insight or meaning to his or her life. Return to 2.13 and try again.

---

## ROLE PLAY FOR EXISTENTIAL THERAPY

Find two others who have also completed this activity unit. Role play brief interviews (anywhere from five to fifteen minutes each) alternating the client, counselor, and observer roles. Record each brief interview on audio- or videotape for later review and evaluation.

- The *counselor* in this role play should practice the techniques of paradoxical intention and dereflection.

- The *client* should provide sufficient information (based on reality) for the counselor to practice paradoxical intention and dereflection.

- The *observer* should note the counselor's attempts to practice these techniques, taking detailed notes on each exchange between counselor and client in the space provided below.

Observer's notes on you as the counselor:

_____

_____

_____

_____

At the conclusion of the brief interview, participants should discuss the performance of the counselor, learning from each other how these specific techniques are properly used. Focusing on positive as well as less effective responses can improve the performance and understanding of these techniques for each participant.

## On Your Own

Once you have completed the above role play, listen to the tape of the interview (on your own) with you as the counselor. Enter your remarks, verbatim, in the spaces provided. Then consider ways in which you could have more accurately demonstrated the techniques (based on the theory) and write these improved responses in the space following each original response.

Original response 1 _____

_____

_____

_____

Improved response _____

_____

_____

_____

Original response 2 _____

_____

_____

_____


Improved response _____

_____

_____

_____


Original response 3 _____

_____

_____

_____


Improved response _____

_____

_____

_____


Original response 4 _____

_____

_____

_____

Improved response _____

_____

_____

_____

Original response 5 _____

_____

_____

_____

Improved response _____

_____

_____

_____

Original response 6 _____

_____

_____

_____

Improved response _____

_____

_____

_____

# Person-Centered Therapy

*Person-Centered* therapy was developed by Carl Rogers, in reaction to what he called "counselor-centered therapy." It was initially described as nondirective counseling, or Rogerian therapy. *Person-Centered* therapy is not problem-solving oriented but seeks instead to help clients know who they really are and to become fully functioning beings. Rogers identified three "necessary and sufficient" conditions for growth and change in clients, and these are the major methods or techniques of *Person-Centered* therapy: *congruence* (in which the therapist's inner experiences and observable outward actions match); *unconditional positive regard* (in which the therapist shows acceptance or deep and genuine caring for the client as a person without reservations, conditions, judgments or evaluations); and *empathic understanding* (in which the therapist enters the place of the client and understands the world from the client's perspective, adopting the client's internal frame of reference). These three conditions are interrelated and may be best understood as general attitudes conveyed to the client by the therapist.

In this Activity Unit, we will cover two *Person-Centered* therapy methods or techniques: *unconditional positive regard* and *empathic understanding*. The same programmed approach to learning effective therapeutic interviewing skills will be used.

# 1. UNCONDITIONAL POSITIVE REGARD

| | | |
|---|---|---|
| **1.1** | *Client:* | *I'm having trouble with my grades in college . . . I've been getting Cs and a couple of Fs . . . and feel terrible about them . . .* |

Choose the most appropriate response:

*Therapist:* *You're feeling badly about the poor grades you've been getting* (Go to 1.2)

*Therapist:* *Why do you think you're doing so poorly academically? What are some of the reasons?* (Go to 1.3)

*Therapist:* *(Remains quiet and waits)* (Go to 1.4)

---

**1.2** *Your Answer:* *You're feeling badly about the poor grades you've been getting.*

Correct. This is a typical response of the Rogerian or *Person-Centered Therapist* who is trying to convey empathy or understanding as well as *unconditional positive regard* to the client, by using a brief summary or paraphrase of what the client is expressing or experiencing. Proceed to 1.5

---

**1.3** *Your Answer:* *Why do you think you're doing so poorly academically? What are some of the reasons?*

This response is more characteristic of a problem-solving approach to therapy that behavior or cognitive therapists may use. It is not the most appropriate response to convey *unconditional positive regard* or empathy. Return to 1.1 and try again.

---

**1.4** *Your Answer:* *(Remains quiet and waits)*

While a *Person-Centered Therapist* may at times remain quiet and wait to show respect and acceptance that are part of *unconditional positive regard*, this response to the client is more typical at this point in the dialogue, of a psychoanalytic therapist who is trying to facilitate free association or further opening up by the client. Return to 1.1 and try again.

---

**1.5** *Client:* *I feel especially bad because my parents are spending tons of money for me to attend an Ivy League school here at Harvard . . . and I am letting them down terribly . . . I'm really afraid of how they'll respond when they find out . . .*

Choose the most appropriate response:

*Therapist:* *Uhmhmm . . . this must be a very hard and painful situation for you to face . . .* (Go to 1.6)

|  |  |  |
|---|---|---|
| *Therapist:* | | *What do you think would be the worst thing your parents could say or do to you if they found out about your poor grades?* (Go to 1.7) |
| *Therapist:* | | *It doesn't matter how much your parents are spending on you, and what your grades end up being as long as you've tried your best. Have you?* (Go to 1.8) |

---

**1.6**    *Your Answer:*    *Uhmhmm . . . this must be a very hard and painful situation for you to face . . .*

Correct. This response does not judge or condemn the client but conveys acceptance as well as caring understanding that are part of *unconditional positive regard*, typical of what a *Person-Centered Therapist* would say. Proceed to 1.9.

---

**1.7**    *Your Answer:*    *What do you think would be the worst thing your parents could say or do to you if they found out about your poor grades?*

This response is more typical of a problem-solving approach to therapy or of a cognitive therapist's attempt to identify the thoughts of the client associated with his or her fears. It is not the best response for a *Person-Centered Therapist* to make to convey *unconditional positive regard*. Return to 1.5 and try again.

---

**1.8**    *Your Answer:*    *It doesn't matter how much your parents are spending on you, and what your grades end up being as long as you've tried your best. Have you?*

This is not a helpful response at all, because it contains strong opinions of the therapist and premature and poor advice-giving. It also ends with confrontation that certainly does not convey *unconditional positive regard*. Return to 1.5 and try again.

---

**1.9**    *Client:*    *. . . This is hard and painful for me . . . but I have no choice because my parents will be asking me about my grades later this week . . . I feel so ashamed . . . they and my other relatives and close friends will think that I'm so stupid . . . I feel like a failure . . . (with tears and pauses, for a few moments) . . .*

Choose the most appropriate response:

*Therapist:*    *On what basis do you say that your parents and relatives and close friends will think you're so stupid?* (Go to 1.10)

> *Therapist:* *What else comes to mind, what other thoughts or feelings? (Go to 1.11)*
>
> *Therapist:* *You feel ashamed and like a failure because you feel you've let your parents and others down . . . their approval is very important to you? . . . (therapist hands over some Kleenex to the client). (Go to 1.12).*

---

**1.10**  *Your Answer:*  *On what basis do you say that your parents and relatives and close friends will think you're so stupid?*

This response is more typical of a cognitive therapist trying to help the client see the evidence or lack of evidence for his or her conclusion that others will think he or she is so stupid. It is not the best response by the *Person-Centered Therapist* seeking to convey *unconditional positive regard* to the client. Return to 1.9 and try again.

---

**1.11**  *Your Answer:*  *What else comes to mind, what other thoughts and feelings?*

This response is more characteristic of a psychoanalytic therapist trying to facilitate further free association by the client. It is not the most appropriate response for conveying *unconditional positive regard*. Return to 1.9 and try again.

---

**1.12**  *Your Answer:*  *You feel ashamed and like a failure because you feel you've let your parents and others down . . . their approval is very important to you? . . . (therapist hands over some Kleenex to the client).*

Correct. The *Person-Centered Therapist* will make such a response, including giving the client some Kleenex, to convey understanding, caring, and *unconditional positive regard* to the client. This response also helps the client see how others' approval seems to be crucial for his or her own sense of self-worth. Proceed to 1.13

---

**1.13**  *Client:*  *I guess I've always depended on others' approval, especially my parents', for my own sense of self-worth or value . . . but I feel it's unfair at times like now . . . I've tried my best yet got poor grades . . . it's only my first term here and I'm still learning the ropes around this big campus . . . I don't really believe I'm that stupid or dumb . . .*

Choose the most appropriate response:

*Therapist:*  *You realize that it's only the first term and you therefore need to give yourself more time to get used to a place like Harvard. Let's discuss how you can cope better and study more efficiently and effectively for the next term . . . (Go to 1.14)*

Therapist:   *You've realized you tend to depend on others' approval for your own sense of value or self-worth . . . but that this is not the best or fairest basis . . . Deep inside you actually feel you're not that dumb or stupid, that given more time you'll be able to do better . . . (Go to 1.15)*

Therapist:   *I'm glad that you can see now that trying your best is all you can do. You can't ask more of yourself than this. Others' approval, even your parents' approval, while nice to have is not essential or necessary for you to feel good about yourself! (Go to 1.16)*

---

**1.14**   *Your Answer:*   *You realize that it's only the first term and you therefore need to give yourself more time to get used to a place like Harvard. Let's discuss how you can cope better and study more efficiently and effectively for the next term.*

This response is more typical of a problem-solving approach that behavior or cognitive therapists may use. It is not the most appropriate response for a *Person-Centered Therapist* to make to convey *unconditional positive regard* to the client. Return to 1.13 and try again.

---

**1.15**   *Your Answer:*   *You've realized you tend to depend on others' approval for your own sense of value or self-worth . . . but that this is not the best or fairest basis . . . Deep inside you actually feel you're not that dumb or stupid, that given more time you'll be able to do better . . .*

Correct. This is a typical response of the *Person-Centered Therapist* to convey both *empathic understanding* as well as *unconditional positive regard* or acceptance to the client.

---

**1.16**   *Your Answer:*   *I'm glad that you can see now that trying your best is all you can do. You can't ask more of yourself than this. Others' approval, even your parents' approval, while nice to have is not essential or necessary for you to feel good about yourself!*

This response is more typical of a cognitive therapist or a rational emotive therapist trying to help the client change his or her thinking. It is a more direct and directive response to restructure or modify the client's thinking. It is not the most appropriate response for the *Person-Centered Therapist* to use to convey *unconditional positive regard* to the client. Return to 1.13 and try again.

## 2. EMPATHIC UNDERSTANDING

---

2.1         Client:    *I've been trying hard for a few months to get a job, after grad-uating from college, but without success! I feel like a failure, like nobody will ever hire me . . . my close friends have all been hired by some company by now . . .*

Choose the most appropriate response:

Therapist:    *On what basis do you say to yourself that you feel like a fail-ure, like nobody will ever hire you?* (Go to 2.2)

Therapist:    *You've tried hard to get a job without success and feel like a failure . . . and kind of hopeless about ever finding a job . . . especially since your peers have all found jobs by now.* (Go to 2.3)

Therapist:    *What else comes to mind?* (Go to 2.4)

---

2.2    Your Answer:    *On what basis do you say to yourself that you feel like a fail-ure, like nobody will ever hire you?*

This response is more characteristic of a cognitive thera-pist trying to help the client see the basis or lack of basis or evidence for his or her thinking that *nobody* will *ever* hire him or her. It is not the most appropriate response for the *Person-Centered Therapist* to use to convey *empathic understanding* to the client. Return to 2.1 and try again.

---

2.3    Your Answer:    *You've tried hard to get a job without success and feel like a failure . . . and kind of hopeless about ever finding a job . . . especially since your peers have all found jobs by now.*

Correct. This response is typical of the *Person-Centered Therapist* who often uses a summary statement or para-phrase of what the client has just said, to convey *empathic understanding* to the client. Proceed to 2.5

---

2.4    Your Answer:    *What else comes to mind?*

This response is more characteristic of a psychoanalytic therapist trying to facilitate free association by the client. It is not the best response for conveying *empathic under-standing* to the client. Return to 2.1 and try again.

---

2.5         Client:    *I guess there's still a chance for me to eventually get a job . . . I can't say for sure that nobody will ever hire me . . . but it sure feels this way because I tried my best for several months already . . . and received tons of rejections! It feels so hopeless and depressing!*

Choose the most appropriate response:

*Therapist:*   *You're feeling quite hopeless and down about the job situation. So far, despite all your best efforts over months, you've received only rejections and lots of them.* (Go to 2.6)

*Therapist:*   *You're right that there's a chance you may still get a job. You can't be absolutely certain that no one will ever hire you!* (Go to 2.7)

*Therapist:*   *Let's discuss how you've gone about looking for jobs, and see if I can help you with some job-seeking skills or tips.* (Go to 2.8)

---

**2.6**   *Your Answer:*   *You're feeling quite hopeless and down about the job situation. So far, despite all your best efforts over months, you've received only rejections and lots of them.*

Correct. The *Person-Centered Therapist* will use such a response to summarize what the client has said or expressed, to convey *empathic understanding* from the client's internal frame of reference, to the client. Proceed to 2.9

---

**2.7**   *Your Answer:*   *You're right that there's a chance you may still get a job. You can't be absolutely certain that no one will ever hire you!*

This response is more typical of a cognitive therapist or rational-emotive therapist trying to help the client replace absolutist, extreme, negative, and unreasonable thinking with more reasonable, rational, balanced and positive ways of thinking. It is not the most appropriate response to convey *empathic understanding* to the client. Return to 2.5 and try again.

---

**2.8**   *Your Answer:*   *Let's discuss how you've gone about looking for jobs, and see if I can help you with some job-seeking skills or tips.*

This response is more typical of a directive, problem-solving approach to therapy that some cognitive or behavior therapists may use. It is not the best response to convey *empathic understanding* to the client. Return to 2.5 and try again.

---

**2.9**   *Client:*   *I'm actually feeling so tired and discouraged that I don't feel like applying for any more jobs! This has been such a blow to my ego . . . I feel pretty deflated and crushed right now . . .*

Choose the most appropriate response:

*Therapist:*   *Uhmhmm . . . this has been very painful and hard for you, for your own sense of self-worth, so much so that you don't feel like trying anymore regarding job applications . . .* (Go to 2.10)

*Therapist:* *Well, let's try to pick up the pieces and move on. What are some other job options or possibilities you haven't explored so far?* (Go to 2.11)

*Therapist:* *Uhmhmm . . .* (Go to 2.12)

---

**2.10** *Your Answer:* *Uhmhmm . . . this has been very painful and hard for you, for your own sense of self-worth, so much so that you don't feel like trying anymore regarding job applications . . .*

Correct. This response is a good example of what the *Person-Centered Therapist* may say to convey *empathic understanding* to the client. Proceed to 2.13

---

**2.11** *Your Answer:* *Well, let's try to pick up the pieces and move on. What are some other job options or possibilities you haven't explored so far?*

This response does not convey *empathic understanding*. Instead it is more typical of a directive, problem-solving approach to therapy. Return to 2.9 and try again.

---

**2.12** *Your Answer:* *Uhmhmm . . .*

This is a brief response from the therapist that acknowledges the client's experience, but it is too brief in this dialogue to convey adequately more *empathic understanding* to the client. Return to 2.9 and try again.

---

**2.13** *Client:* *I guess I'm feeling pretty depressed over this whole lousy situation! . . . Maybe I'm feeling too sorry for myself too . . . this is such a tough and stinking position to be in!*

Choose the most appropriate response:

*Therapist:* *What else is happening in your life, besides this lousy job situation?* (Go to 2.14)

*Therapist:* *This is really hard for you . . . you're feeling really lousy . . . kind of stuck?* (Go to 2.15)

*Therapist:* *(Remains quiet and waits)* (Go to 2.16)

---

**2.14** *Your Answer:* *What else is happening in your life, besides this lousy job situation?*

This response can be seen as an example of dereflection, a technique used at times by existential therapists or logotherapists to refocus the client's attention away from negative rumination on to something else more pleasant or favorable. It is not the most appropriate response for a *Person-Centered Therapist* to make to convey more *empathic understanding* to the client. Return to 2.13 and try again.

---

**2.15**   *Your Answer:*   *This is really hard for you . . . you're feeling really lousy . . . kind of stuck?*

Correct. This response is typical of what the *Person-Centered Therapist* may say to convey further *empathic understanding* and support to the client.

---

**2.16**   *Your Answer:*   *(Remains quiet and waits)*

This response is sometimes used by *Person-Centered Therapists* to give the client more time to open up more, but in this dialogue, it is not the best response to convey further *empathic understanding* to the client. This response is more characteristic of a psychoanalytic therapist waiting for more free association or material to be brought up by the client. Return to 2.13 and try again.

---

## ROLE PLAY FOR PERSON-CENTERED THERAPY

Find two others who have also completed this activity unit. Role play brief interviews (anywhere from five to fifteen minutes each) alternating the client, counselor, and observer roles. Record each brief interview on audio- or videotape for later review and evaluation.

- The *counselor* in this role play should practice the techniques of unconditional positive regard and empathic understanding.

- The *client* should provide sufficient information (based on reality) for the counselor to practice unconditional positive regard and empathic understanding.

- The *observer* should note the counselor's attempts to practice these techniques, taking detailed notes on each exchange between counselor and client in the space provided below.

Observer's notes on you as the counselor:

_____

_____

_____

_____

At the conclusion of the brief interview, participants should discuss the performance of the counselor, learning from each other how these specific techniques are properly used. Focusing on positive as well as less effective responses can improve the performance and understanding of these techniques for each participant.

## On Your Own

Once you have completed the above role play, listen to the tape of the interview (on your own) with you as the counselor. Enter your remarks, verbatim, in the spaces provided. Then consider ways in which you could have more accurately demonstrated the techniques (based on the theory) and write these improved responses in the space following each original response.

Original response 1 _____

_____

_____

_____

Improved response _____

_____

_____

_____

Original response 2 _____

_____

_____

_____

Improved response _____

_____

_____

_____

Original response 3 _____

_____

_____

_____


Improved response _____

_____

_____

_____


Original response 4 _____

_____

_____

_____


Improved response _____

_____

_____

_____


Original response 5 _____

_____

_____

_____


Improved response _____

_____

_____

_____

Original response 6 _____

_____

_____

_____

Improved response _____

_____

_____

_____

# Gestalt Therapy

Gestalt therapy was developed by Frederick or "Fritz" Pearls. The Gestalt Therapist plays an extremely active role in trying to provoke clients into greater awareness, assuming that clients who are more aware will solve their own problems in their own time. There are many Gestalt therapy techniques, all of which are more experiential rather than verbal. Gestalt therapy is about doing rather than saying. A general "rule" of Gestalt therapy is that communication is to be between equals in the present tense. Among the many Gestalt therapy techniques are the following: *dream work (experiential), converting questions to statements, using personal pronouns, assuming responsibility, playing the projection, the empty chair, making the rounds, exaggeration, and confrontation.*

In this Activity Unit, we will cover two Gestalt Therapy techniques: *assuming responsibility* (in which clients are encouraged to conclude all expressions of feelings or beliefs with, "And I take responsibility for it." and to change "can't" to "won't", and "but" to "and"), and the *empty chair* (in which clients are encouraged to picture an absent person sitting in the empty chair across from them and to engage in a dialogue with that person, moving back and forth from chair to chair). The same programmed approach to learning effective therapeutic interviewing skills will be used.

# 1. ASSUMING RESPONSIBILITY

| | | |
|---|---|---|
| **1.1** | *Client:* | *I didn't do well in my M.B.A. program this past term . . . I got Bs and Cs when I usually get mostly As . . . the courses were not that interesting and some of the professors were lousy!* |

Choose the most appropriate response:

| | |
|---|---|
| *Therapist:* | *Your grades were not as good this past term but you feel this is partly due to some lousy professors and courses . . .* (Go to 1.2) |
| *Therapist:* | *Let's review your study skills . . . tell me how you go about preparing for course assignments and exams . . .* (Go to 1.3) |
| *Therapist:* | *Please end your statements with "And I take responsibility for it." (Go to 1.4)* |

---

**1.2**    *Your Answer:*    *Your grades were not as good this past term but you feel this is partly due to some lousy professors and courses . . .*

This response is more typical of a Person-Centered therapist trying to convey empathy to a client. It is not the most appropriate response for the Gestalt Therapist to make in order to help the client in assuming responsibility. Return to 1.1 and try again.

---

**1.3**    *Your Answer:*    *Let's review your study skills . . . tell me how you go about preparing for course assignments and exams . . .*

This response is typical of a direct, problem-solving approach to therapy that emphasizes skills training. It is not the most appropriate response to facilitate the client's assuming responsibility in Gestalt therapy. Return to 1.1 and try again.

---

**1.4**    *Your Answer:*    *Please end your statements with "And I take responsibility for it."*

Correct. This is a common response or technique used by the Gestalt Therapist to encourage or direct the client to assume responsibility for his or her own feelings or beliefs. Proceed to 1.5

---

**1.5**    *Client:*    *It feels strange to do this but I'll try . . . I didn't do well this past term and got some poor grades . . . And I take responsibility for it! The courses were not all that interesting and there were some lousy professors . . . And I take responsibility for it!*

Choose the most appropriate response:

Therapist: *Tell me how you feel as you repeatedly tell yourself "And I take responsibility for it!"* (Go to 1.6)

Therapist: *(Remains quiet and waits)* (Go to 1.7)

Therapist: *It feels weird for you saying "And I take responsibility for it" after every expression of your feelings or beliefs.* (Go to 1.8)

---

**1.6**   Your Answer:   *Tell me how you feel as you repeatedly tell yourself "And I take responsibility for it!"*

Correct. The Gestalt Therapist uses "How" or "What" questions and not "Why?" questions because "Why?" questions tend to lead to intellectualization and blocking of awareness or feelings. This response also continues to focus on assuming responsibility for the client. Proceed to 1.9

---

**1.7**   Your Answer:   *(Remains quiet and waits)*

This response is more typical of a psychoanalytic therapist trying to facilitate free association by the client. It is too passive for the Gestalt Therapist who is usually very active and who is trying to encourage the client in *assuming responsibility*. Return to 1.5 and try again.

---

**1.8**   Your Answer:   *It feels weird for you saying "And I take responsibility for it" after every expression of your feelings or beliefs.*

This response is more typical of a Person-Centered therapist trying to convey empathic understanding to the client. It is not the most appropriate response for the Gestalt Therapist to use to actively continue the focus on *assuming responsibility* on the part of the client. Return to 1.5 and try again.

---

**1.9**          Client:   *I feel strange a bit still . . . but I am more aware now of my responsibility or my part in getting the poor grades . . . I can't blame it all on the lousy professors or uninteresting courses.*

Choose the most appropriate response:

Therapist: *Good . . . so let's see what your responsibility is and how we can help you change, for example, improve your study skills?* (Go to 1.10)

Therapist: *You feel you are partly responsible for your poor grades . . .* (Go to 1.11)

| | | |
|---|---|---|
| | *Therapist:* | *You are becoming more aware of feeling responsible for your grades . . .* (Go to 1.12) |

**1.10**  *Your Answer:*  *Good . . . so let's see what your responsibility is and how we can help you change, for example, improve your study skills?*

This response is more problem-solving oriented and is not the most appropriate response for the Gestalt Therapist to use to continue the focus on assuming responsibility on the part of the client. Return to 1.9 and try again.

**1.11**  *Your Answer:*  *You feel you are partly responsible for your poor grades . . .*

This response is a summary statement that reflects empathy for the client. It is not the best response for the Gestalt Therapist to use to actively encourage the client to continue focusing on *assuming responsibility*. Return to 1.9 and try again.

**1.12**  *Your Answer:*  *You are becoming more aware of feeling responsible for your grades . . .*

Correct. The Gestalt Therapist uses the present tense to briefly summarize the client's experience of greater awareness of his or her responsibility for his or her grades, and therefore continues the focus on assuming responsibility on the part of the client. Proceed to 1.13

**1.13**  *Client:*  *I can't really blame myself either for my poor grades. I don't feel good about them but some of the professors were really lousy!*

*Therapist:*  *Please change the word "can't" in what you just said to "won't."* (Go to 1.14)

*Therapist:*  *You feel part of the blame for your poor grades rests on the professors who were lousy.* (Go to 1.15)

*Therapist:*  *Why do you think some of the professors were lousy?* (Go to 1.6)

**1.14**  *Your Answer:*  *Please change the word "can't" in what you just said to "won't".*

Correct. The Gestalt Therapist actively and directly encourages the client to change his or her statement to *"I won't really blame myself . . ."* so that he or she can *assume responsibility* for his or her feelings and beliefs. This assuming of responsibility is aimed at helping the client see himself or herself as having some internal strength rather than depending on external controls.

---

**1.15**   *Your Answer:*   *You feel part of the blame for your poor grades rests on the professors who were lousy.*

This is a response that conveys empathic understanding to the client. It is not the most appropriate response for the Gestalt Therapist to make to help the client stay focused on *assuming responsibility*. Return to 1.13 and try again.

---

**1.16**   *Your Answer:*   *Why do you think some of the professors were lousy?*

This response is not typical of the Gestalt Therapist who usually avoids "Why?" questions because they tend to lead to intellectualization and blocking of feelings or deeper awareness of what's happening or what the client is experiencing in the here and now. It is therefore not the most appropriate response to help the client continue to focus on *assuming responsibility*. Return to 1.13 and try again.

---

## 2. EMPTY CHAIR

---

**2.1**         *Client:*   *I've been feeling very frustrated with my father lately. He smokes too much and I'm afraid he'll get lung cancer, but it's so difficult to talk to him openly about this.*

Choose the most appropriate response.
*Therapist:*   *Why is it so difficult to talk to your father?* (Go to 2.2)
*Therapist:*   *You want to talk to your father about his smoking too much but it's not easy to do this.* (Go to 2.3)
*Therapist:*   *Let me suggest that you imagine your father sitting in the empty chair across from you. Tell him what you want to say to him, and then switch chairs and be your father and say what he will say back to you. Okay?* (Go to 2.4)

---

**2.2**   *Your Answer:*   *Why is it so difficult to talk to your father?*

This response is not typical of the Gestalt Therapist who usually avoids asking "Why?" questions because they tend to lead to intellectualization and blocking of further awareness. Return to 2.1 and try again.

---

**2.3**    *Your Answer:*    *You want to talk to your father about his smoking too much but it's not easy to do this.*

This response is a good one for conveying empathy to the client but it is more typical of a Person-Centered therapist. It is not the most appropriate response for the Gestalt Therapist wanting to use the *Empty Chair* technique with the client. Return to 2.1 and try again.

---

**2.4**    *Your Answer:*    *Let me suggest that you imagine your father sitting in the empty chair across from you. Tell him what you want to say to him, and then switch chairs and be your father and say what he will say back to you. Okay?*

Correct. The Gestalt Therapist will make such a response in order to introduce the *Empty Chair* technique to the client to help him or her role-play the way he or she would like to behave toward his or her father. Also switching roles and chairs will help the client be more aware of his or her father's perspective. Proceed to 2.5

---

**2.5**    *Client:*    *This feels kind of weird using the empty chair for my father who is not here. I can't do it!*

Choose the most appropriate response:

*Therapist:*    *You feel you can't do the role-play using the empty chair - it feels too strange or awkward for you.* (Go to 2.6)

*Therapist:*    *Please change the word "can't" to "won't" and make your statement again!* (Go to 2.7)

*Therapist:*    *(Remains quiet and waits)* (Go to 2.8)

---

**2.6**    *Your Answer:*    *You feel you can't do the role-play using the empty chair . . . it feels too strange or awkward for you.*

This response is more typical of a Person-Centered therapist trying to convey empathic understanding to the client. It is not the best response to encourage the client to go on with the *Empty Chair* technique. Return to 2.5 and try again.

---

**2.7**    *Your Answer:*    *Please change the word "can't" to "won't" and make your statement again!*

Correct. The Gestalt Therapist is active and directly suggests to the client a change of wording from "can't" to "won't" to help the client assume responsibility, so that they can go on with the *Empty Chair* technique. Proceed to 2.9

**2.8**    *Your Answer:*    *(Remains quiet and waits)*

This response is more typical of a psychoanalytic therapist trying to facilitate free association by the client. It is
too passive and inappropriate a response for a Gestalt
Therapist trying to help the client go on with the *Empty
Chair* technique. Return to 2.5 and try again.

---

**2.9**    *Client:*    *Well, . . . I "won't" do it! I guess I'll have to decide whether I
will or won't do it. It does feel awkward but I guess if I really
want to, I can give it a shot . . . Alright, let me try, but don't
laugh at me!*

Choose the most appropriate response:

*Therapist:*    *You've realized you can at least give it a try, not you can't do
it! That's good . . . so go ahead and speak to your father sitting
in the empty chair in front of you.* (Go to 2.10)

*Therapist:*    *You're willing to give it a try but you don't want to be embarrassed or laughed at.* (Go to 2.11)

*Therapist:*    *Why are you afraid that I might laugh at you?* (Go to 2.12)

---

**2.10**    *Your Answer:*    *You've realized you can at least give it a try, not you can't do
it! That's good . . . so go ahead and speak to your father sitting
in the empty chair in front of you.*

Correct. The Gestalt Therapist will use such a response to
actively encourage the client to go on and try the *Empty
Chair* technique. Proceed to 2.13

---

**2.11**    *Your Answer:*    *You're willing to give it a try but you don't want to be embarrassed or laughed at.*

This response is good for conveying empathy to the
client. It is not the most appropriate response for the
Gestalt Therapist to make to encourage the client to go
on and try the *Empty Chair* technique. Return to 2.9 and
try again.

---

**2.12**    *Your Answer:*    *Why are you afraid that I might laugh at you?*

This response is more typical of a psychoanalytic therapist
or a cognitive therapist interested in exploring further the
thoughts and feelings of the client. It is not the most
appropriate response for the Gestalt Therapist interested
in encouraging the client to try the *Empty Chair* technique.
Also, "Why?" questions are usually avoided by the
Gestalt Therapist. Return to 2.9 and try again.

| 2.13 | *Client:* | *Alright, here goes . . . Dad, I've been meaning to talk to you for some time now . . . this is hard for me to bring up to you because I love and respect you . . . but your smoking so much is really bothering me . . . I'm afraid you'll get lung cancer or something soon. You know what I mean? . . . (pauses and gets teary)* |

Choose the most appropriate response:

| | *Therapist:* | *That's great! I believe you did really well and you are ready to talk to your father!* (Go to 2.14) |
| | *Therapist:* | *You're doing well . . . it's painful though . . . try to be your father now and switch chairs and roles and see what happens, okay?* (Go to 2.15) |
| | *Therapist:* | *Did you say all you wanted to say? Let's do it again if you feel it'll be helpful.* (Go to 2.16) |

---

| 2.14 | *Your Answer:* | *That's great! I believe you did really well and you are ready to talk to your father!* |

This response contains premature closure and focuses more on the adequacy of the client's skills in talking to his or her father. It is not the most appropriate response for the Gestalt Therapist to use to encourage the client to go on with the *Empty Chair* technique. Return to 2.13 and try again.

---

| 2.15 | *Your Answer:* | *You're doing well . . . it's painful though . . . try to be your father now and switch chairs and roles and see what happens, okay?* |

Correct. The Gestalt Therapist will encourage the client on his or her progress but also convey empathy regarding the pain of the situation for the client. The Gestalt Therapist will go on and direct the client to the next step of the *Empty Chair* technique.

---

| 2.16 | *Your Answer:* | *Did you say all you wanted to say? Let's do it again if you feel it'll be helpful.* |

This response focuses mainly on skills training and further practice. It is not sufficiently empathic and is not the most appropriate response for the Gestalt Therapist to make to help the client go on with the *Empty Chair* technique. Return to 2.13 and try again.

---

## ROLE PLAY FOR GESTALT THERAPY

Find two others who have also completed this activity unit. Role play brief interviews (anywhere from five to fifteen minutes each) alternating the client, counselor, and observer roles. Record each brief interview on audio- or videotape for later review and evaluation.

- The *counselor* in this role play should practice the techniques of assuming responsibility and the empty chair.

- The *client* should provide sufficient information (based on reality) for the counselor to practice assuming responsibility and the empty chair.

- The *observer* should note the counselor's attempts to practice these techniques, taking detailed notes on each exchange between counselor and client in the space provided below.

Observer's notes on you as the counselor:

_____

_____

_____

_____

At the conclusion of the brief interview, participants should discuss the performance of the counselor, learning from each other how these specific techniques are properly used. Focusing on positive as well as less effective responses can improve the performance and understanding of these techniques for each participant.

## On Your Own

Once you have completed the above role play, listen to the tape of the interview (on your own) with you as the counselor. Enter your remarks, verbatim, in the spaces provided. Then consider ways in which you could have more accurately demonstrated the techniques (based on the theory) and write these improved responses in the space following each original response.

Original response 1  _____

_____

_____

_____

Improved response _____

_____

_____

_____

Original response 2 _____

_____

_____

_____

Improved response _____

_____

_____

_____

Original response 3 _____

_____

_____

_____

Improved response _____

_____

_____

_____

Original response 4 _____

_____

_____

_____

Improved response _____

_____

_____

_____

Original response 5 _____

_____

_____

_____

Improved response _____

_____

_____

_____

Original response 6 _____

_____

_____

_____

Improved response _____

_____

_____

_____

# Transactional Analysis

Transactional Analysis (TA) was originally developed by Eric Berne, who merged, mixed, and synthesized the therapeutic approaches of Freud, Adler, and Rogers. Berne viewed personality as consisting of three conscious or pre-conscious ego states (each an organized psychological system of feelings, thoughts, and behaviors): the Parent, the Adult, and the Child. The TA Therapist tries to help clients achieve autonomy or responsibility and control of their lives - to free one's Adult from the negative influences of the Child and Parent. The TA Therapist also attempts to help clients analyze their relation-ships by discovering their predominant Life Positions (e.g., "I'm okay-you're okay," or "I'm okay-you're not okay," etc.), and the "games" they tend to play to avoid intimacy.

The TA Therapist functions very much like a teacher explaining key TA ideas such as structural analysis, script analysis, and game analysis. He or she acts as a catalyst to enable clients to mobilize their resources and make full and effective use of all three ego states in order to live game-free.

TA has a number of major methods or techniques including the following: initial *contracting* between the TA Therapist and client specifying goals of the client, what the therapist and client will do, and criteria for determining when the goals have been reached; *structural analysis* to help the client identify ego states (Adult, Critical Parent, Nurturing Parent, Free or Natural Child, and Adapted Child) and how they function; *functional analysis* which is a didactic method to describe transactions to the client; *game analysis* to help the client see what ways of game-playing he or she may be involved in; and *script analysis* aimed at examining the client's life direction, usually set at an early age.

In this Activity Unit, we will cover two TA therapy techniques that are often used: *initial contracting* between the therapist and client and *structural analysis*. The same programmed approach to learning effective therapeutic interviewing skills, covering one skill at a time, will be used.

# 1. CONTRACTING

**1.1**          *Client:*      *I'm tired of always having to be the "superman" in my fam-
                               ily — the breadwinner, the leader, the handyman, the caring
                               father for my two young children, the loving husband and
                               great lover for my wife, the productive worker at the office,
                               and on and on . . . I am not happy with my life as it is and I
                               really want to change . . . I'm tired and fed up!*

                               Choose the most appropriate response:

              *Therapist:*     *You've had enough of having to be a super-duper, always pro-
                               ductive man in all areas of your life, and really want a change
                               at this time.* (Go to 1.1)

              *Therapist:*     *Sounds like you really want a change in your life at this time.
                               As we start therapy, our first step is to set up a contract. I
                               would like you to state specific beliefs, feelings, and behaviors
                               that you would like to change in order to achieve your goals.
                               We will also discuss your role and mine in therapy, okay?* (Go
                               to 1.3)

              *Therapist:*     *What else comes to mind?* (Go to 1.4)

---

**1.2**   *Your Answer:*    *You've had enough of having to be a super-duper, always pro-
                            ductive man in all areas of your life, and really want a change
                            at this time.*

                            This is a good response for conveying empathy to the
                            client, but it is not the most appropriate response for a
                            TA Therapist to make to help the client set up an initial
                            contract that is specific and not vague or too general.
                            Return to 1.1 and try again.

---

**1.3**   *Your Answer:*    *Sounds like you really want a change in your life at this time.
                            As we start therapy, our first step is to set up a contract. I
                            would like you to state specific beliefs, feelings, and behaviors
                            that you would like to change in order to achieve your goals.
                            We will also discuss your role and mine in therapy, okay?*

                            Correct. The TA Therapist gets right into *contracting* with
                            the client and explains what needs to be done to come up
                            with a clear and specific contract for change, by making
                            such a response. Proceed to 1.5

---

**1.4**   *Your Answer:*    *What else comes to mind?*

                            This response is more typical of a psychoanalytic thera-
                            pist interested in facilitating free association by the
                            client. It is not the most appropriate response for a TA

Therapist to make to help the client come up with a specific *contract* for change. Return to 1.1 and try again.

---

**1.5**          *Client:*        *I'm not sure what my goals are . . . except I want to be a much happier person who can be more spontaneous . . . who can enjoy life more and throw caution to the wind more often!*

Choose the most appropriate response:

*Therapist:*     *You seem to feel stuck in your life now, and you really want to be freer and happier and more adventurous*          (Go to 1.6)

*Therapist:*     *(Remains quiet and waits)* (Go to 1.7)

*Therapist:*     *Your overall goal is to be a happier person. You want to enjoy life more and throw caution to the wind more often . . . can you give me a couple of more concrete or specific examples as to what you mean by this?* (Go to 1.8)

---

**1.6**   *Your Answer:*   *You seem to feel stuck in your life now, and you really want to be freer and happier and more adventurous . . .*

This response is more typical of a Person-Centered therapist wanting to convey empathic understanding to the client. It is not the most appropriate response for the TA Therapist conducting *contracting* as specifically as possible with the client. Return to 1.5 and try again.

---

**1.7**   *Your Answer:*   *(Remains quiet and waits)*

This response or lack of responding is more typical of a psychoanalytic therapist waiting for more material to emerge or trying to facilitate further free association from the client. It is not an appropriate response for the TA Therapist conducting *contracting* with the client. Return to 1.5 and try again.

---

**1.8**   *Your Answer:*   *Your overall goal is to be a happier person. You want to enjoy life more and throw caution to the wind more often . . . can you give me a couple of more concrete or specific examples as to what you mean by this?*

Correct. This response is characteristic of the TA Therapist who summarizes briefly what the client has expressed, but goes on to ask for more concrete, specific examples of the changes he is desiring, in order to continue the initial process of *contracting* with the client. Proceed to 1.9

---

**1.9**          *Client:*     *Well . . . one thing that I've been thinking of for awhile is to take a longer vacation and go with my wife on the cruise to Alaska and not worry about all the overtime pay I'll be losing! . . . And be able to just leave the kids with my parents for a week or two and not feel guilty about it! I want to change my thinking, my tendency to feel so responsible all the time for everyone else . . .*

Choose the most appropriate response:

*Therapist:*     *You said it! Why don't you just do it for once? Have you talked to your wife about this wish of yours?* (Go to 1.10)

*Therapist:*     *Good . . . so more specifically, you want to change your thinking, from rigid, legalistic and constraining to freer, more spontaneous, and less guilt-ridden . . . so that, for example, you'll really be able to go on that Alaska cruise with your wife, without the kids! What else would you like to change?* (Go to 1.11)

*Therapist:*     *You've felt too hemmed in and constricted with caring for others so much . . . you feel it's time to take care of yourself too . . . and the cruise with your wife is where you would love to start . . .* (Go to 1.12)

---

**1.10**  *Your Answer:*     *You said it! Why don't you just do it for once? Have you talked to your wife about this wish of yours?*

This is an affirming and encouraging response to the client, but a bit premature and too opinionated on the part of the therapist. It is also not the best response for the TA Therapist to make to further the process of specific *contracting* with the client. Return to 1.9 and try again.

---

**1.11**  *Your Answer:*     *Good . . . so more specifically, you want to change your thinking, from rigid, legalistic and constraining to freer, more spontaneous, and less guilt-ridden . . . so that, for example, you'll really be able to go on that Alaska cruise with your wife, without the kids! What else would you like to change?*

Correct. This response is typical of a TA Therapist who summarizes with empathy what the client has expressed, emphasizing what is specific or concrete, and then proceeds to ask another question to further the process of initial *contracting* with the client. Proceed to 1.13

---

**1.12**  *Your Answer:*     *You've felt too hemmed in and constricted with caring for others so much . . . you feel it's time to take care of yourself too . . . and the cruise with your wife is where you would love to start . . .*

This is a good response for conveying empathic understanding and unconditional positive regard to the client, but it is more typical of a Person-Centered therapist. It is not the best response for a TA Therapist to use to facilitate the process of specific *contracting* with the client. Return to 1.9 and try again.

---

| | | |
|---|---|---|
| **1.13** | *Client:* | *Mmm . . . well, I guess another area of change I would like to see is in my relationship with my wife. I feel that I am often more like a parent or father to her than an equal partner, because she depends on me so much for so many things. When I try to talk to her about this, it doesn't work or get anywhere. I wish we could relate more adult-to-adult . . . but don't get me wrong, she is a good and loving wife and mother!* |

Choose the most appropriate response:

*Therapist:*   *Who does your wife remind you of?* (Go to 1.14)

*Therapist:*   *You want a more mature and equal relationship with your wife but you get nowhere whenever you try to discuss this with her . . . this has been frustrating for you.* (Go to 1.15)

*Therapist:*   *Okay, sounds like you have another specific area of change you would like to see. You want a more adult-to-adult relationship with your wife, instead of feeling like a parent to her. Before we go on discussing other specific changes or goals you may like to achieve, let me briefly explain that my role in therapy will be quite active, like a teacher and trainer, and I expect you to participate actively as well in your efforts to change. Any questions or comments so far, before we go on and discuss what particular changes you would like to see in your interactions with your wife that would reflect a more equal, adult relationship?* (Go to 1.16)

---

**1.14**   *Your Answer:*   *Who does your wife remind you of?*

This response is one that a psychoanalytic therapist may use in the process of interpreting transference and helping the client gain further insight into unconscious processes. It is not an appropriate response at this point for the TA Therapist to make to continue specific *contracting* with the client. Return to 1.13 and try again.

---

**1.15**   *Your Answer:*   *You want a more mature and equal relationship with your wife but you get nowhere whenever you try to discuss this with her . . . this has been frustrating for you.*

This is a good response for summarizing what the client has expressed and conveying empathy to him. It is not the best response for the TA Therapist to use to proceed with initial *contracting* with the client. Return to 1.13 and try again.

---

**1.16**   *Your Answer:*   *Okay, sounds like you have another specific area of change you would like to see. You want a more adult-to-adult relationship with your wife, instead of feeling like a parent to her. Before we go on discussing other specific changes or goals you may like to achieve, let me briefly explain that my role in therapy will be quite active, like a teacher and trainer, and I expect you to participate actively as well in your efforts to change. Any questions or comments so far, before we go on and discuss what particular changes you would like to see in your interactions with your wife that would reflect a more equal, adult relationship?*

Correct. Although this is a pretty long response, it is quite typical of the TA Therapist to summarize another specific goal or area of change, explain briefly the roles of therapist and client, and then return to asking for even more concrete examples of changes the client wants to see in this new area of interactions with his wife. These interchanges between the TA Therapist and client will go on until a clear and specific *contract* with a few goals and changes described by the client, can be agreed upon by both therapist and client.

---

## 2. STRUCTURAL ANALYSIS

**2.1**        *Client:*     *About my relationship with my wife . . . we really do love each other very much, and we get along okay overall . . . but I'm frustrated by my feeling that I'm more like a father or parent to her because she depends on me to do most things around the house, and has to have my opinions before she can even make the simplest of decisions . . . I definitely want a more mature, equal and adult-to-adult relationship with her.*

Choose the most appropriate response:
*Therapist:*   *Let's pause here for me to explain further a few basic ideas or concepts from Transactional Analysis, as I assume my therapist's role as a teacher for awhile. These concepts are crucial for understanding how you and your wife interact and relate with each other, and eventually how to change your interactions or transactions to healthier ones. As you can see on the board here*

*before you, I've drawn three circles with P standing for Parent, A for Adult, and C for Child, respectively. These are the three basic concepts for describing our personality or ego states . . . (therapist goes on to define P, A, and C, as well as the Critical Parent versus the Nurturant Parent, and the Free or Natural Child versus the Adapted Child) . . . Any questions or comments so far, before we try to apply these concepts to you and your wife?* (Go to 2.2)

Therapist:    *You sound frustrated and dissatisfied with your having to be like a parent to your wife. You want a more equal and adult marital relationship.* (Go to 2.3)

Therapist:    *Well, let's discuss how you can achieve a better and more adult relationship with your wife . . . Let's brainstorm some ideas.* (Go to 2.4)

---

**2.2**    *Your Answer:*    *Let's pause here for me to explain further a few basic ideas or concepts from Transactional Analysis, as I assume my therapist's role as a teacher for awhile. These concepts are crucial for understanding how you and your wife interact and relate with each other, and eventually how to change your interactions or transactions to healthier ones. As you can see on the board here before you, I've drawn three circles with P standing for Parent, A for Adult, and C for Child, respectively. These are the three basic concepts for describing our personality or ego states . . . (therapist goes on to define P, A, and C, as well as the Critical Parent versus the Nurturant Parent, and the Free or Natural Child versus the Adapted Child) . . . Any questions or comments so far, before we try to apply these concepts to you and your wife?*

Correct. While this is a long response, it is typical of what the TA Therapist does when he or she begins to teach TA concepts like Parent, Adult, and Child, didactically, often using helpful tools like a board and diagrams to the client, in conducting *Structural Analysis*. The *application* of the key TA concepts to the client's problem is ultimately what is crucial, after giving the client a chance to ask questions or have further clarifications, if need be. Proceed to 2.5

---

**2.3**    *Your Answer:*    *You sound frustrated and dissatisfied with your having to be like a parent to your wife. You want a more equal and adult marital relationship.*

This is a good response to convey empathy to the client, but it is not the best response to use for the TA Therapist conducting *Structural Analysis* with the client where basic TA concepts are usually taught didactically and directly. Return to 2.1 and try again.

---

**2.4**    *Your Answer:*    *Well, let's discuss how you can achieve a better and more adult relationship with your wife . . . Let's brainstorm some ideas . . .*

This response is a direct, problem-solving approach, which is not the most appropriate response for a TA Therapist to make at this point, because it is too premature. TA concepts need to be taught and discussed in Structural Analysis before solutions are explored. Return to 2.1 and try again.

---

**2.5**    *Client:*    *Well . . . I've noticed that when my wife kids around with me, like teasing me in a sweet way, and I respond likewise and tease her back nicely, things go fine. But there are times when I'm trying to talk to her about a serious financial decision and we need to problem-solve as two adults and she continues with her teasing, that I start getting upset. I then start to scold her a bit, and she tends to withdraw after that.*

Choose the most appropriate response:
*Therapist:*    *Then how do you feel?* (Go to 2.6)
*Therapist:*    *What do you say to her when she withdraws?* (Go to 2.7)
*Therapist:*    *That's a good example of an interaction between you and your wife that we can use TA concepts to better understand. When you and your wife both tease each other in a nice way, what ego states are functioning?* (Go to 2.8)

---

**2.6**    *Your Answer:*    *Then how do you feel?*

This is a good question for helping the client to open up more and share his feelings in response to his wife's withdrawal, a question often used by Person-Centered therapists. It is not the best question, however, for a TA Therapist to use to further conduct *Structural Analysis* with the client. Return to 2.5 and try again.

---

**2.7**    *Your Answer:*    *What do you say to her when she withdraws?*

This response is more typical of a behavior or cognitive therapist or a systemically oriented therapist interested in elucidating the behavioral patterns or sequences of communication between a couple. It is not the best response for the TA Therapist who wants to go on with *Structural Analysis* and help the client *identify* the ego states involved in particular interactions with his wife. Return to 2.5 and try again.

**2.8**   *Your Answer:*   *That's a good example of an interaction between you and your wife that we can use TA concepts to better understand. When you and your wife both tease each other in a nice way, what ego states are functioning?*

Correct. This response is characteristic of what the TA Therapist might say to encourage the client to apply TA concepts to better understand his interactions or transactions with his wife. Proceed to 2.9

---

**2.9**   *Client:*   *We must both be acting from our Child states when we tease each other like that . . . and we do enjoy it and it's fun and funny . . . but not all the time!*

Choose the most appropriate response:

*Therapist:*   *Okay, that's good . . . you've identified the Child-Child interaction or transaction and it goes well as long as you stay at that level . . . When you get serious and want to discuss financial matters what ego state are you functioning from, and your wife when she continues to sweetly tease you then? (Go to 2.10)*

*Therapist:*   *(Remains quiet and waits) (Go to 2.11)*

*Therapist:*   *Why not all the time? (Go to 2.12)*

---

**2.10**   *Your Answer:*   *Okay, that's good . . . you've identified the Child-Child interaction or transaction and it goes well as long as you stay at that level . . . When you get serious and want to discuss financial matters what ego state are you functioning from, and your wife when she continues to sweetly tease you then?*

Correct. The TA Therapist encourages the client's correct identification of TA ego states, and asks further questions to help him go on with the task of *Structural Analysis* and identification of other ego states involved in his interactions with his wife. Proceed to 2.13

---

**2.11**   *Your Answer:*   *(Remains quiet and waits)*

This passive response is more typical of a psychoanalytic therapist trying to facilitate free association by the client, or a Person-Centered or Existential therapist waiting empathically for the client to open up more. It is not the most appropriate response for the TA Therapist to use, to actively proceed with the task of *Structural Analysis* with the client. Return to 2.9 and try again.

---

**2.12**   *Your Answer:*   *Why not all the time?*

This response is more typical of a therapist interested in exploring further the thoughts and feelings of the client, although "Why?" questions may not be the most helpful ones to use. This response is not the most appropriate one for the TA Therapist conducting *Structural Analysis* with the client. Return to 2.9 and try again.

---

**2.13**        *Client:*   *I guess I'm functioning from my Adult state when I want to have a serious discussion about money matters, and my wife is still continuing from her Child State when she carries on with the teasing. And when I get angry a bit and scold her, I guess I'm sure acting like the Parent in me . . . and she withdraws like a shamed Child! I'm getting the hang of these TA concepts!*

Choose the most appropriate response:

*Therapist:*   *Good . . . you're getting the hang of it! Now that you've accurately identified the ego states involved in these interactions with your wife, I want to move on and do some Transactional or Functional Analysis with you and help you see how particular crossed transactions as I draw them here on the board cause problems for you and your wife . . . (Go to 2.14)*

*Therapist:*   *Just because you can label or name the ego states in your interactions with your wife does not mean anything yet! You still need to learn how to behave differently! (Go to 2.15)*

*Therapist:*   *How are you feeling now, and what else comes to mind? (Go to 2.16)*

---

**2.14**   *Your Answer:*   *Good . . . you're getting the hang of it! Now that you've accurately identified the ego states involved in these interactions with your wife, I want to move on and do some Transactional or Functional Analysis with you and help you see how particular crossed transactions as I draw them here on the board cause problems for you and your wife . . .*

Correct. This response is typical of the TA Therapist doing *Structural Analysis* with the client, and beginning to move on to *Transactional or Functional Analysis* so that the client can gain further insight into crossed transactions and how eventually to change them to healthier ones. *Game analysis* and *script analysis* are also often used eventually by the TA Therapist to help the client gain more insight and to change, according to the goals and contract agreed upon initially.

**2.15**   *Your Answer:*   *Just because you can label or name the ego states in your inter-actions with your wife does not mean anything yet! You still need to learn how to behave differently!*

This response is not a helpful one, although it contains some truth. It is not the best response for the TA Therapist to use to encourage the client and to further the task of *Structural Analysis* before proceeding to *Transactional or Functional Analysis*. Return to 2.13 and try again.

---

**2.16**   *Your Answer:*   *How are you feeling now, and what else comes to mind?*

This response is typical of therapists (e.g., psychoana-lytic, Person-Centered, or Cognitive) interested in help-ing the client to explore his feelings and thoughts further. It is not the best response for the TA Therapist proceed-ing with *Structural Analysis* with the client and beginning to do some *Transactional or Functional Analysis* as well. Return to 2.13 and try again.

---

## ROLE PLAY FOR TRANSACTIONAL ANALYSIS

Find two others who have also completed this activity unit. Role play brief interviews (anywhere from five to fifteen minutes each) alternating the client, counselor, and observer roles. Record each brief interview on audio- or video-tape for later review and evaluation.

- The *counselor* in this role play should practice the techniques of initial contracting and structural analysis.

- The *client* should provide sufficient information (based on reality) for the counselor to practice initial contracting and structural analysis.

- The *observer* should note the counselor's attempts to practice these tech-niques, taking detailed notes on each exchange between counselor and client in the space provided below.

Observer's notes on you as the counselor:

_____

_____

_____

_____

At the conclusion of the brief interview, participants should discuss the performance of the counselor, learning from each other how these specific techniques are properly used. Focusing on positive as well as less effective responses can improve the performance and understanding of these techniques for each participant.

## On Your Own

Once you have completed the above role play, listen to the tape of the interview (on your own) with you as the counselor. Enter your remarks, verbatim, in the spaces provided. Then consider ways in which you could have more accurately demonstrated the techniques (based on the theory) and write these improved responses in the space following each original response.

Original response 1 _____

_____

_____

_____

Improved response _____

_____

_____

_____

Original response 2 _____

_____

_____

_____

Improved response _____

_____

_____

_____

Original response 3 _____

_____

_____

_____

Improved response _____

_____

_____

_____

Original response 4 _____

_____

_____

_____

Improved response _____

_____

_____

_____

Original response 5 _____

_____

_____

_____

Improved response _____

_____

_____

_____

Original response 6 _____

_____

_____

_____

Improved response _____

_____

_____

_____

# *Behavioral Therapy*

Behavior therapy came into its own in the 1950s with Joseph Wolpe's advent of systematic desensitization, but its development as a school of therapy is also associated with others such as B.F. Skinner, Hans Eysenck, Albert Bandura and Arnold Lazarus. Behavior therapy is based mainly on three learning paradigms: respondent learning, operant conditioning, and social modeling. Its goal is to extinguish the client's identified maladaptive behavior and to introduce or strengthen adaptive behavior leading to a productive life. The Behavior Therapist is usually very active and directive in therapy, serving as a consultant, a supporter, a resource, and as a model. Behavior therapy as a process has four major steps: accurately defining the problem, gathering a developmental history of the client, setting specific goals, and determining the best methods for change.

The major task of behavior therapy is to resolve the client' symptoms. There are literally dozens and dozens of behavior therapy techniques. Some of the most widely used methods include the following: *behavioral assessment* (specifying an individualized treatment plan), *positive reinforcement* (reward for positive behavior), *token economies* (using tokens to be exchanged for rewards or privileges), *assertiveness training* (enabling clients to more freely express their thoughts and feelings), *modeling* (learning through observing the behavior of another), *relaxation training* (discriminating between tense and relaxed muscle groups to relax upon cue), *systematic desensitization* (pairing of a neutral stimulus with one that already elicits fear), and *flooding* (maximizing the anxious state of a client for eventual extinction of the anxiety).

In this Activity Unit we will cover two behavior therapy techniques that are commonly used: *assertiveness training* and *relaxation training*. The same programmed approach to learning effective therapeutic interviewing skills, covering one skill at a time, will be used.

## 1. ASSERTIVENESS TRAINING

---

| | | |
|---|---|---|
| **1.1** | *Client:* | *I have a really hard time saying "No" to people who make all kinds of requests of me. I want to help but I'm feeling overwhelmed by all the things and projects I've committed myself to, by saying "Yes" to almost every request made of me. I'm feeling anxious and somewhat resentful but I can't get myself to say "No" . . . I'm not sure how to say it and I don't want to hurt people's feelings.* |

Choose the most appropriate response:

*Therapist:* *What are you afraid might happen if you say "No" to people? (Go to 1.2)*

*Therapist:* *You really struggle with not being able to turn down people's requests or demands of you. You're actually feeling overwhelmed with anxiety and some resentment. (Go to 1.3)*

*Therapist:* *I see . . . It seems to me that you do want to be able to say "No" to people at times, but you're not quite sure what to say or whether you'll be able to do it. Do you think it'll be helpful if we practice in a role-play several times, saying "No" nicely but firmly to people's requests or demands of you? (Go to 1.4)*

---

**1.2**   *Your Answer:*   *What are you afraid might happen if you say "No" to people?*

This is a response often used by therapists such as Cognitive therapists to identify the specific thoughts the client might have that are associated with his or her fears so that eventually cognitive restructuring of negative thinking can be conducted. It is not the best response for the Behavior Therapist to use in order to guide the client into *assertiveness training* per se. Return to 1.1 and try again.

---

**1.3**   *Your Answer:*   *You really struggle with not being able to turn down people's requests or demands of you. You're actually feeling overwhelmed with anxiety and some resentment.*

This response summarizes what the client has expressed and conveys empathy to the client. It is not the most appropriate response for the Behavior Therapist to use to guide the client into *assertiveness training*. Return to 1.1 and try again.

---

**1.4**   *Your Answer:*   *I see . . . It seems to me that you do want to be able to say "No" to people at times, but you're not quite sure what to say or whether you'll be able to do it. Do you think it'll be helpful if* *we practice in a role-play several times, saying "No" nicely but firmly to people's requests or demands of you?*

Correct. This response is typical of the Behavior Therapist who is trying to guide the client into *assertiveness training* by suggesting role-playing assertiveness skills for turning down requests or demands from others. This response also reflects some empathy for the client and collaborating with the client by asking him or her whether the intervention suggested sounds like it might be helpful, rather than imposing it on the client. Proceed to 1.5

---

**1.5**   Client:   *Sometimes I think I know what to say but I get anxious and don't want to hurt people's feelings . . . but usually I'm not really sure what to say or how to say it. I'm willing to try whatever you suggest in a role-play so that I can practice or learn what to say . . . I'm a little nervous about the role-play though.*

Choose the most appropriate response:

Therapist:   *(Remains quiet and waits)* (Go to 1.6)

Therapist:   *Why are you nervous about the role-play? What thoughts and feelings come to mind?* (Go to 1.7)

Therapist:   *Most people do get a bit nervous about role-playing, but they usually get over it very quickly. Let me suggest that you role-play yourself and I role-play a friend of yours making a request or demand of you . . . Are you ready? Okay, let's try the first role-play   "Hey, I really need your help. Could you please stand in for me next Sunday as an usher at church? . . . I really want to go on this weekend fishing trip . . . Please?"* (Go to 1.8)

---

**1.6**   Your Answer:   *(Remains quiet and waits)*

This passive response is more typical of a psychoanalytic therapist trying to facilitate free association by the client. It is not an appropriate response for the Behavior Therapist who has just begun *assertiveness training* with the client. Return to 1.5 and try again.

---

**1.7**   Your Answer:   *Why are you nervous about the role-play? What thoughts and feelings come to mind?*

This response is more typical of a psychoanalytic therapist or a Cognitive therapist interested in exploring further the client's thoughts and feelings associated with the role-play. It is not the most appropriate response for the Behavior Therapist who wants to proceed with *assertiveness training* with the client. Return to 1.5 and try again.

---

**1.8**   *Your Answer:*   *Most people do get a bit nervous about role-playing, but they usually get over it very quickly. Let me suggest that you role-play yourself and I role-play a friend of yours making a request or demand of you . . . Are you ready? Okay, let's try the first role-play . . . "Hey, I really need your help. Could you please stand in for me next Sunday as an usher at church? . . . I really want to go on this weekend fishing trip . . . Please?"*

Correct. This response is typical of what the Behavior Therapist would say to a client, to reassure the client of the normality of having some initial nervousness about role-playing, and yet encouraging the client to go on with the role-play, giving clear instructions to the client, and then starting the role-play. This is the initial part of *assertiveness training*. Proceed to 1.9

---

**1.9**          *Client:*   *Okay . . . let me try . . . here goes . . . "Well . . . I'm kind of busy next Sunday and I would rather not have to usher . . . but I know the fishing trip is really special to you . . . so I'll step in unless you can find someone else . . . "*

Choose the most appropriate response:
*Therapist:*   *It's hard for you to come right out and just say "No!"* (Go to 1.10)
*Therapist:*   *(Remains quiet and waits)* (Go to 1.11)
*Therapist:*   *That's not bad, not bad at all! Sounds like you said some of what you wanted to, about being busy yourself and preferring not to have to usher, but then you backed off from saying a full and firm "No." How do you feel about what you said, and how might we improve on it?* (Go to 1.12)

---

**1.10**   *Your Answer:*   *It's hard for you to come right out and just say "No!"*

This is a response that conveys empathy to the client but it is not the best response for the Behavior Therapist to use to proceed with *assertiveness training* with the client. Return to 1.9 and try again.

**1.11**  *Your Answer:*  *(Remains quiet and waits)*

This passive response or lack of response, more typical of a psychoanalytic therapist, is not an appropriate one for the Behavior Therapist conducting *assertiveness training* with the client. Return to 1.9 and try again.

---

**1.12**  *Your Answer:*  *That's not bad, not bad at all! Sounds like you said some of what you wanted to, about being busy yourself and preferring not to have to usher, but then you backed off from saying a full and firm "No." How do you feel about what you said, and how might we improve on it?*

Correct. This response is characteristic of the Behavior Therapist who wants to encourage the client by giving positive feedback on what was done well in the role-play, but also giving gentle corrective feedback on what still needs to be improved. The therapist ends with a question to enlist collaboration from the client rather than jumping in and telling the client exactly what to say. Proceed to 1.13

---

**1.13**  *Client:*  *Well, I feel it wasn't a bad first attempt! And I'm feeling a lot less nervous about role-playing. I guess I should not back off at all ... Let me try again ... "I'm sorry but I'm really busy next Sunday and so I can't usher for you. You may be able to find someone else to do it ..." How's that?*

Choose the most appropriate response:

*Therapist:*  *You're feeling better now about the role-playing and are willing to try to improve on saying "No" to people. (Go to 1.14)*

*Therapist:*  *Very good! You're right about not backing off, and not saying too much more after a clear and firm "No" and you did exactly that! Let's try it again one more time, for practice, okay? Here goes ... (Go to 1.15)*

*Therapist:*  *What do you think? How do you feel about it? (Go to 1.16)*

---

**1.14**  *Your Answer:*  *You're feeling better now about the role-playing and are willing to try to improve on saying "No" to people.*
This response summarizes what the client may be feeling, to convey empathic understanding to the client. It is not the most appropriate response for the Behavior Therapist who is in the process of conducting *assertiveness training* with the client. Return to 1.13 and try again.

---

**1.15**    *Your Answer:*    *Very good! You're right about not backing off, and not saying too much more after a clear and firm "No" and you did exactly that! Let's try it again one more time, for practice, okay? Here goes . . .*

Correct. This response is typical of the Behavior Therapist conducting *assertiveness training* with the client, with the use of praise or positive reinforcement, feedback, and some coaching, and another role-play, for further practice and skills building.

---

**1.16**    *Your Answer:*    *What do you think? How do you feel about it?*

This response is useful for further exploration of the client's thoughts and feelings about the role-play just completed. While it *may* also be used by the Behavior Therapist, it is not the best response for continuing *assertiveness training* with the client. Return to 1.13 and try again.

---

## 2. RELAXATION TRAINING

---

**2.1**        *Client:*    *I feel tense often, and I have been having trouble falling asleep recently. I just don't seem to be able to unwind and relax sufficiently to fall asleep.*

Choose the most appropriate response:

*Therapist:*    *(Remains quiet and waits)* (Go to 2.2)

*Therapist:*    *You've been having trouble with insomnia and tension.* (Go to 2.3)

*Therapist:*    *Before I discuss relaxation training which can be of help to you for tension reduction and insomnia treatment, let me ask you what you've tried so far to relax and unwind?* (Go to 2.4)

---

**2.2**    *Your Answer:*    *(Remains quiet and waits)*

This passive response is more characteristic of a psychoanalytic therapist. It is not an appropriate response for the Behavior Therapist who is trying to introduce *relaxation training* to the client with tension and insomnia problems. Return to 2.1 and try again.

---

**2.3**    *Your Answer:*    *You've been having trouble with insomnia and tension.*

This is a response for summarizing what the client has expressed and for conveying empathy to the client. It is not the best response for the Behavior Therapist trying to introduce the client to *relaxation training*. Return to 2.1 and try again.

---

**2.4**    *Your Answer:*    *Before I discuss relaxation training which can be of help to you for tension reduction and insomnia treatment, let me ask you what you've tried so far to relax and unwind?*

Correct. The Behavior Therapist will often make such a response to introduce the intervention of *relaxation training* but ask what the client has tried so far, before going into the detailed instructions of relaxation training. The client might already have tried one or two of the relaxation techniques without much benefit, and therefore the Behavior Therapist can suggest other relaxation techniques the client has not tried before or just a bit. Proceed to 2.5

---

**2.5**    *Client:*    Well . . . I've tried to drink some warm milk, even some alcohol or a "night-cap," listening to soft music, but none of these have helped . . . I end up tossing and turning in bed, feeling tense and frustrated, often for a couple of hours.

Choose the most appropriate response:

*Therapist:*    *What do you think about when you feel tense and can't sleep at night?* (Go to 2.6)

*Therapist:*    *Okay . . . sounds like you have not tried to do a series of relaxation exercises like tensing and relaxing your muscles, telling yourself to relax and unwind or using calming self-talk, and imagining pleasant scenes such as lying on the beach in Hawaii, if you like the beach or Hawaii that is!* (Go to 2.7)

*Therapist:*    *What else comes to mind now as you're telling me about your insomnia?* (Go to 2.8)

---

**2.6**    *Your Answer:*    *What do you think about when you feel tense and can't sleep at night?*

This response is typical of a Cognitive therapist interested in identifying the thoughts that are associated with the client's tension and insomnia, so that cognitive restructuring of such maladaptive thinking can be eventually conducted. It is not the best response for the Behavior Therapist who wants to proceed with *relaxation training* with the client. Return to 2.5 and try again.

**2.7**     *Your Answer:*     *Okay . . . sounds like you have not tried to do a series of relax-*
                                *ation exercises like tensing and relaxing your muscles, telling*
                                *yourself to relax and unwind or using calming self-talk, and*
                                *imagining pleasant scenes such as lying on the beach in*
                                *Hawaii, if you like the beach or Hawaii that is!*

                                Correct. The Behavior Therapist uses a response like this
                                to further introduce and briefly describe some of the
                                *relaxation techniques* that will be taught to the client, since
                                the client does not seem to have used such techniques
                                systematically yet. Proceed to 2.9

---

**2.8**     *Your Answer:*     *What else comes to mind now as you're telling me about your*
                                *insomnia?*

                                This response is more typical of a psychoanalytic thera-
                                pist trying to facilitate free association by the client. It is
                                not the most appropriate response for the Behavior
                                Therapist who is proceeding with *relaxation training* with
                                the client. Return to 2.5 and try again.

---

**2.9**     *Client:*          *I guess I haven't put it all in a package like that . . . I sure*
                                *would like to learn how to relax better and more quickly, so I'm*
                                *ready for the relaxation training.*

                                Choose the most appropriate response:
            *Therapist:*        *You seem motivated to learn relaxation techniques . . . sounds*
                                *like you really want to overcome the insomnia and tension . . .*
                                *(Go to 2.10)*
            *Therapist:*        *Are you sure? (Go to 2.11)*
            *Therapist:*        *Good . . . let me describe briefly the progressive muscle relax-*
                                *ation exercises we'll be using for 4 major muscle groups . . . I'll*
                                *start with your arm muscles and I want you later to tense*
                                *them like this by flexing your arms or biceps hard and holding*
                                *the tension for 7-10 seconds by counting slowly up to 5, and*
                                *then letting your arms flop down and go limp as you tell your-*
                                *self to "Relax, unwind, letting go of all the tension, allowing*
                                *the muscles to smooth out . . ." for 20 seconds or so, and imag-*
                                *ine a pleasant scene, before repeating this exercise. We'll even-*
                                *tually do each exercise a total of four times. I'll give you the*
                                *instructions for the other 3 major muscle groups - your head*
                                *and neck muscles, the upper body muscles including your*
                                *shoulders, chest, and abdomen, and your leg muscles - a little*
                                *later. Any questions about the arm muscles? Okay, go ahead*
                                *and try it out once . . . just for practice . . . Good . . . Let's go*
                                *on to the head and neck muscles . . . (Go to 2.12)*

**2.10**   *Your Answer:*   *You seem motivated to learn relaxation techniques . . . sounds like you really want to overcome the insomnia and tension . . .*

This response conveys empathic understanding to the client but is not the best response for the Behavior Therapist to make to go on with *relaxation training* for the client. Return to 2.9 and try again.

---

**2.11**   *Your Answer:*   *Are you sure?*

This is not a helpful question for any therapist to ask at this point. Questioning the client's motivation is not an appropriate response for the Behavior Therapist who is interested instead in motivating the client for *relaxation training*. Return to 2.9 and try again.

---

**2.12**   *Your Answer:*   *Good . . . let me describe briefly the progressive muscle relaxation exercises we'll be using for 4 major muscle groups . . . I'll start with your arm muscles and I want you later to tense them like this by flexing your arms or biceps hard and holding the tension for 7-10 seconds by counting slowly up to 5, and then letting your arms flop down and go limp as you tell yourself to "Relax, unwind, letting go of all the tension, allowing the muscles to smooth out . . ." for 20 seconds or so, and imagine a pleasant scene, before repeating this exercise. We'll eventually do each exercise a total of four times. I'll give you the instructions for the other 3 major muscle groups - your head and neck muscles, the upper body muscles including your shoulders, chest, and abdomen, and your leg muscles - a little later. Any questions about the arm muscles? Okay, go ahead and try it out once . . . just for practice . . . Good . . . Let's go on to the head and neck muscles . . .*

Correct. This long response is typical of the Behavior Therapist giving specific instructions for relaxation exercises so that the client can learn and later practice such exercises in the session and at home. *Relaxation training* has therefore begun. Proceed to 2.13

---

**2.13**   *Client:*   *. . . Wow, all these 4 major exercises seem to work pretty good for me, but I've just tried each of them once . . . you said we'll do each a total of 4 times, so are you going to guide me now through the whole package?*

Choose the most appropriate response:

*Therapist:*   *Good . . . and yes I'll be guiding you now through a 10-15 minute session of relaxation training proper. You now know how to do each of the 4 major exercises for progressive muscle relaxation, alternately tensing and relaxing your muscles. Now sit back as comfortably as you can, close your eyes, and follow my instructions . . .* (Go to 2.14)

Therapist:    *(Remains quiet and waits)* (Go to 2.15)
Therapist:    *You seem to be really keen to go through the whole package of relaxation exercises fully.* (Go to 2.16)

---

**2.14**  *Your Answer:*    *Good . . . and yes I'll be guiding you now through a 10-15 minute session of relaxation training proper. You now know how to do each of the 4 major exercises for progressive muscle relaxation, alternately tensing and relaxing your muscles. Now sit back as comfortably as you can, close your eyes, and follow my instructions . . .*

Correct. This response is typical of the Behavior Therapist conducting *relaxation training* with the client, giving clear instructions to the client and guiding the client through the whole package of progressive muscle relaxation exercises for 10-15 minutes. Homework relaxation exercises are usually also prescribed, and the client will be asked to use them at bedtime to help reduce tension and overcome insomnia. Other behavioral methods for treating insomnia will also be covered, such as stimulus control methods (e.g., getting out of bed after a few moments of sleeplessness instead of staying in bed tossing and turning for hours, getting back into bed only when feeling very tired and sleepy, etc.)

---

**2.15**  *Your Answer:*    *(Remains quiet and waits)*

This passive response or lack of response is definitely inappropriate for the Behavior Therapist at this point of conducting *relaxation training* with the client where more specific instructions need to be given. Return to 2.13 and try again.

---

**2.16**  *Your Answer:*    *You seem to be really keen to go through the whole package of relaxation exercises fully.*

This is a response that summarizes the client's experience with empathic understanding, but it is not a sufficient response for the Behavior Therapist to make in order to continue doing *relaxation training* with the client where more specific instructions are needed. Return to 2.13 and try again.

---

## ROLE PLAY FOR BEHAVIORAL THERAPY

Find two others who have also completed this activity unit. Role play brief interviews (anywhere from five to fifteen minutes each) alternating the client, counselor, and observer roles. Record each brief interview on audio- or video-tape for later review and evaluation.

- The *counselor* in this role play should practice the techniques of assertiveness training and relaxation training.

- The *client* should provide sufficient information (based on reality) for the counselor to practice assertiveness training and relaxation training.

- The *observer* should note the counselor's attempts to practice these techniques, taking detailed notes on each exchange between counselor and client in the space provided below.

  Observer's notes on you as the counselor:

  _____

  _____

  _____

  _____

At the conclusion of the brief interview, participants should discuss the performance of the counselor, learning from each other how these specific techniques are properly used. Focusing on positive as well as less effective responses can improve the performance and understanding of these techniques for each participant.


## On Your Own

Once you have completed the above role play, listen to the tape of the interview (on your own) with you as the counselor. Enter your remarks, verbatim, in the spaces provided. Then consider ways in which you could have more accurately demonstrated the techniques (based on the theory) and write these improved responses in the space following each original response.

  Original response 1  _____

  _____

  _____

  _____

Improved response _____

_____

_____

_____

Original response 2 _____

_____

_____

_____

Improved response _____

_____

_____

_____

Original response 3 _____

_____

_____

_____

Improved response _____

_____

_____

_____

Original response 4 _____

_____

_____

_____

Improved response _____

_____

_____

_____

Original response 5 _____

_____

_____

_____

Improved response _____

_____

_____

_____

Original response 6 _____

_____

_____

_____

Improved response _____

_____

_____

_____

# Cognitive Therapies

Cognitive therapies are widely used and well known today. The major ones include Rational-Emotive Therapy or RET developed by Albert Ellis, Cognitive Therapy by Aaron Beck, and Cognitive-Behavior Modification by Donald Meichenbaum. Cognitive therapies are also often called Cognitive-Behavioral Therapies.

As in Behavior Therapy, Cognitive Therapies contain literally dozens and dozens of therapeutic techniques, often including both cognitive and behavioral ones. The basic approach in Cognitive Therapies, including RET, is to help clients identify and change their irrational, distorted, unreasonable, inaccurate ways of thinking to more rational, reasonable, balanced, and accurate ways of thinking, because such irrational beliefs or thoughts often underlie problem feelings such as anxiety, anger, and depression, as well as maladaptive behaviors. The Cognitive Therapist or Rational-Emotive Therapist often assumes a very active role as teacher, trainer, consultant, or coach, but usually in a collaborative relationship with the client.

Among the many therapeutic techniques of RET are the following: *use of the A-B-C theory of RET* (where A stands for the *Activating Event*, B for the client's irrational *Beliefs*, and C for the *Consequences* whether emotional or behavioral for the client as a result of holding on to such irrational Beliefs), *disputation* (of irrational beliefs or distorted thinking), *countering* and *action homework*. Three major types of interventions from the Cognitive Therapies, especially the Cognitive-Behavioral Therapies, are: *coping skills training* (in which clients are assisted in developing cognitive and behavioral skills for dealing with challenging or stressful situations): *cognitive restructuring* (which attempts to directly help the client to modify maladaptive thought patterns); and *problem-solving training* (in which the client's general capacity for understanding and dealing with challenging problems is expanded).

In this Activity Unit, we will cover two techniques from the Cognitive Therapies that are widely used: *Use of the A-B-C Theory of RET (Ellis)* and

*Cognitive restructuring (Beck).* The same programmed approach to learning effective therapeutic interviewing skills, covering one skill at a time, will be used.

## 1. USE OF THE A-B-C THEORY OF RET (ELLIS)

1.1          Client:     *I've been feeling discouraged and depressed in the last few weeks, mainly because I've not had any success at all in getting a date with a woman. I've tried calling at least five different women that I would like to get to know better, but they all turned me down for a date.*

                             Choose the most appropriate response:

      Therapist:    *It's been hard and painful for you to have several women turn you down for a date . . . you're actually feeling pretty down and discouraged.* (Go to 1.2)

      Therapist:    *You said you've been feeling depressed and discouraged because you've been turned down repeatedly by women. But if you pause to think more carefully, you'll see that your feelings of discouragement and depression (C or Consequences) are not really caused by being turned down for dates (A or Activating Event). The B in between refers to your Beliefs or what you are saying to yourself as triggered or activated by A. This is the A-B-C view of human functioning that I would like you to learn and use in understanding how you tend to get stuck in lousy feelings because of your irrational thoughts or beliefs (B). Tell me now what are the beliefs you have that are triggered by your being turned down repeatedly for a date . . .* (Go to 1.3)

      Therapist:    *(Remains quiet and waits)* (Go to 1.4)

1.2    Your Answer:    *It's been hard and painful for you to have several women turn you down for a date . . . you're actually feeling pretty down and discouraged.*

                             This is a good response for conveying empathic understanding to the client. It is *not* the most appropriate response for the Cognitive Therapist to make to help the client quickly learn how to use the A-B-C theory of human behavior. Return to 1.1 and try again.

1.3    Your Answer:    *You said you've been feeling depressed and discouraged because you've been turned down repeatedly by women. But if you pause to think more carefully, you'll see that your feelings of discouragement and depression (C or Consequences) are not really caused by being turned down for dates (A or Activating*

*Event). The B in between refers to your Beliefs or what you are saying to yourself as triggered or activated by A. This is the A-B-C view of human functioning that I would like you to learn and use in understanding how you tend to get stuck in lousy feelings because of your irrational thoughts or beliefs (B). Tell me now what are the beliefs you have that are triggered by your being turned down repeatedly for a date . . .*

Correct. This rather lengthy response is characteristic of the Cognitive Therapist or Rational-Emotive Therapist at this point when the therapist is trying to teach the basics of the A-B-C theory of human functioning to the client. Proceed to 1.5

---

**1.4**   *Your Answer:*   *(Remains quiet and waits)*

This passive response is more typical of a psychoanalytic therapist. It is too passive for the Cognitive Therapist or Rational-Emotive Therapist who is trying to didactically teach the client the A-B-C theory of human functioning. Return to 1.1 and try again.

---

**1.5**          *Client:*   *Well . . . I'm not sure if I would say I have irrational beliefs but I do think to myself after being rejected again for a date, that I'm not attractive enough, that there's something wrong with me, and that it's terrible for me to be rejected . . .*

Choose the most appropriate response:

*Therapist:*   *So you have several Beliefs or Bs that focus on how unattractive and deficient you are and how terrible or horrible it is to be rejected. How do all these beliefs make you feel? (Go to 1.6)*

*Therapist:*   *You seem to feel inferior, with much self-doubt, after being turned down for dates. Let's discuss further your feelings of inferiority and how to deal with this important issue. (Go to 1.7)*

*Therapist:*   *You feel it's terrible to be rejected . . . (Go to 1.8)*

---

**1.6**   *Your Answer:*   *So you have several Beliefs or Bs that focus on how unattractive and deficient you are and how terrible or horrible it is to be rejected. How do all these beliefs make you feel?*

Correct. The Cognitive Therapist or Rational-Emotive Therapist will summarize the irrational beliefs and then help the client to see how they lead to problem feelings by asking a direct question as in this response. Proceed to 1.9

| 1.7 | *Your Answer:* | *You seem to feel inferior, with much self-doubt, after being turned down for dates. Let's discuss further your feelings of inferiority and how to deal with this important issue.* |
|---|---|---|

This response focuses on the feelings of inferiority and the issue of a possible "inferiority complex." It is more typical of an Adlerian therapist than of a Cognitive or Rational-Emotive Therapist trying to teach the client the A-B-C view of human functioning. Return to 1.5 and try again.

| 1.8 | *Your Answer:* | *You feel it's terrible to be rejected . . .* |
|---|---|---|

This is a brief response to convey empathic understanding to the client, a response more typical of a Person-Centered therapist than of the Cognitive or Rational-Emotive Therapist trying to didactically teach the client the A-B-C theory of human functioning. Return to 1.5 and try again.

| 1.9 | *Client:* | *I guess I feel lousy and . . . it hurts deep inside . . . and I feel I can't take this anymore . . . Mmm . . . I'm beginning to see how my beliefs and negative thoughts actually affect my feelings . . .* |
|---|---|---|

Choose the most appropriate response:

*Therapist:*   *You're realizing how your negative thoughts affect your feelings but it still hurts deeply.* (Go to 1.10)

*Therapist:*   *Good . . . you can see now more clearly how your irrational and negative thoughts or beliefs (B) can cause you to feel lousy and down (C). It is not really the Activating Event or A of being turned down for dates per se that makes you feel depressed. It's your thinking in between! Let's take another example from your life to see if you can put your experience into the A-B-C categories.* (Go to 1.11)

*Therapist:*   *What else comes to mind?* (Go to 1.12)

| 1.10 | *Your Answer:* | *You're realizing how your negative thoughts affect your feelings but it still hurts deeply.* |
|---|---|---|

This is a response for conveying empathic understanding to the client. It is not the best response for the Cognitive or Rational-Emotive Therapist to use to continue to teach the client the A-B-C theory of human functioning. Return to 1.9 and try again.

**1.11**   *Your Answer:*   *Good . . . you can see now more clearly how your irrational and negative thoughts or beliefs (B) can cause you to feel lousy and down (C). It is not really the Activating Event or A of being turned down for dates per se that makes you feel depressed. It's your thinking in between! Let's take another example from your life to see if you can put your experience into the A-B-C categories.*

Correct. The Cognitive or Rational-Emotive Therapist will continue to reinforce the A-B-C view, and then ask the client for another example from his life so that he can apply the A-B-C categories himself. Proceed to 1.13

---

**1.12**   *Your Answer:*   *What else comes to mind?*

This is a brief response often used by a psychoanalytic therapist to facilitate further free association by the client. It is not the most appropriate response for the Cognitive or Rational-Emotive Therapist to use for teaching the client the A-B-C theory of human functioning. Return to 1.9 and try again.

---

**1.13**   *Client:*   *Last week I felt depressed for a couple of days because I got a poor grade, a B, on a class test. I guess the Activating Event (A) here would be my getting a poor grade and the Consequences (C) would be my feeling depressed. The B or Beliefs in between are more difficult to pin down but . . . I do recall thinking it's terrible to have a grade of B, I should be getting straight As and do perfectly all the time, otherwise I'm not worth much and people would not think highly of me . . .*

Choose the most appropriate response:

*Therapist:*   *You seem to be struggling with a deep sense of inferiority so much so that you feel you have to perform well and get straight As all the time to have people's respect and approval. (Go to 1.14)*

*Therapist:*   *It's hard for you to think that people may not think highly of you . . . (Go to 1.15)*

*Therapist:*   *Good . . . you're beginning to see how the A-B-C theory can help you to understand what irrational beliefs or thoughts may be causing you to feel terrible or down. The next step is to help you dispute as strongly as you can, such irrational thoughts or beliefs so you can begin to feel better . . . (Go to 1.16)*

**1.14**   *Your Answer:*   *You seem to be struggling with a deep sense of inferiority so much so that you feel you need to perform well and get straight As all the time to have people's respect and approval.*

This response is more typical of an Adlerian therapist focusing on the "inferiority complex" of the client. It is not the most appropriate response for the Cognitive or Rational-Emotive Therapist to use to further teach the A-B-C theory to the client and proceed to disputation of irrational beliefs. Return to 1.13 and try again.

---

**1.15**   *Your Answer:*   *It's hard for you to think that people may not think highly of you . . .*

This response is for conveying empathy to the client, but it is not the best response for the Cognitive or Rational-Emotive Therapist to use to further teach the A-B-C theory to the client. Return to 1.13 and try again.

---

**1.16**   *Your Answer:*   *Good . . . you're beginning to see how the A-B-C theory can help you to understand what irrational beliefs or thoughts may be causing you to feel terrible or down. The next step is to help you dispute as strongly as you can, such irrational thoughts or beliefs so you can begin to feel better . . .*

Correct. This is a response typical of the Cognitive or Rational-Emotive Therapist trying to didactically teach the A-B-C theory to the client and move on to disputation of irrational beliefs, which is at the core of RET.

---

## 2. COGNITIVE RESTRUCTURING (BECK)

---

**2.1**        *Client:*   *I'm feeling depressed again this week . . . I'm really tired of this struggle with depression . . .*

Choose the most appropriate response:

*Therapist:*   *(Keeps quiet and waits)* (Go to 2.2)
*Therapist:*   *Uhmhmm . . . it's hard to keep on struggling with feeling down . . .* (Go to 2.3)
*Therapist:*   *Can you tell me what goes through your mind, what you're thinking about when you feel depressed like this?* (Go to 2.4)

**2.2**   *Your Answer:*   *(Keeps quiet and waits)*

This response is more typical of a psychoanalytic therapist trying to facilitate free association by the client. It is not the best response in conducting *cognitive restructuring* of maladaptive thinking in the client. Return to 2.1 and try again.

---

**2.3**   *Your Answer:*   *Uhmhmm . . . it's hard to keep on struggling with feeling down . . .*

This is a response that conveys empathic understanding to the client, and is more typical of the Person-Centered therapist, although the Cognitive Therapist may also use such a response at times to convey empathy. However, it is not the best response for the Cognitive Therapist to make in order to proceed with *cognitive restructuring* of the client's maladaptive, negative, or distorted thinking that often underlies depression. Return to 2.1 and try again.

---

**2.4**   *Your Answer:*   *Can you tell me what goes through your mind, what you're thinking about when you feel depressed like this?*

Correct. This response is typical of the Cognitive Therapist who is trying to help the client identify specific thoughts that are associated with the depressive feelings in the initial stage of *cognitive restructuring*. Proceed to 2.5

---

**2.5**            *Client:*   *Well, . . . I guess I thought a lot about the poor grade I got in a course . . . it was a C, and I started doubting my intelligence or ability to get through college . . . I also felt no one will really respect me now . . . my C stands for catastrophic for me . . . I really feel down and discouraged about it.*

Choose the most appropriate response:

*Therapist:*   *You feel really down because you're thinking that getting the C is terrible or catastrophic . . . that it means you're not intelligent and you may not make it through college . . . that people won't respect you anymore . . . do you think this is a fair and reasonable conclusion with strong evidence for it or is there another way of thinking about your C grade? (Go to 2.6)*

*Therapist:*   *Getting that C has really affected you, and you feel pretty lousy and down about it. (Go to 2.7)*

*Therapist:*   *What else comes to mind? (Go to 2.8)*

2.6    *Your Answer:*    *You feel really down because you're thinking that getting the*
                         *C is terrible or catastrophic . . . that it means you're not intel-*
                         *ligent and you may not make it through college . . . that people*
                         *won't respect you anymore . . . do you think this is a fair and*
                         *reasonable conclusion with strong evidence for it or is there*
                         *another way of thinking about your C grade?*

                         Correct. This response is typical of what the Cognitive
                         Therapist would say to help the client begin to challenge
                         the maladaptive, distorted thinking and look at things
                         from an alternative perspective, what is sometimes
                         called "alternative therapy" in *cognitive restructuring*.
                         Proceed to 2.9

---

2.7    *Your Answer:*    *Getting that C has really affected you, and you feel pretty*
                         *lousy and down about it.*

                         This response is for conveying empathic understanding
                         to the client and is more typical of the Person-Centered
                         therapist. It is not the best response for the Cognitive
                         Therapist to make at this point in conducting *cognitive
                         restructuring* of maladaptive thinking with the client.
                         Return to 2.5 and try again.

---

2.8    *Your Answer:*    *What else comes to mind?*

                         This response is more characteristic of the psychoana-
                         lytic therapist trying to facilitate further free association
                         by the client. It is not the best response for the Cognitive
                         Therapist to use at this point in conducting *cognitive
                         restructuring* of maladaptive thinking with the client.
                         Return to 2.5 and try again.

---

2.9         *Client:*    *I guess I don't have any hard evidence that people won't*
                         *respect me anymore because of my C grade . . . I just feel they*
                         *might . . . and since you asked me whether there's another way*
                         *of looking at things, I guess I'm not that dumb after all,*
                         *because my other grades have been mainly Bs and even a cou-*
                         *ple of As . . . I just hate that C! But it's really not the end of*
                         *the world, and my overall GPA is still half-decent . . . yeah I*
                         *can see it a bit differently now, kind of putting the C in proper*
                         *perspective . . . and I'm feeling a bit better . . .*

                         Choose the most appropriate response:
            *Therapist:*  *As you think about it more, you seem to be feeling better . . .*
                         *(Go to 2.10)*
            *Therapist:*  *(Remains quiet and waits) (Go to 2.11)*

> *Therapist:*   *So you can see now that you really don't have strong or hard evidence that people won't respect you at all just because of your C grade . . . in fact you have other evidence to remind you that you're actually not doing that badly in your studies. You are able to think in a different way, to put the C in proper perspective, so that you're saying to yourself that while you don't like the C, you can live with it, it's not the end of the world. You seem to be feeling better as a result . . . Good! Now let me ask you another question. Suppose, just suppose that you do have evidence that people, at least your close friends, do not respect you anymore because of your C grade. So what if this is true, what does this mean to you? (Go to 2.12)*

---

**2.10**   *Your Answer:*   *As you think about it more, you seem to be feeling better . . .*

This is a brief summary response to convey empathy to the client. It is more characteristic of a Person-Centered therapist but is not the best response for the Cognitive Therapist to use to further facilitate the process of *cognitive restructuring* of the client's maladaptive thinking. Return to 2.9 and try again.

---

**2.11**   *Your Answer:*   *(Remains quiet and waits)*

This passive response or lack of a response is more typical of a psychoanalytic therapist who is trying to facilitate further free association by the client. It is not the best response for the Cognitive Therapist to make to further facilitate the process of *cognitive restructuring* of the client's maladaptive thinking. Return 2.9 and try again.

---

**2.12**   *Your Answer:*   *So you can see now that you really don't have strong or hard evidence that people won't respect you at all just because of your C grade . . . in fact you have other evidence to remind you that you're actually not doing that badly in your studies. You are able to think in a different way, to put the C in proper perspective, so that you're saying to yourself that while you don't like the C, you can live with it, it's not the end of the world. You seem to be feeling better as a result . . . Good! Now let me ask you another question. Suppose, just suppose that you do have evidence that people, at least your close friends, do not respect you anymore because of your C grade. So what if this is true, what does this mean to you?*

Correct. This pretty long response is typical of what the Cognitive Therapist would say to convey empathy to the client but also summarize and reinforce the change in thinking or perspective about the C - first to realize there is no hard evidence or basis for concluding that people will not respect the client anymore because of the poor grade, and second to see that one C in the context of mostly Bs and a couple of As is not that bad. The Cognitive Therapist goes one step further by asking the crucial *"So What If . . . "* question to help the client identify his or her basic assumptions and deeper beliefs about the need to have other people's approval and respect all the time (in order to feel self-worth?). Proceed to 2.13

---

**2.13**      *Client:*     *Well . . . if my close friends really do not respect me anymore because of my C, then I will feel pretty lousy and depressed . . . It will mean that I'm not up to par, that I'm not smart or good enough and this is terrible! I need people's approval and respect for me to feel that I'm worth something for my own self-respect and self-worth . . . maybe I'm too dependent on others but I really feel the need for their validation!*

                 Choose the most appropriate response:

     *Therapist:*    *Other people really affect your own sense of self-worth and your feelings overall . . .* (Go to 2.14)

     *Therapist:*    *So, it seems that your sense of self-worth is very dependent on getting other people's approval or respect . . . if you don't have it, then you feel you're not worth much, you're not somebody, that this is almost like the end of the world for you . . . do you see any problems with this basic assumption or view of life for you?* (Go to 2.15)

     *Therapist:*    *Uhmmmm . . . you really struggle with having to get people's approval or respect.* (Go to 2.16)

---

**2.14**   *Your Answer:*    *Other people really affect your own sense of self-worth and your feelings overall . . .*

This response is more typical of the Person-Centered therapist trying to convey empathic understanding to the client. It is not the most appropriate response for the Cognitive Therapist to make to go on with further *cognitive restructuring* of the client's maladaptive thinking. Return to 2.13 and try again.

---

**2.15**   *Your Answer:*    *So, it seems that your sense of self-worth is very dependent on getting other people's approval or respect . . . if you don't have it, then you feel you're not worth much, you're not somebody, that this is almost like the end of the world for you . . . do you see any problems with this basic assumption or view of life for you?*

Correct. The Cognitive Therapist will often make a response like this one in order to summarize the maladaptive basic assumption or way of thinking that the client has just described, and help the client to begin challenging it by asking the question at the end of this response. This gets at the very heart of *cognitive restructuring* of the client's maladaptive thinking, a major or crucial part of the cognitive therapies.

**2.16**   *Your Answer:*   *Uhmmmmm . . . you really struggle with having to get people's approval or respect.*

This is a brief response for conveying empathic understanding to the client that is more typical of a Person-Centered therapist. It is not the most appropriate response for the Cognitive Therapist at this point of conducting further *cognitive restructuring* of the client's maladaptive thinking. Return to 2.13 and try again.

## ROLE PLAY FOR COGNITIVE THERAPIES

Find two others who have also completed this activity unit. Role play brief interviews (anywhere from five to fifteen minutes each) alternating the client, counselor, and observer roles. Record each brief interview on audio- or video-tape for later review and evaluation.

- The *counselor* in this role play should practice the techniques of using the A-B-C theory of RET (Ellis) and cognitive restructuring (Beck).

- The *client* should provide sufficient information (based on reality) for the counselor to practice the A-B-C theory of RET and cognitive restructuring.

- The *observer* should note the counselor's attempts to practice these techniques, taking detailed notes on each exchange between counselor and client in the space provided below.

Observer's notes on you as the counselor:

_____

_____

_____

_____

At the conclusion of the brief interview, participants should discuss the performance of the counselor, learning from each other how these specific techniques are properly used. Focusing on positive as well as less effective responses can improve the performance and understanding of these techniques for each participant.

## On Your Own

Once you have completed the above role play, listen to the tape of the interview (on your own) with you as the counselor. Enter your remarks, verbatim, in the spaces provided. Then consider ways in which you could have more accurately demonstrated the techniques (based on the theory) and write these improved responses in the space following each original response.

Original response 1 _____

_____

_____

_____

Improved response _____

_____

_____

_____

Original response 2 _____

_____

_____

_____

Improved response _____

_____

_____

_____

Original response 3 _____

_____

_____

_____


Improved response _____

_____

_____

_____


Original response 4 _____

_____

_____

_____


Improved response _____

_____

_____

_____


Original response 5 _____

_____

_____

_____


Improved response _____

_____

_____

_____

Original response 6 _____

_____

_____

_____

Improved response _____

_____

_____

_____

# Reality Therapy

Reality Therapy was developed by William Glasser in the early 1960s. It is based on Control Theory and sometimes these two terms are used interchangeably. The primary goal of Reality Therapy is to help clients identify and change self-defeating behavior, make appropriate choices in facing reality, and develop a sense of responsibility. The Reality Therapist seeks to establish a solid emotional relationship with the client by being tough, interested, warm, understanding, sensitive, and genuine.

Glasser outlines eight general procedures for Reality Therapists to use: establishing a caring rapport, focusing on behavior (not feelings), focusing on the present (not the past), making a specific plan, getting a commitment, accepting no excuses, eliminating punishment, and never giving up. With regard to specific therapeutic techniques or methods, the following are among the more widely used ones in Reality Therapy: *structuring, confrontation, contracts, instruction, Skillful Questioning* (the central question being "Does your present behavior enable you to get what you want now, and will it take you in the direction you want to go?"), *Emphasizing Choice* (e.g., by turning adjectives and nouns into verbs), *role playing, support, constructive debate, humor, self-disclosure, positive addictions*, and *assessment* of client's progress.

In this Activity Unit, we will cover two Reality Therapy techniques that are often used: *Skillful Questioning* and *Emphasizing Choice*. The same programmed approach to learning effective therapeutic interviewing skills, covering one skill or technique at a time, will be used.

# 1. SKILLFUL QUESTIONING

| | | |
|---|---|---|
| 1.1 | Client (male): | *. . . There's so much anger in me . . . when I get angry at some-one I just let him have it by shouting at him and even hitting him if I feel like it, even if he's a member of my own gang. It makes me feel powerful, in control and in charge, and special . . . for awhile at least, until I get into trouble with the police again.* |

Choose the most appropriate response:

| | |
|---|---|
| Therapist: | *(Remains quiet and waits)* (Go to 1.2) |
| Therapist: | *Although your expressions of anger tend to get you into trou-ble with the law, you feel good for awhile because of the power and control you experience.* (Go to 1.3) |
| Therapist: | *Do you think that what you're doing, blowing up at people you're angry at, is helping you or hurting you?* (Go to 1.4) |

---

**1.2**    Your Answer:    *(Remains quiet and waits)*

This passive response is more characteristic of a psycho-analytic therapist wanting to encourage free association by the client. It is too passive and not the best response for the Reality Therapist to make in using *Skillful Questioning* to help the client face reality and be more responsible in the choices he makes in his life. Return to 1.1 and try again.

---

**1.3**    Your Answer:    *Although your expressions of anger tend to get you into trou-ble with the law, you feel good for awhile because of the power and control you experience.*

This response conveys empathic understanding to the client and is more characteristic of a Person-Centered therapist. It is not the most appropriate response for the Reality Therapist to make in using *Skillful Questioning* to help the client face reality and develop responsibility. Return to 1.1 and try again.

---

**1.4**    Your Answer:    *Do you think that what you're doing, blowing up at people you're angry at, is helping you or hurting you?*

Correct. The Reality Therapist begins the *Skillful Questioning* intervention by asking the client whether his behavior of blowing up at people he is angry at is really helping or hurting him. Other questions will follow. Proceed to 1.5

---

**1.5**              Client:     *Well . . . I do feel good and powerful for awhile, but I guess get-*
*ting into trouble with the law or police so often is not really good*
*for me . . . I'm getting a pretty bad record! Also, I'm losing some*
*of my close friends when I fight with them like this . . .*

Choose the most appropriate response:
Therapist:   *So, you can see that what you're doing actually ends up hurt-*
*ing you, even if you feel good at first for awhile. Is what you*
*are doing now, what you want to be doing . . . in the months*
*and years ahead of you? (Go to 1.6)*
Therapist:   *What other thoughts and feelings come to mind? (Go to 1.7)*
Therapist:   *You realize that getting into trouble with the law is not good*
*for you, . . . you're getting a bad record . . . and you are also*
*losing some close buddies . . . (Go to 1.8)*

---

**1.6**   Your Answer:   *So, you can see that what you're doing actually ends up hurt-*
*ing you, even if you feel good at first for awhile. Is what you*
*are doing now, what you want to be doing . . . in the months*
*and years ahead of you?*

Correct. This response is typical of what the Reality
Therapist would say to summarize what the client has
expressed and gently confront him with the self-destruc-
tiveness of his present angry behavior, and then go on to
asking him another key question about his future in
*Skillful Questioning* of the client. Proceed to 1.9

---

**1.7**   Your Answer:   *What other thoughts and feelings come to mind?*

This response or question is more typical of a psychoanalytic therapist or a cognitive therapist interested in further exploring the client's thoughts and feelings. It is not
the most appropriate response or question for the Reality
Therapist to use in further *Skillful Questioning* of the
client to help him face reality and develop responsibility.
Return to 1.5 and try again.

---

**1.8**   Your Answer:   *You realize that getting into trouble with the law is not good*
*for you, . . . you're getting a bad record . . . and you are also*
*losing some close buddies . . .*

This response conveys empathic understanding to the
client and is more typical of a Person-Centered therapist. It
is not the best response for the Reality Therapist to use in
*Skillful Questioning* of the client. Return to 1.5 and try again.

---

1.9        *Client:*        *Well . . . I still like the feeling of power and control . . . but I*
*guess I don't really want to continue to be so angry at people*
*. . . if you can help me to control my anger better, and yet still*
*experience some power and feel special about myself . . . I'm*
*open to that.*

Choose the most appropriate response:

*Therapist:*        *More specifically, what are you expecting or hoping I'll be able*
*to do for you at this point?* (Go to 1.10)

*Therapist:*        *You seem to want to control your anger better but still experi-*
*ence power and feel special about yourself . . . and you want me*
*to help you do this.* (Go to 1.11)

*Therapist:*        *You seem open to change . . . to finding ways of feeling special*
*about yourself and be in control, and yet not blow up in anger*
*so often. How committed do you think you are to therapy here*
*with me and to really changing your behavior?* (Go to 1.12)

---

1.10        *Your Answer:*        *More specifically, what are you expecting or hoping I'll be able*
*to do for you at this point?*

This response is more typical of a cognitive therapist or
behavior therapist interested in finding out the client's
specific expectations of the therapist and therapy in the
process of change. It is not the best response for the
Reality Therapist in the midst of *Skillful Questioning* of
the client, and trying to help the client assess his commitment to therapy and to change in his life and behavior. Return to 1.9 and try again.

---

1.11        *Your Answer:*        *You seem to want to control your anger better but still experi-*
*ence power and feel special about yourself . . . and you want me*
*to help you do this.*

This response is a good summary for conveying empathy to the client. It is more typical of a Person-Centered
therapist, but it is not the best response for the Reality
Therapist to make in further *Skillful Questioning* of the
client. Return to 1.9 and try again.

---

1.12        *Your Answer:*        *You seem open to change . . . to finding ways of feeling special*
*about yourself and be in control, and yet not blow up in anger*
*so often. How committed do you think you are to therapy here*
*with me and to really changing your behavior?*

Correct. This response is typical of the Reality Therapist
conducting *Skillful Questioning* of the client and focusing
on his level of commitment to therapy and to personal

change, before embarking on a more specific behavior change program. Proceed to 1.13

---

**1.13**           *Client:*       *That's why I'm here! I've gotten into trouble with the law too often and will go to jail if something doesn't happen. I'll give it my best shot if you can help me in some practical way.*

Choose the most appropriate response:

*Therapist:*    *Okay, that's a deal! Let me begin by reminding you that you always have a choice — to change or not to change, to behave or act in ways that do not hurt you and others or that do hurt or harm you and others. Now what are some things you have done that make you feel special and in control and yet you do not choose to "anger" yourself?* (Go to 1.14)

*Therapist:*    *Good . . . now let me explain to you an anger control program that you'll be practicing with my help. It'll involve learning to relax by taking slow deep breaths, using calming self-talk such as "Take it easy . . . slow down . . . don't take it personally . . . ," and thinking or imagining pleasant scenes like a sunset.* (Go to 1.15)

*Therapist:*    *(Remains quiet and waits)* (Go to 1.16)

---

**1.14**   *Your Answer:*   *Okay, that's a deal! Let me begin by reminding you that you always have a choice - to change or not to change, to behave or act in ways that do not hurt you and others or that do hurt or harm you and others. Now what are some things you have done that make you feel special and in control and yet you do not choose to "anger" yourself?*

Correct. The Reality Therapist will use a response like this to confirm the client's commitment to therapy and to change, and to remind the client of choice and responsibility always before him. His needs to feel unique or special, and to have control are acknowledged as legitimate, but the Reality Therapist helps the client to think of more realistic and responsible ways of meeting them. The Reality Therapist also begins to change "anger" from a noun into a verb, a technique that the next section will cover in more detail.

---

**1.15**   *Your Answer:*   *Good . . . now let me explain to you an anger control program that you'll be practicing with my help. It'll involve learning to relax by taking slow deep breaths, using calming self-talk such as "Take it easy . . . slow down . . . don't take it personally . . . ," and thinking or imagining pleasant scenes like a sunset.*

This response is more typical of a behavior or cognitive therapist starting to teach the client specific coping skills for anger control. Some of these skills may also be used by the Reality Therapist eventually, but this response is not the most appropriate one for the Reality Therapist to use at this ending point of *Skillful Questioning* of the client. Return to 1.13 and try again.

---

**1.16**  *Your Answer:*    *(Remains quiet and waits)*

This passive response is more typical of a psychoanalytic therapist. It is not the most appropriate response for the Reality Therapist wrapping up *Skillful Questioning* of the client and trying to help him see the need to make choices always in a realistic and responsible way, so that his needs for feeling special and having some control can be met without hurting others or himself. Return to 1.13 and try again.

---

## 2. EMPHASIZING CHOICE

---

**2.1**       *Client:*    *When I get angry, it's very hard for me to control myself. I just lash out at whoever has offended me usually in words, but sometimes physically too. But like I said, the anger makes me feel powerful and special.*

Choose the most appropriate response:

*Therapist:*  *Anger is a very powerful emotion for you, and you seem to have mixed feelings about it . . . wanting to control it and yet enjoying its power and control over others . . .* (Go to 2.2)

*Therapist:*  *Uhmmmm . . .* (Go to 2.3)

*Therapist:*  *I know that we often speak of our feelings such as anger as if they just happen to us, that we have no choice at all. But the truth is that we always have a choice . . . and it may help you to remember this by saying "When I'm angering myself" rather than "When I get angry" or "When anger hits me." Change the word into a verb, "angering." Try that now . . .* (Go to 2.4)

---

**2.2**  *Your Answer:*    *Anger is a very powerful emotion for you, and you seem to have mixed feelings about it . . . wanting to control it and yet enjoying its power and control over others . . .*

This response conveys empathic understanding to the client, and is more characteristic of a Person-Centered therapist. It is not the most appropriate response for the Reality Therapist to make in *Emphasizing Choice* to the client, and encouraging him to choose responsibly and realistically. Return to 2.1 and try again.

---

**2.3**   *Your Answer:*   *Uhmmmm . . .*

This brief and passive response may be used by a psychoanalytic therapist to encourage the client to go on and open up more or free associate, or by a Person-Centered therapist to communicate unconditional positive regard and empathic understanding. It is not the best response for the Reality Therapist to use in *Emphasizing Choice* to the client. Return to 2.1 and try again.

---

**2.4**   *Your Answer:*   *I know that we often speak of our feelings such as anger as if they just happen to us, that we have no choice at all. But the truth is that we always have a choice . . . and it may help you to remember this by saying "When I'm angering myself" rather than "When I get angry" or "When anger hits me." Change the word into a verb, "angering." Try that now . . .*

Correct. This response is what the Reality Therapist would usually use to convey to the client the reality of choice that is ever present, and to encourage him to choose responsibly. A specific technique here is to change nouns or adjectives like "anger" or "angry" into verbs such as "angering," in *Emphasizing Choice* to the client. Proceed to 2.5

---

**2.5**   *Client:*   *It's hard . . . I'm used to saying "When the anger hits me" but let me try . . . When I'm angering myself and feel so upset I sometimes end up hitting others physically, usually slapping them on the face . . .*

Choose the most appropriate response:

*Therapist:*   *(Remains quiet and waits)* (Go to 2.6)

*Therapist:*   *I know it's hard but keep on going . . . I would like you this time to use not only "angering" but "bullying" and "hurting" in place of "anger," "angry," or "hitting" or "slapping" . . .* (Go to 2.7)

*Therapist:*   *When you get so angry, you hit others physically . . . it's difficult at that point to control yourself.* (Go to 2.8)

---

2.6      *Your Answer:*      *(Remains quiet and waits)*

This passive response or lack of verbal response is more typical of a psychoanalytic therapist trying to facilitate further free association or opening up by the client. It is not the most appropriate response for the Reality Therapist to make in *Emphasizing Choice* to the client and helping him to assume more personal responsibility for his "angering" himself. Return to 2.5 and try again.

---

2.7      *Your Answer:*      *I know it's hard but keep on going . . . I would like you this time to use not only "angering" but "bullying" and "hurting" in place of "anger," "angry," or "hitting" or "slapping" . . .*

Correct. This response is typical of the Reality Therapist who wants to continue *Emphasizing Choice* to the client, by suggesting more verbs he can use to develop a deeper sense of personal responsibility and choice in his anger experiences or "angering." Proceed to 2.9

---

2.8      *Your Answer:*      *When you get so angry, you hit others physically . . . it's difficult at that point to control yourself . . .*

This response is more typical of the Person-Centered therapist who is trying to communicate empathic understanding to the client. It is not the best response for the Reality Therapist to make in *Emphasizing Choice* to the client regarding his "angering" or anger experiences. Return to 2.5 and try again.

---

2.9                 *Client:*      *This is difficult but I'll try . . . When I'm angering myself I sometimes have so much angering that I end up bullying and hurting others . . .*
Choose the most appropriate response:
                 *Therapist:*      *Good . . . now that you are able to say you are angering yourself and ending up bullying and hurting others, how do you feel?* (Go to 2.10)
                 *Therapist:*      *Uhmmmm . . .* (Go to 2.11)
                 *Therapist:*      *What else comes to mind, as you say that?* (Go to 2.12)

---

2.10      *Your Answer:*      *Good . . . now that you are able to say you are angering yourself and ending up bullying and hurting others, how do you feel?*

Correct. The Reality Therapist will often make such a response to reinforce the client's efforts at using verbs such as angering, bullying, hurting rather than anger or angry, and then ask the client how he feels to determine whether he has begun to feel more responsibility for his angering or anger experiences and the need to make better choices that do not hurt others while meeting his needs for uniqueness and power. Proceed to 2.13

---

**2.11**   *Your Answer:*   *Uhmmmm . . .*

This brief response is more typical of a Person-Centered therapist wanting to convey unconditional positive regard and some empathic understanding to the client. It is not the most appropriate response for the Reality Therapist to make in continuing *Emphasizing Choice* to the client. Return to 2.9 and try again.

---

**2.12**   *Your Answer:*   *What else comes to mind, as you say that?*

This response is more characteristic of a psychoanalytic therapist trying to facilitate further free association by the client. It is not the best response for the Reality Therapist to use in continuing with *Emphasizing Choice* to the client. Return to 2.9 and try again.

---

**2.13**   *Client:*   *Well . . . I guess I do feel I have more choice and control or responsibility for my anger or angering . . . that I can choose to control the anger more rather than choose to let it get worse . . . and I feel badly for hurting and bullying others . . . I guess I need to find other better ways of feeling special about myself or having some power than in bullying or hurting others, especially my friends . . .*

Choose the most appropriate response:

*Therapist:*   *You've done really well . . . you realize now that you do have some choice in your angering. You don't want to continue to bully or hurt others in your angering yourself. Your needs for feeling unique or special and having some power or control in your life are valid needs. Let's discuss some other ways that are not hurtful to yourself or others that you can use to meet such needs. For example . . .* (Go to 2.14)

*Therapist:*   *Let's brainstorm other better ways as you said . . .* (Go to 2.15)

*Therapist:*   *(Remains quiet and waits)* (Go to 2.16)

**2.14**  *Your Answer:*  *You've done really well . . . you realize now that you do have some choice in your angering. You don't want to continue to bully or hurt others in your angering yourself. Your needs for feeling unique or special and having some power or control in your life are valid needs. Let's discuss some other ways that are not hurtful to yourself or others that you can use to meet such needs. For example . . .*

Correct. The Reality Therapist will make such a response to continue *Emphasizing Choice* to the client by reinforcing what the client has said and learned so far, and by encouraging the client to think of other better and more responsible and realistic ways of meeting his needs for feeling unique and having some control or power in his life without hurting himself or others. The Reality Therapist can either wait for the client to come up with the first idea or the therapist can suggest one to start the discussion (e.g., get involved in a positive addiction such as joining or leading a football team, or lifting weights and competing in a body building contest, etc.).

---

**2.15**  *Your Answer:*  *Let's brainstorm other better ways as you said . . .*

This response is a direct, problem-solving approach to the client's struggle or problem. It is a bit too brief and premature a response for the Reality Therapist to use, since the Reality Therapist wants to first reinforce choice and responsibility for the client before going on to brainstorm or suggest better ways of meeting his needs for a sense of uniqueness and control or power in his life, for example, developing "positive addictions." Return to 2.13 and try again.

---

**2.16**  *Your Answer:*  *(Remains quiet and waits)*

This passive response is more characteristics of a psychoanalytic therapist trying to facilitate further free association by the client. It is not the most appropriate response for the Reality Therapist to use in continuing *Emphasizing Choice* to the client. Return to 2.13 and try again.

## ROLE PLAY FOR REALITY THERAPY

Find two others who have also completed this activity unit. Role play brief interviews (anywhere from five to fifteen minutes each) alternating the client, counselor, and observer roles. Record each brief interview on audio- or video-tape for later review and evaluation.

- The *counselor* in this role play should practice the techniques of skillful questioning and emphasizing choice.

- The *client* should provide sufficient information (based on reality) for the counselor to practice skillful questioning and emphasizing choice.

- The *observer* should note the counselor's attempts to practice these techniques, taking detailed notes on each exchange between counselor and client in the space provided below.

Observer's notes on you as the counselor:

_____

_____

_____

_____

At the conclusion of the brief interview, participants should discuss the performance of the counselor, learning from each other how these specific techniques are properly used. Focusing on positive as well as less effective responses can improve the performance and understanding of these techniques for each participant.

## On Your Own

Once you have completed the above role play, listen to the tape of the interview (on your own) with you as the counselor. Enter your remarks, verbatim, in the spaces provided. Then consider ways in which you could have more accurately demonstrated the techniques (based on the theory) and write these improved responses in the space following each original response.

Original response 1 _____

_____

_____

_____

Improved response _____

_____

_____

_____

Original response 2 _____

_____

_____

_____

Improved response _____

_____

_____

_____

Original response 3 _____

_____

_____

_____

Improved response _____

_____

_____

_____

Original response 4 _____

_____

_____

_____

Improved response _____

_____

_____

_____

Original response 5 _____

_____

_____

_____

Improved response _____

_____

_____

_____

Original response 6 _____

_____

_____

_____

Improved response _____

_____

_____

_____